To

_____

From

_____

Date

_____

Be still, and know that I am God.

PSALM 46:10 NIV

A 365 MORNING LIGHT
DEVOTIONAL

ALONE IN

PRESENCE

Daily Meditations to Draw Close to Him

summerside

Summerside Press™
Minneapolis, MN 55378
www.summersidepress.com

Alone in God's Presence
© 2013 by Summerside Press

ISBN 978-1-60936-749-7

For Bible version information, see appendix after December 31.

The "Plan for Bible Reading" was created by Scottish minister Robert Murray M'Cheyne (1813–1843).

Devotional writing by Dwight Clough, Rebecca Currington, Marcia Ford, Beth Lueders, Deborah Webb in association with Snapdragon Groupˢᴹ, Tulsa, OK, USA.

Edited by Barbara Farmer

Cover and interior design by Jeff Jansen | aestheticsoup.net

Summerside Press is an inspirational publisher offering fresh, irresistible books to uplift the heart and engage the mind.

Printed in China.

What would you pay for an audience with the great Creator, the one who threw the stars out into the great expanse of space and created a world teeming with life? If He were to establish a location here on earth and invite those who wished to come and speak with Him, lines, many miles long, would quickly form. Who among us wouldn't be willing to wait days, weeks for a few moments alone in His presence. Oh the things we would say, the questions we would ask.

Would you be surprised to learn that God has indeed agreed to spend time alone with whomever wishes to do so? He is not, of course, waiting in some earthly location. But through His Holy Spirit He has made Himself accessible to us here on earth. When we pour out our hearts, He hears us—each and every time. No need to travel to a faraway place. No need to wait patiently in line. There is no fee to pay; no ticket is required. He is as close to you as your breath—and He is waiting. Waiting for you to open the door and let Him in, waiting to comfort, strengthen, encourage, enlighten, defend, and provide.

This Morning Light devotional, *Alone in God's Presence,* was created to encourage you to reach out to Him and experience the wonder of His presence each morning, right where you are. We hope you will see 365 opportunities to draw close to God, to linger there, and to receive what you need from Him. We have also added a Bible Reader's Guide to help you know Him better through the systematic reading of His Word. May this devotional be a great adventure of discovery for you— an investment that will change your life forever.

THE AUTHORS

January 1

SEEKING INTIMACY WITH GOD

Set your mind and heart to seek the LORD your God.

—1 CHRONICLES 22:19 NRSV

THOSE OF US WHO HAVE GOALS quickly discover that setting the goal is only the beginning. The diligence required to reach your goal is the most demanding part of the journey. For example, deciding to be a professional golfer is the easier part. The determination to make it a reality will consume the better part of your life.

What about goals that are of a more private and personal nature? For instance, how do you reach the goal of becoming a friend of God? Just as is true in any friendship, to become intimate with God you must learn to engage with Him with your intellect and your emotions. And since you can't meet with Him face to face you must seek Him where He can be found.

First, discover God with your mind. Seek Him by reading about Him in the Bible, inspirational books, stories, and testimonials. Listen to godly teachers and preachers. Ask family and friends about their experiences with God.

The more you know about Him, the more you will experience God with your heart. Speak to Him in prayer and wait for the quiet impression of His Spirit speaking to your heart. Don't be afraid to talk to Him about anything. He already knows you inside and out.

January 2

IF FEELINGS COULD TALK

Bring joy to your servant, for to you, O Lord, I lift up my soul.

—**PSALM 86:4** NIV

IF YOUR FEELINGS COULD TALK, WHAT would they say?

Like children who blurt out whatever is on their minds, feelings convey the very contents of our souls. *I am deeply loved. I'm ugly. No one cares. Life is beautiful. Things are going my way. I'm trapped and all alone. Life is unfair.*

Those messages and those beliefs may or may not be true; they may or may not reflect reality. But they are there, and deep inside we have reasons for coming to those conclusions.

All of this provides an opportunity for God to reveal His truth. As you come into His presence and let your feelings talk, you hold these buried messages up to Him, and, if you can, you tell Him how you came to your conclusions. Then you look up into the face of God and ask, "Is it true? Am I really ugly? Will I never amount to anything? What is the truth?"

That is when the transformation comes. That is when you learn the soul-cleansing truth. It is the truth for you and for all of us. We really are beautiful, deeply loved, fully capable sons and daughters of God.

January 3

YOUR DISTINCTIVE GIFTS

There are different kinds of gifts, but the same Spirit.
There are different kinds of service, but the same Lord.

—1 CORINTHIANS 12:4-5 NIV

AS YOU SPEND TIME ALONE WITH God, you will increasingly desire to find new ways to serve Him, ways to spread His love to the people in your immediate circle and beyond. You will long to discover your God-given gifts

Maybe you already know where your talents lie. If you have the voice of an angel, for example, it's likely that you've been singing praises to God for some time now. But many people whose talents aren't so obvious often wonder if they even have a gift. Meanwhile, they're among the first to lend a helping hand, organize a special event, or encourage others to believe God's promises—not realizing that the work they're already doing reveals the talent they have been given.

If you are yearning to be of service to the One you are growing closer and closer to each day, look at what you are already doing. Welcoming people into your home and providing for their needs and their comfort shows that you have the gift of hospitality; if people confide in you about the problems in their lives, you likely have the gift of wisdom. God's gifts are not hidden. Look around you and you will see them.

January 4

FILL 'ER UP, GOD

*Saul's son Jonathan went to David at Horesh
and helped him find strength in God.*

—1 SAMUEL 23:16 NIV

SOME DAYS IT DOESN'T TAKE MUCH to push your physical, emotional, and spiritual tanks toward empty. A fussy child, a displeased boss, a short-tempered spouse, and your own critical self-talk leave you feeling drained. You know the drill. Demands and interruptions squeeze out your enthusiasm, and you wilt in exhaustion.

The good thing is: none of this surprises God. He knows everything that crosses your path each day, and He knows just how much pressure and fatigue you can handle. One of the wonderful joys in following Him is He knows just when and how to refill your tank.

A stockpile of encouragement and perspective may come in the form of a loving friend who offers a hand and an understanding heart, or laughter via a greeting card may erase your weariness. God continually surprises His children with everyday boosters. A surefire way to find strength before you enter the thick of each day is to set aside some quiet moments alone to talk to God and listen for His voice. As your loving Provider, He is eager to sustain you no matter what you'll face. What comfort it is to know that His "service station" is open 24/7.

January 5

REASONING WITH GOD

"Let us reason together," says the LORD.

—ISAIAH 1:18 NASB

GOD WANTS TO ENGAGE YOU RIGHT where you are. Do you have objections to the journey of faith? God wants to look over your list of grievances with you. Have Christian leaders disappointed you? God wants to know about it. Does the way of faith seem irrelevant or impractical? God wants to hear about it.

God loves to listen to you. He wants to hear what's on your heart. But He also wants to reason with you. He wants to speak His truth into your life. He wants your trust, even when things seem unreasonable. He wants to offer you grace to help you make sense of your world.

In your time alone with God, take a few minutes to talk things over. You may discover a side of God you have never experienced before. These conversations with God will help you see your world in a new light. Any falsehoods you believed will begin to fall away so what is true may endure. As your misconceptions about God are removed, the gentle sweetness of God's offer to you will become apparent. You will find yourself changed, and your old ways won't make sense to you anymore. You will find in God something new and far better.

January 6

WORTH THE WAIT

Since ancient times no one has heard,
no ear has perceived, no eye has seen any God besides you,
who acts on behalf of those who wait for him.
—ISAIAH 64:4 NIV

WAITING IS NOT THE STRONGEST SUIT for the majority of us. We fidget in lines anticipating concert doors to open, we squirm in seats eager for doctors to see us. Toss in delays in traffic and at airports and we can feel extra-edgy. We live in an increasingly instantaneous society, and sometimes when we find our schedules gridlocked, we try to force God's hand to hurry up, abandoning His counsel to wait with patience.

Our propensity for wanting speedy resolutions and smooth-sailing agendas is nothing new to God. He's watched His children press for more in less time since He first created Adam and Eve. As He's watched our restlessness, He's remained steadfastly patient and ever ready to calm our uneasy spirits.

During life's slowdowns, it's wise to take a deep breath and let your thoughts turn heavenward. Your even-keeled God knows just how to orchestrate everything you need to get through each day. What relief to know that He is acutely aware of each millisecond of today…and tomorrow. As God carefully unfolds the minutes and hours of your life, give thanks that He is always worth the wait.

A LONG-TERM LOVE

Love must be sincere. Hate what is evil; cling to
what is good. Be devoted to one another in brotherly love.
Honor one another above yourselves.

—ROMANS 12:9-10 NIV

THINK BACK TO YOUR CHILDHOOD MEMORIES. Do you recall your first friend? What was it about that person that drew you in? Would you still be friends today if you had stayed in touch?

As children we have little control over whether our relationships will remain intact. Families move from city to city, and sometimes those early friendships fall through the cracks, making room for new ones.

But as adults, we have more control over our ability to remain faithful in friendship, technology being what it is and transportation closing the geographical gap.

Many times in Scripture God speaks to the issue of faithfulness in friendships, particularly friendship with Him and those within the community of faith. Why does it matter to Him? It is important to God because love is the reason we live. It is the central core of our existence on the earth, and it gives meaning to all of life.

Because love is the defining characteristic of God, you will find that love begins to define you as you move deeper and deeper into His heart. Your identity begins to conform to His as you spend more and more time in His presence.

To really know God is to love like God.

January 8

GOD IS NO GENIE

This is the confidence we have in approaching God:
that if we ask anything according to his will, he hears us.
And if we know that he hears us—whatever we ask—
we know that we have what we asked of him.

—1 JOHN 5:14-15 NIV

THE MAGICAL IDEA OF A GENIE granting three wishes has long captivated people. If only we could summon an all-powerful servant to deliver our requests.

King Solomon in early Israel actually met his magical genie in a dream, only the mystical granter of wishes was no imaginary genie. He was God, Creator of the universe, who asked the new king, "What do you want? Ask, and I will give it to you!"

Wow! Imagine God asking you what you want and promising to give it to you. Would you ask for an easy life? To see your family living in success and contentment?

Solomon simply asked for an understanding heart. Just think of what you could do with the ability to discern the best in every situation, to quickly weed out the good from the bad. What would life look like if you could better understand others…or yourself…or even God?

God is not a wish-granting genie. Far better, He is the great Almighty. He owes you nothing, but He loves you with an unfailing love. Reach out to Him by faith, knowing that He desires to bless your life with good gifts.

January 9

THE UNIQUENESS OF GOD

O Lord, there is no one like you—there is no other God.
In fact, we have never even heard of another god like you!
—1 CHRONICLES 17:20 TLB

WHAT DO YOU CONSIDER YOUR MOST distinguishing characteristic? Would it be your dimples? Or is it your naturally
curly hair?

Maybe you would say that your uniqueness is more of an internal
issue as opposed to something physical. So, for instance, your dis-
tinctiveness might be your ability to draw a complete stranger into an
intimate conversation.

Have you ever considered the uniqueness of the God whom Jesus
called "Father," He whom the kings of ancient Israel called "LORD"?
Have you ever pondered how distinctly different are those who diligently follow this God?

The most distinguishing characteristic of God is love, which includes
every expression of love that occurs within the context of a relationship:
grace, gentleness, mercy, understanding, kindness, joy, and affection.
He is the God who tenderly watches over the weak, who bends from
His lofty dwelling place to live among the helpless, who hurries to
forgive and rushes to rescue people from their self-imposed despair.

Is that what you think of when you think of God? Love is His
distinguishing characteristic, and as His child you will grow to resem-
ble Him. The more you know Him, the more you'll become like Him.
His love will make you distinctly different.

January 10

REAL FAITH

*Let us draw near to God with a sincere heart
in full assurance of faith.*
—HEBREWS 10:22 NIV

WOULD YOU BE SURPRISED TO LEARN that God isn't all that religious? God is practical and deeply interested in all the details of your life. Yes, God can be experienced in beautiful songs and inspiring messages, but sometimes we are just looking for a little help, a little encouragement, a little comfort along the way.

The real life of faith isn't confined to Sunday mornings. Far from it! The place God wants to be is right where you are, in the traffic jam running late for an appointment, at the bedside of a sick child, on the phone with a friend. A child rushes back to her mother to share new discoveries, to hide from danger, to pour out her tangled emotions. As children of God, we also rush back to our Father for all these things.

What do you need today? A dose of direction? A teaspoon of clarity? A full cup of joy? God is found in the details, in the practical stuff of your life. Through these everyday connections a relationship is forged that will withstand the stress when crisis comes. The defining moment in your life is now; this moment could shape your eternal relationship with God.

January 11

PLAIN SPEAKING

My message and my preaching were very plain. Rather than using clever and persuasive speeches, I relied only on the power of the Holy Spirit. I did this so you would trust not in human wisdom but in the power of God.

—1 CORINTHIANS 2:4-5 NLT

IF YOU'VE EVER BEEN AFRAID TO talk about God to your friends, coworkers, or even family members, you're not alone. Lots of people hesitate to tell others about what God is doing in their lives. In some cases, that hesitation stems from a mistaken belief that they have to have all the answers to every faith-related question—and they have to express those answers with eloquence and certainty.

Relax. Few people, if any, expect you to speak with the authority or the public voice of a gifted preacher. More importantly, God doesn't expect that of you either. He knows your strengths and weaknesses, and He provides everything you need to do what He has called you to do, including telling others about Him.

So—what is God doing in your life? Answer that question as if you're talking to your best friend; that's how you can talk to anyone about God. Simply speak from your heart, relying on God's Spirit to help you express your love of God in a way that could very well transform another person's life. There's no need to ever be concerned about trying to use elegant, impressive speech when you're talking about God. He Himself is impressive enough.

January 12

JOY IN GOD

Let the light of your face shine upon us, O Lord.
You have filled my heart with greater joy than
when their grain and new wine abound.

—Psalm 4:6-7 niv

RISING UP AT MORNING'S FIRST LIGHT, anticipation fills my heart as I prepare to sit with God during the earliest moments of the day, basking in His sunlight. I turn on a lamp, wash the sleep from my eyes, and pour my first cup of coffee, running through the day's agenda in my mind briefly as I settle into my chair.

I am aware that the disposition of my heart is bent toward one direction or another as a result of yesterday's events and today's pressures. Somewhere in the tension between the two, I open myself up to God and let His light shine in on me, washing over my inner being with rejuvenation and joy.

I sense His countenance in the gentleness of the rising sun— His joy in creation coming alive with the dawn's new light. I join Him in rejoicing over the simple pleasures of nature: the dew sparkling on the grass, the cheerful song of the birds perched on a limb nearby, the gentle breeze wafting through the window by my chair.

Prayers of thanksgiving and praise well up in my heart and find expression in spontaneous worship without effort. I have awakened to find that God is already awake to me.

WISDOM IN THE HEART

*The whole world sought audience with Solomon
to hear the wisdom God had put in his heart.*
—1 KINGS 10:24 NIV

IN TODAY'S WORLD, SUCCESS IS MEASURED by wealth, status, and power. Lists boasting the globe's wealthiest individuals and organizations are published broadly for public perusal. By contrast, in the most sophisticated ancient civilizations success was measured in terms of wisdom, and people came from all over the world to drink deeply from the well of wise men. Isn't it curious that time has so eroded our values that we now promote material wealth as the most coveted commodity, while attaining wisdom doesn't even rate an honorable mention?

What would be different in your life if the pursuit of wisdom became your highest priority? How would it make a difference in the lives of others? How would you go about seeking wisdom?

True wisdom has only one source—God. There are, however, many facets of wisdom and various ways to obtain it. One of the most effective ways is to seek the presence of God regularly. You can obtain an audience with God through pondering on His Word, worship, or prayer. The important thing is to become aware that you are with God, yielding to Him in sincere humility. Being in the presence of God is where true renovation of the heart begins, bringing wisdom in its wake.

January 14

FRAGILE, BUT LOVED

Drink from the brook and eat what the ravens bring you,
for I have commanded them to bring you food.
—1 KINGS 17:4 NLT

THINK FOR A MOMENT ABOUT HOW fragile we are. To stay alive we need the perfect combination of oxygen and nitrogen in the air we breathe, just the right amount of water and other chemicals in our bodies, a steady supply of the right proteins and other nutrients to sustain us. Dangers abound. Mishaps and microbes threaten us. Bombs and bacteria can kill us.

Why would God design us humans to be so...breakable? Does He delight in dangling us over danger? After shaping stars and building continents, did He run out of durable building supplies when He fashioned us from the dust? Doesn't He realize that it can be really scary sometimes to be human?

Maybe God does understand our fears. Maybe He knows even better than we do how susceptible we are to harm. But when our backs are up against the wall, does that mean God is cornered also?

Absolutely not! God never runs out of options, and every one of our vulnerabilities is an opportunity for Him to express His creative love for us.

Ask Him for what you need. He's always listening. His solution may not be what you imagined, but it will always be more than enough.

January 15

A PASSION FOR RIGHTEOUSNESS

Who is there to harm you if you prove zealous for what
is good? But even if you should suffer for the sake of
righteousness, you are blessed.
—1 PETER 3:13-14 NASB

IT'S NOT UNUSUAL TO MEET PEOPLE who are passionate about certain things in life, like sports, music, movies, or chocolate. But to find someone who is passionate about righteousness—the pursuit of all that is good and holy—well, that's a rarity. While many people may acknowledge the need for righteousness, very few actually pursue it with wholehearted devotion and zeal. And that's not surprising, because a passion for righteousness often comes at a high cost.

In parts of the world where persecution is the norm, that price may be the very life of a follower of Christ. In westernized countries, severe persecution is rarely seen, but still, you may be concerned that your zeal for God could jeopardize the close relationships you have with friends and family.

The time you spend alone with God serves to strengthen and prepare you for the negativity you may receive from loved ones who don't share your enthusiasm for God. You can't expect those who don't know God to rejoice with you over what He is doing in your life, but you can expect God to bless you as you continue to pursue all that is good and holy.

January 16

POURING OUT YOUR HEART

*"Oh no, sir!" she replied. "I haven't been drinking wine
or anything stronger. But I am very discouraged, and I was
pouring out my heart to the LORD."*
—1 Samuel 1:15 NLT

SOME DAYS IT DOESN'T TAKE MUCH for a person to sink into despair. You make a costly error at work. Your teen lashes out at you. A close friend is moving away. The doctor's report is less than favorable. Discouragement looms around the corner every time the sun comes up, and sometimes this pesky foe knocks on your door before you're even out of bed in the morning.

Hannah from the ancient country of Ephraim had plenty of reasons to wallow in gloom. She could not bear children, but her husband's other wife could and often taunted her for her inability to conceive. Plus, the other wife's sons were respected Jewish priests. Hannah felt like a worthless woman, a useless wife. So what did Hannah do? She turned her discouragement into prayer. Hannah poured out her heart to God.

Have you tried this purging of your emotions before God? It's simply talking things out honestly with Him or writing down all your troubling thoughts. Go ahead, try it. God can handle anything you're thinking and feeling. He always knows what you're facing, and He understands your discouragement. Like He did with Hannah, He'll be listening to your every word and planning ways to uplift you.

January 17

OWNERSHIP AND INGENUITY

Yours, O Lord, is the greatness, the power, the glory, the victory, and the majesty. Everything in the heavens and on earth is yours, O Lord, and this is your kingdom.
—1 CHRONICLES 29:11 NLT

WHAT WAS YOUR MOST RECENT PURCHASE? A framed print, a dress, or maybe a car? Did you at first experience a certain pride of ownership, as though your purchase sparkled like a new penny?

More importantly, what was your most recent creation? A letter you wrote, a bed of flowers you landscaped, something you built with your own two hands? Did you feel the distinct gratification that comes with the experience of innovation or design? There is nothing like it.

That very kind of warmth glows within the heart of God concerning His creation. It is His design—His engineering—that brought the earth and its inhabitants into being. It is His genius and His loyalty that maintains it. It is His lavish generosity that makes it bring forth abundant resources that sustain our lives and our desires. It is His constant care and concern that keeps the cycle of life in perpetual motion. Imagine the sense of accomplishment and joy He must feel when He considers what He has done.

One way to express your appreciation for all God has done is to simply take the time to acknowledge Him and applaud Him in your heart.

January 18

LEVERAGE

What do we have?

—1 SAMUEL 9:7 NIV

A SEEMINGLY TRIFLING INCIDENT CAN CHANGE a life. Walking off a troop ship, a young soldier was singled out at random for an assignment. He stepped away from his companions and never saw them again. Every one of his shipmates was killed; he alone returned home alive.

You never know what you have in your hands. David had a stone, but it toppled the monster Goliath and stopped evil plans to enslave a nation. A young boy had a lunch bag with some bread and fish in it. But, in the hands of Jesus, that lunch fed five thousand.

Small things can make a big difference. Self-defense experts call this principle leverage. With the right leverage, a small person can deflect an attack from a much larger person. A slight turn of the wrist, a pivot at the waist, and a dangerous attacker is tossed harmlessly aside.

What can God do with what you have in your hands? The bits and pieces of your life may appear mundane, but in God's hands they are tools that can change eternity. Offer your words, your work, whatever you have in front of you to Him, and see what miracle He will do.

FINDING CONTENTMENT

Godliness with contentment is great gain.
For we brought nothing into the world, and we can take
nothing out of it. But if we have food and clothing,
we will be content with that.
—1 TIMOTHY 6:6-8 NIV

IN A CULTURE THAT CONTINUALLY PROMOTES the idea that more is better, finding contentment feels like an uphill battle. There's always something that lures you into thinking that if you only had that, if you could only go there, if you could just live the way they do, then you'd be satisfied.

But people who have found true contentment know that acquiring "more" never satisfies. True contentment comes when you realize that in your life with God, you already have everything you'll ever need and then some. Becoming content with your life isn't an impossible goal to strive for; it's a reality that's available to you now.

Gratitude for what God has already given you is an essential element in learning to be content. Thank God for His provision, and rest in the knowledge that He will continue to provide. Ask Him to make you more aware each day of the abundance you already have, appreciating how little it takes to lead a truly satisfied life.

When you view your possessions—and your desire for more—from God's perspective, you will also begin to identify those things in your life that have eternal value—and you'll discover that *that* is where true contentment lies.

CHOOSING GOD

*Choose this day whom you will serve...but as for me
and my household, we will serve the LORD.*

—JOSHUA 24:15 NRSV

IN OUR CULTURE, INDIVIDUALITY AND PERSONAL choices are celebrated. And what's the harm? Having choices empowers. In a typical day, you are free to choose what you wear, what you eat, and what you want to do with your time. Each day you have dozens of choices to make.

What you may not realize is that God paid an enormous price in order to preserve your right to live as you choose. Though He is often perceived as a bit of a bully, handing down mandates in the form of commandments to those who follow Him, that is far from the truth. After all, He could have forced you to listen to Him, follow Him, obey Him. He could have, but He didn't. He created you with a will and gave you the right to choose—even when you choose against Him.

God does not bully or coerce. Those who turn to Him do so in response to His love. They see in His commandments not a God who coldly issues orders, but a God who wishes to spare us the grief and heartache that follow selfishness and greed. When it comes to going your own way or going God's way—which will you choose?

January 21

ALWAYS SECURE

*We all have different gifts, each of which came
because of the grace God gave us.*
—ROMANS 12:6 NCV

WHETHER OR NOT YOU HOLD HIGHER degrees of education or years of experience, you will eventually find yourself in the company of someone by whom you feel dwarfed in terms of intellect or ability. Some people respond to this feeling by over-reaching, attempting to cover for their insufficiency with lofty words or arrogance, though the cover-up never works. Others seem to flounder, losing their nerve completely, failing to operate even at their normal capacity. And still others seethe with envy and resentment, wasting precious energy on unproductive emotions.

It's likely that the problem is a simple misunderstanding. We may fail to realize that God grants to each of us certain strengths that resonate with His eternal purposes for our lives. Rather than feeling inferior or insecure, we should rejoice in the gifts of others, realizing that in truth we are simply different—what we lack in one area, we make up for in another. It isn't about one person being better, but rather God's deep desire that we realize our need for each other.

Don't hesitate to admire someone for the gifts God has given. Doing so does not diminish you in any way. As you spend time alone with God, your own special gifts and abilities will shine forth.

STARTING SMALL

They will greet you and give you two loaves of bread,
which you shall accept from their hand.

—1 SAMUEL 10:4 ESV

YOU ARE CALLED INTO GREATNESS. AS a royal son or daughter of God, you are engineered for eternity, designed to make a difference. No one can take your place in God's heart, in His Kingdom, in His family. All through eternity, you will still be bringing delight to God and smiles to the faces of your brothers and sisters who dearly love you. Filled with the wisdom of the ages, every word that comes from your mouth will impart encouragement and life to those around you.

But don't expect to start out with a limousine and bodyguards. The path to your true potential seldom starts with glitter and glamour, nor does it begin with an infinitely complex problem to solve. Instead, it starts right where you are, with the mundane stuff of everyday life. There you form the strength of character that God requires for the great assignments He has waiting for you. A simple act of obedience, a kind word, a selfless deed…these are the building blocks of greatness. Every day, as you spend time with God, He is fashioning you for your ultimate destiny. You are being trained to rule. We start small, but we don't stay there.

January 23

GENEROSITY OF SPIRIT

*Remember this: Whoever sows sparingly will also
reap sparingly, and whoever sows generously
will also reap generously.*

—2 CORINTHIANS 9:6 NIV

GENEROSITY IS A QUALITY THAT EVERYONE seems to admire. Some people may not understand it ("Why would she give so much money to *that* charity?"), but still, few people would find any real fault with those who give generously to others.

You don't need a huge bank account or an embarrassment of riches to be a generous giver. Generosity takes many forms, some of which have nothing to do with finances. When you are alone with God, ask Him to show you how you can become generous; He may show you that you already *are*. Do you volunteer with a charity? Do you listen compassionately to your friends when they're pouring out their hearts to you? Do you share encouragement from God's Word with someone who needs it? In short, do you give of your time, talents, and energy even when it's inconvenient to do so?

That's generosity of spirit, and just about everyone can have it— including those who are homebound but spend their time in prayer for others and those who have little but share what they have with those who have less. By cultivating a generous spirit, you discover even more ways you can enrich the lives of others. And as you reflect God's spirit of love, you'll be drawn closer to Him.

January 24

GOD HAS AN APP FOR THAT

*David said, "The L*ORD *who delivered me from the paw of the lion and from the paw of the bear, He will deliver me from the hand of this Philistine." And Saul said to David, "Go, and may the L*ORD *be with you."*

—1 SAMUEL 17:37 NASB

A PLETHORA OF TECHNICAL OPTIONS IS easily available to lift us out of a tight spot or distract us in uncomfortable situations. We can glide our finger over a touch screen and instantly learn how to administer first aid. If we're lonely or upset we can get lost online or in an on-demand movie without leaving the sofa. With all these immediate conveniences, one may wonder if we still need God that much.

The truth is, we need God today just as much as anyone ever did throughout the ages. We may even need Him more. Our culture's ever-evolving technology appears to make us more self-sufficient, more capable, more in control. In reality, these externals can prevent us from relying upon God and abiding in His presence.

The Bible is full of accounts of individuals who trusted God to rescue them from harm or to lend a consoling ear. They earnestly turned to their Deliverer. You can do the same. Through His Word and His presence, God has an app for everything. Just glide your fingers through the pages of the Bible, or even over an e-book reader touch screen, and He'll meet you with fresh courage, strength, and guidance for living life to the fullest. He has the latest technology for meeting your needs today.

POWER WITH GOD

God has surely listened and heard my voice in prayer.
—**PSALM 66:19 NIV**

IF YOU ARE A PARENT, YOU'RE familiar with the uniqueness of each of your children's voices. Not merely an aural issue, each one's voice has a distinctive effect upon your heart because each relationship stands on its own, having a singular impact upon your life.

So it is in God's experience, as well. When you come into the presence of God, He recognizes you as the individual that you are— unique in all the world. The sound of your voice tugs with familiarity upon His heart, and He draws near to you to listen to what is on your heart. Delighting in your presence, He hushes the heavenly host to hear the petitions you bring. And pleased with every indication of your increasing trust, He receives your praise and gratitude, responding in Spirit with peace and joy.

At some point in your growing friendship with God, you come to discover a staggering sense of power in prayer. You might find that this is especially true when your prayers are a heartfelt request on someone else's behalf. Compassion for others and prayerful intercession are a powerful combination, having the capacity to cause things to stir in the depths of heaven. Recognizing such a connection, you pray all the more.

January 26

GOD KNOWS BEST

Teach me to do your will, for you are my God.
Let your good spirit lead me on a level path.
—PSALM 143:10 NRSV

SOONER OR LATER WE WILL ALL encounter a command from God that doesn't make sense. God's requirement may seem outdated, or too difficult, or not in our best interest. It may seem like we must choose between goodness and happiness. It may seem that God doesn't care, that He is arbitrary, that He doesn't really know what we need. It may seem confusing. And then, perhaps something deep inside of us says "no" to God.

We who are parents see this in action. We try to give our children the moral reason behind our directions. But sometimes, especially when children are very young, we just need to say, "Mommy and Daddy know best."

Why do we say "no" to God? Ultimately, it's because we think that we know better than God what is best. But we are not more righteous than God. There are always good reasons behind His instructions, but those reasons are not always available to us. Often the reasons will become clear after we obey. Sometimes they become clear as the decades unfold and we have the perspective of life. In some cases, we will need to wait until we stand before Him. But, in the end, God's requirements will always make sense.

LIFE-CHANGING WORD

*No prophecy of Scripture is a matter of private opinion.
And why? Because it's not something concocted in the
human heart. Prophecy resulted when the Holy Spirit
prompted men and women to speak God's word.*

—2 PETER 1:20-21 MSG

WHAT'S YOUR PERSPECTIVE ON THE BIBLE? Do you think of it as an important work of literature, more historical than relevant? Is it a great religious text for use by pastors and in church settings? Or is it your guiding light, a treasury of spiritual truth that illuminates your life with its limitless wisdom?

There's a reason the Bible has withstood the test of time and every bit of criticism leveled at it: The Bible is unique in all of literature, because it was written by God, not just by human beings. Humans wrote down the words, but those words were inspired by the Spirit of God. Many scholars who have sought to tear it apart with their criticism have ended up embracing it as they discovered its life-changing power for themselves.

The Bible's transformational power is also available to you. Developing the habit of reading the Bible will enrich your life. It will offer you guidance on a daily basis and strengthen your relationship with God. You'll realize it's worth it to replace time spent surfing the Internet or watching television with Bible reading. Its impact on your life will prove to be priceless and immeasurable.

LOVE COVERS ALL

Most of all, love each other as if your life depended on it.
Love makes up for practically anything.

—I PETER 4:8 MSG

YOU KNOW HOW MISCOMMUNICATION AND MISTAKES can fuel the flames of a smoldering misunderstanding. Words somehow turn heated. Feelings quickly singe. Maybe that's why God emphasizes love so much in the Bible. He knows us all too well. Like the gentle father that He is, He reminds us that first and foremost we are to love one another. It is love that will keep us faithful, keep us joyful, keep us tuned in to heavenly things.

You may never have considered all the things love can do. When someone speaks unfavorably about you, love can kindle forgiveness. When a person deeply wounds you, love can bring healing. When you blow it and offend someone, love can help you find your way to remorse and forgiveness. Love can make friends of enemies and break the bonds of prejudice.

But you can't generate restorative love on your own. It takes God's long-suffering, gentle love to cool the heat of anger and heal broken hearts. His love reaches further than you could ever imagine. It has been called the mightiest force in all the universe. Give it first place in all your relationships.

FOUND OUT

Eventually God will bring everything that we do out into the open and judge it according to its hidden intent, whether it's good or evil.

—ECCLESIASTES 12:14 MSG

A YOUNG WOMAN APPROACHED THE MANAGER'S booth at the local grocery store and requested an application for employment.

"You shop here regularly, don't you?" the manager asked.

"Yes, I've been a customer ever since we moved to town," she nodded, smiling.

"I regret that I can't hire you," he responded mournfully. "Just last week, I saw you hide a carton of ice cream on a dry goods shelf behind some cereal boxes. Several items in my inventory would have spoiled had I not witnessed it."

"But I decided not to buy it," she stammered, "and I couldn't afford to go all the way back to the freezer section. I was in a hurry."

"Likewise, I can't afford to hire someone who doesn't have integrity in small ways, for such a person will never be able to muster integrity when faced with a bigger temptation," he finished.

The only way to feel complete comfort in your private moments alone with God is to conform to His character, not only in the open, but also in the secret places of your heart. Practice being a person of integrity in the most private dimension—where nobody sees and nobody knows. When you are comfortable in God's presence, you will be comfortable wherever you are.

January 30

THE FINGERPRINTS OF GOD

If this plan or this work is of men, it will come to nothing.

—ACTS 5:38 NKJV

HOW DO YOU TELL THE DIFFERENCE between the work of God and mere human effort? For those of us who live in cold climates, we know what it means to wrestle with snow. A heavy snowfall can cripple a city, and it can take hours or even days to dig ourselves out. We get up, walk outside, and hear the sounds of shovels scraping sidewalks, snow plows grinding over asphalt, and snow blowers roaring as they throw snow into great piles on either side of the driveway. Yet, when it thaws, God effortlessly and silently removes the snow without any huffing or puffing.

In the same way, the work of God seldom attracts a lot of attention. Typically, it isn't noisy or flashy. Most of the time, the work of God comes in the form of quiet miracles, gentle transformations, invisible works of wonder. But the results are lasting change. The great enterprises of men rise and fall, then they fade from our memory. But the fingerprints of God are on the eternal. The work He does through His children is inspired as they spend time alone with Him and then go out to touch the world.

NOT A WORRY

Don't fret or worry. Instead of worrying, pray.
Let petitions and praises shape your worries into prayers,
letting God know your concerns.
—PHILIPPIANS 4:6 MSG

WORRY IS ONE OF THE BIGGEST time-wasters in life, yet it's a challenge to master the art of worry-free living. Even though worrying does not produce a single positive outcome, it's a practice that's often indulged in by otherwise highly productive people. So why do people worry when there's no point to it?

One reason we worry is that it gives us a false sense of control over an uncontrollable situation. Here's an example: Your daughter is driving home from college several hundred miles away. She should have arrived hours earlier; it's late and stormy, she's not answering her cell phone, and you're worried sick. What else can you do? Worry seems to be the only thing you *can* do.

But wait. There is something else you can do: You can sit quietly in the presence of God, allowing Him to give you what the Bible calls the "peace which surpasses all understanding" (Philippians 4:7). It's a peace so deep and profound that it's unexplainable. In fact, when it sweeps over you, you may feel incredulous ("Wait! I should be worrying!"). Let it come. Let it assure you that whatever the situation may be, it is in God's powerful and protective hands—and so are you.

EYES OF FAITH

O our God, will You not judge them? For we have no power
against this great multitude that is coming against us;
nor do we know what to do, but our eyes are upon You.
—2 CHRONICLES 20:12 NKJV

ADMITTING THAT YOU'RE STUCK AND DON'T know exactly
what to do is a humbling experience. Pride puffs its chest when
you find yourself squirming in a bind. "I can figure this out eventually.
I know I can fix this," you mumble to yourself when struggling to solve
a dilemma. You're hard-wired to be independent and master personal
challenges—to a point. Some things in life you are just not meant to
figure out completely.

Try as you will, you won't succeed at understanding why some
people die young and others suffer long in their older years. You won't
fully comprehend the mysteries of the cosmos or all the intricacies of
human genetics. You weren't designed to be a know-it-all. That honor
belongs to God.

Your job is to open your mind and heart to God's leading and
steady your eyes of faith on Him. It's actually freeing to admit you're
stuck and don't have everything neatly arranged and operating as you
please. Go ahead...try turning from your problems right now and
gazing at God. Even surrender the things you seem to have under
control. Developing a heavenward focus is one thing worth trying out.

February 2

THE FAITH TO CELEBRATE

Elijah said to Ahab, "Go and enjoy a good meal!
For I hear a mighty rainstorm coming!"
—1 KINGS 18:41 TLB

THOUGH THINGS DON'T ALWAYS GO AS planned, we find security in knowing that there are some things we can count on—like the sunrise, for instance. Very few of us go to sleep worrying about whether the sun will come up in the morning.

Even more than the rising of the sun, you can count on God's faithfulness in every day and in any circumstance. That doesn't mean that everything will happen according to your wishes, but it does mean that God can and will work with everything that happens.

The next time you find yourself in a situation where things aren't going your way, accept it as an opportunity to engage with God in exercising true faith. Go to Him in prayer and ask Him for insight and understanding regarding your circumstances, realizing that His will can be accomplished through adversity as well as ease.

As you gain more insight and understanding, you'll move deeper into faith and begin to celebrate the outcome in advance. Those who know God know that He will champion His people. It's just a matter of time. So even if things aren't exactly as you wish, trust the Lord enough to rejoice in what lies ahead.

HIDING PLACES

Yes, he has hidden himself.
—1 SAMUEL 10:22 NIV

ALL OF US HIDE. ALL OF us have said things, done things, and thought things that we don't want others to know about. We would rather forget these things ever happened. Most of us have had things done to us that we don't want to remember. Driven by shame or guilt or fear, we hide. We hide from each other. We hide from ourselves. And we try to hide from God.

But God knows all our hiding places. God alone knows all of our hidden hurts and faults. He knows our most embarrassing moments. He knows all about the things that are so painful to think about that we hide them even from ourselves.

This is why, even long after we have come to faith in Christ, Jesus is still knocking at the doors inside our soul. He's inviting us to come out of hiding and share our deepest secrets with Him.

Why would He do that? Does He delight in exposing our faults? Nothing could be further from the truth! Rather, He is gently showing us that He can be trusted with our darkest secrets. He is inviting us to discover the healing and transforming power of His presence in our places of pain.

THE PATH OF FORGIVENESS

Be gentle and ready to forgive; never hold grudges.
Remember, the Lord forgave you, so you must forgive others.
—COLOSSIANS 3:13 TLB

ONE OF THE HEAVIEST BURDENS PEOPLE carry around with them is an unforgiving heart—and it's a burden that they often don't recognize. They seldom consider the damage they are doing to themselves by their failure to forgive someone who has hurt them. It's been said that refusing to forgive is like drinking poison and waiting for the one who hurt you to die.

When you consider everything for which God has forgiven you, it's not unreasonable for Him to expect you to forgive others, whether or not you feel like it. Forgiveness is an act of your will and not your emotions. Yes, it's rooted in love, but in your love for God and His love for you rather than in your love for others. You may not "feel" love for the person you need to forgive, but you can extend forgiveness when you realize that doing so is an act of obedience to God.

The path of forgiveness is one that takes the high road. It's on that road that you can lay down the heavy burdens you've been carrying around and—perhaps for the first time in a long time—experience the freedom that comes with a truly forgiving heart.

THE ULTIMATE CHAMPION

The LORD says this to you:
"Don't be afraid or discouraged because of this large army.
The battle is not your battle, it is God's."

—2 CHRONICLES 20:15 NCV

MUHAMMAD ALI. SUGAR RAY LEONARD. OSCAR De La Hoya. All professional boxing champs who know how to dodge and pummel their opponents in the ring. But when it comes to fighting it out with the Devil, we can only go undefeated with God's help.

Our sly challenger counterpunches and crosses us with an on-slaught of lies, fears, and criticisms that can instantly buckle us to our knees. Satan smirks when we're knocked out cold early in the fight because we're not prepared.

We don't need to face battles and even obstacles in our life alone. God never intended for us to go head to head with the Enemy. Jesus already did that by dying on the cross, taking Satan to the ropes, and being crowned the ultimate Champion over all the universe.

When we invite God to go before us in our daily skirmishes, He is eager to protect us against the Enemy's tactics. When we are jabbed with insults, God doesn't want us to punch back. When we feel like a failure, He wants us to remember our real worth. Let's choose our battles carefully and let God fight it out with the Devil on our behalf.

February 6

LISTENING FOR THE LORD

*The LORD came and stood there and called
as he had before, "Samuel, Samuel!"
Samuel said, "Speak, LORD.
I am your servant and I am listening."*
—1 SAMUEL 3:10 NCV

NONE OF US LIKES TO WAIT. One of our most difficult spiritual challenges can be to wait for the Lord to give us direction: where to live, what occupation to pursue, whom to marry, and the like. Waiting leaves you in a state of limbo when what you really want to do is get on with the business of living.

Is it possible that the delay in guidance could be because we are asking the wrong questions? Instead of asking, "Whom shall I marry?" or "What career should I choose?" we might try moving the focus of our inquiry off of ourselves and onto God. For instance, we could ask, "Lord, what are You doing now in which I might participate?"

Knowing that God is such a caring Father, you learn that you can entrust your life to Him, confident that He will watch over every detail and concern. It actually frees you to become engaged in what He is up to.

Why not risk it? Why not tell the Lord that you are ready to hear whatever is on His mind, then wait and see where He leads you. It is possible that His aspirations are far more exciting than yours.

THE CURE FOR WORRY

Do not worry about tomorrow.

—MATTHEW 6:34 NKJV

ALL OF US WORRY AT TIMES. It's part of the human condition. But, when we worry, God engages us with three important questions that we need to answer in His presence.

First: "What are you afraid of?" Take your time. Let your fears talk. Share them with God. By sharing your fears with God, you give Him opportunity to deal with them. Discover the reassurance He wants to bring to you. Sometimes this reassurance comes in one miraculous moment. Sometimes it comes bit by bit over time.

Second: "What do you want?" God satisfies our desires with good things. Many times He's just waiting for us to ask. Asking God for something better takes us out of complaint mode and reorients us toward a more hopeful future. Don't be afraid to ask. Remember, it's not the size of your request but the size of your God that matters.

Third: "What is true?" Our circumstances can sometimes blind us to reality. We need to come back to the unshakable certainty of God's promises and His character as revealed in His Word. This frees us up to celebrate the inevitable triumph of God's goodness in our lives.

GREATER TRUST, FEWER FEARS

Be strong, courageous, and firm; fear not nor be in terror before them, for it is the Lord your God Who goes with you; He will not fail you or forsake you.

—DEUTERONOMY 31:6 AMP

D O YOU FULLY REALIZE THAT GOD is always with you and that you can always trust Him? One evidence of your faith in God is the extent to which you've handed over your fears to Him. The more you trust Him, the fewer fears you should have.

Maybe you're still riddled with fear. What can you do about it? How can you learn to trust God more? When it comes to trust, your relationship with God isn't all that different from your relationship with a close friend or spouse. Early on in a friendship, you share information about yourself a little bit at a time. As you learn to trust the other person more, you share deeper thoughts and intimate secrets, knowing your friend will carefully guard them.

One way to develop a greater trust in God and allow Him to allay your fears is to immerse yourself in His Word, particularly those passages that reassure you of His constant presence with you, His protection over you, and His care for you at all times and in every circumstance. The biblical truth about God's concern for you is your greatest and most effective weapon against the fears that plague you.

PERFORMANCE REVIEW

He lived well before GOD, doing the right thing for the most part. But he wasn't wholeheartedly devoted to God.

—2 CHRONICLES 25:2 MSG

PRACTICALLY EVERY DAY YOU ZIP THROUGH performance routines. You like certain things to eat, you prefer a certain shampoo, and you drive certain streets. There's just something about having life ordered to your liking.

As a daily habit, you also strive to do the right things. You try to treat others with kindness and you long to know God on a deeper level. But sometimes in the ebb and flow of living, you can step onto a treadmill of going through the motions—particularly in living well before God.

Without realizing it, your friendship with God can slip into a confined pattern of on-the-go prayers and a speedy look at a Bible verse. Or, you can obey His guidelines, but your heart is ho-hum toward truly resting in His presence. If outwardly you lean toward performing for God while inwardly you fuss a bit, take heart. Even if your passion for the things of God wanes and wobbles now and then, God steadily enjoys you and holds you with an unwavering grip.

So hand God the things that lull you into a robotic spiritual performer and watch with expectancy as the living God recharges your devotion into a vibrant relationship with Him.

WHAT'S WOOING YOUR HEART?

For when Solomon was old, his wives turned his heart away after other gods; and his heart was not wholly devoted to the LORD his God, as the heart of David his father had been.
—1 KINGS 11:4 NASB

A MYRIAD OF DISTRACTIONS SPINS AROUND you every day. Your growing to-do list. Your bodily aches and pains. Your family responsibilities. Your workload. Your home's maintenance. Toss in a dizzying ride on a financial roller coaster or the aftermath of a shipwrecked relationship, and you're whirling in a mess of commotion and emotion.

When life hurls too many disruptions at you, somehow an eager devotion to know God can slip to the back burner. It's tough to set your heart on the things of heaven when the things of earth scream for your attention. King Solomon was considered the world's wisest man, yet even he waned in his passion for his Creator. Sure, he still went through a few outward motions of seeking after the Almighty, but his wives who followed pagan gods distracted him by insisting he follow their empty rituals.

What's wooing your heart these days? Is something standing in the way of your devotion to God? If so, ask God to help you retune your priorities and silence the distractions. He will if you ask Him to. It won't be an instant fix, and it won't be easy, but you will get there if you set your heart on it.

February 11

STANDING ALONE

Keep alert, stand firm in your faith, be courageous,
be strong. Let all that you do be done in love.
—1 CORINTHIANS 16:13-14 NRSV

WHAT IS IT LIKE TO STAND alone? How can one person stand against a tsunami of evil? From Joan of Arc to Martin Luther King Jr., history is full of ordinary people who changed their world.

In fact, many great people needed to be shown how ordinary they were before they were allowed to accomplish anything great. Often these people worked alone for many years before anyone joined them. Moses, for example, worked as a shepherd for forty years before he freed his people from slavery.

What gave these people the courage and the audacity to stand alone? Were they born leaders? Did they have some special DNA that gave them superpowers? The real difference is that they knew their God. They trusted Him. They knew they could depend on Him.

As you spend time alone with God and grow to know Him better, you will become aware of what He is asking you to do. He will help you identify your voice of encouragement, of confrontation, of healing. He will show you where you can make a difference. It may be your solitary voice that will transform a family, a culture, a nation. You may be poised to change history.

February 12

HUMILITY: A SIGN OF STRENGTH

*Always be humble and gentle. Be patient with each other,
making allowance for each other's faults because of
your love.*

—EPHESIANS 4:2 NLT

THERE IS A MISCONCEPTION THAT HUMILITY is a sign of weakness. In fact, humility is a sign of great strength, the strength of character that enables a person to step aside and allow the limelight to fall on someone else. It's characteristic of the kind of person who routinely says, "You first."

Although the Bible tells us that God rewards the humble, a truly humble person would never seek a reward. Genuine humility isn't the kind of trait people pursue because of its perks; rather, it reveals what's already in a person's heart—the gratitude, joy, love, and compassion that are cultivated in time spent with God. Those qualities can't be manufactured. It takes time to ferret out the subtle forms of pride that may be hidden from one's own view but are all too apparent to other people. When you ask God's Spirit to expose areas of pride in your life, you can shorten that time considerably.

True humility doesn't come easily, especially in a culture that devalues it. Humility requires ignoring society's perspective and submitting yourself—and every aspect of your life—to God, who can be trusted with everything you give Him.

BEHIND THE SCENES

The Lord stood with me and strengthened me.

—2 TIMOTHY 4:17 NASB

ONE QUICK GLANCE AROUND YOUR HOME and you'll no doubt see treasured photos of loved ones. There are posed portraits of everyone dressed up, adorable snapshots of the kids, silly close-ups with your best friends.

Photos of those most dear to us remind us of the preciousness of life and the camaraderie of kindred spirits. The people whose photos you display are typically the individuals you count on. When you need advice, they point you to solutions. When you need a little tenderness, they offer a warm embrace. How encouraging it is to ponder the blessings of people who support you through thick and thin.

But have you given much thought lately to God standing with you and strengthening you? If you were to look more intently at your treasured photos, would you see Him in the smiling faces? Or even see Jesus laughing as He pokes His head between you and your friends? This week as you notice your framed photos, why not pause a few seconds and think not just about the people you see, but about the One who has been by your side from the beginning. He is the one faithfully standing with you and undergirding you—even if it's often behind the scenes.

THE LOVE LAVISHED ON YOU

The amazing grace of the Master, Jesus Christ,
the extravagant love of God, the intimate friendship
of the Holy Spirit, be with all of you.
—2 CORINTHIANS 13:14 MSG

HAVE YOU EVER SPENT TIME JUST thinking about the love God has lavished on you? It can be utterly overwhelming to meditate on the love of God, especially when you realize just how undeserved His love is. In the presence of His love, you confront the feebleness of your love for Him.

But God wants you to meditate on His love, particularly when you feel least deserving of it, because He wants you to understand—to the extent that anyone on earth can—how deep and profound His love is. He knows that flawed humans have a flawed grasp of genuine love, but by sitting quietly in His presence and reflecting on nothing but His awesome love for you, you can catch a glimpse of the great and magnificent love that He will pour out on you throughout eternity.

Accept God's generous love for you without hesitation and without question. He knows you're undeserving of that love, and He knows you can't possibly return an equal measure of love to Him. But that's what His grace is all about. He *chooses* to lavish an abundance of undeserved, unrequited love on every one of His people, including you.

THE BATTLE IS THE LORD'S

*Everyone assembled here will know that the LORD
rescues his people, but not with sword and spear.
This is the LORD's battle.*

—1 SAMUEL 17:47 NLT

THERE IS AN UNDERCURRENT OF ANXIETY these days related to the constant threat of a nuclear holocaust, particularly with the increasing conflict in the Middle East and the spread of terrorism. This generation has had to learn to cope with the power derived from the science of splitting atoms, the advancement in technology that makes it such a threat to the human race, and the evil that perpetrates violent schemes.

The good news is that the ultimate power to create or destroy life does not rest with mankind. Man did not originate his own existence, nor does man have the authority to annihilate the race. The breath of God—which first filled the nostrils of Adam—has been passed through generation after generation, only once having hung by the bare thread of possible extinction as decreed by God Himself (Genesis 7).

There is one critical contingency that determines how you will deal with this constant threat of disaster: faith in God. It is faith in God's omniscient power, learned in times alone with Him, that will keep your heart still in the tumultuous days we live in. Knowing Him intimately, knowing that the battles are His, is your safe haven in the storm.

February 16

WHAT CAN GOD DO?

*Nothing can hinder the L*ORD *from saving
by many or by few.*
—1 SAMUEL 14:6 ESV

HOW DO WE GET THE RIGHT perspective on our circumstances? The Bible is full of stories of people whose backs were up against the wall. They faced certain death, slavery, oppression, and every kind of trouble. Often they had nothing—no weapons to fight an overwhelming enemy, no food to feed their families, no cure for their diseases, no money to pay their taxes, no hope that life could ever again be right. In their darkest moments, they discovered a God whose love and power went far beyond their wildest expectations.

Spend time immersed in these stories. During your time with God, soak up these inspiring passages, and the faith of these men and women of God will begin to enter your soul. This faith strengthens you to face all circumstances: the bills you can't pay, the people you can't change, the addictions you can't tame, the diseases you can't cure, the grief that won't go away. The floodgates are opened, the life-giving water quenches the thirst in your heart, restoring the hope that was lost.

What can God do? Every life is meant to be an answer to that question. Your problems are not permanent. God's provision is. You will experience His deliverance.

ACCESSING THE WISDOM OF GOD

*Look carefully then how you walk! Live purposefully
and worthily and accurately, not as the unwise and witless,
but as wise (sensible, intelligent people).*

—EPHESIANS 5:15 AMP

REMEMBER THE COUNTRY SONG TITLED "LOOKIN' for Love"?
Substitute the word "wisdom" for "love," and you have a pretty
accurate description of what the world is doing now and has been
doing for millennia. It's lookin' for wisdom in all the wrong places.

The wisdom of the ages can be summed up in one book: the Bible.
Any time you need to make a significant decision, the answer is available to you in the pages of that one book. That doesn't mean, of course,
that the exact answer will be there; it won't tell you if you should go
to Dartmouth or Yale, or whether you should relocate to Miami or
Houston. But it will give you the principles you need to consider
whenever you're about to make an important decision—and it will
warn you when you're about to veer off course.

In some ways, it's amazing that people don't consult the wisdom
of God more often. But you can be among those who know where to
look for answers when life gets complicated and problems don't have
clear-cut answers.

God loves you and He wants you to reap the benefits of
making good choices for your life. That's why He gave you a book
filled with wisdom.

RUN FOR THE HILLS

Be strong and courageous. Don't be frightened or terrified....
Someone greater is on our side.

—2 CHRONICLES 32:7 GWT

FEAR CAN CLAW AT OUR MINDS and hearts and squeeze the joy out of life. If we stop to think about it, most of us fear dozens of things every single day. We fear being late for work, we fear being involved in a car accident, we fear the disapproval of others. Some of us dread dental appointments, financial slowdowns, and aging. Fear is cloaked in big and small packages that unexpectedly and frequently arrive on our doorstep.

Yet our fear, worry, and apprehension are no surprise to God. Although He doesn't experience trepidation at anything, He understands us when we balk at challenges or panic when pained. Countless times throughout His Word, God confidently reassures us that we can gain courage and "fear not." Yet He doesn't just command our bravery, He nudges us to let go of our anxiety and apprehensions by shifting our thinking.

How do we practically deal with those never-ending fears? By remembering throughout the day that we are not alone because God—who is infinitely greater than any intimidating person or any daunting situation—is right beside us. When reminded that God is constantly on our side, we can stand up to our fears and watch our worry take a run for the hills.

THE BUNDLE OF LIFE

*Should anyone rise up to pursue you and to seek your life,
then the life of my lord shall be bound in the bundle of the
living with the LORD your God.*

—1 SAMUEL 25:29 NASB

THERE IS SOMETHING CURIOUSLY CONTAGIOUS ABOUT life in community. People thrive in the mainstream of communication, service to others, shared pain, and blended joy. In fact, the very meaning of being human requires that you have others with whom you can interact humanely.

The ability to thrive in community begins with God. Being in relationship with God orients you to understand your place among others—your purpose among the living. You discover your values by spending time with God in the counsel of His Word, and you discover your worth in worship. The truth is we can't really know who we are with others until we have discovered who we are with God.

So who are you in God's eyes? You are His child—His precious child. Because you are human, He cherishes you above all other created things. You have His imprint on you, which means that in the very core of your existence, you are remarkably like Him—loving, nurturing, creative, adventuresome, truthful, respectful, generous, kind, patient, and unselfish. Spending time with God breathes fresh life into those God-like characteristics, reviving the resemblance between the Father and the child.

Recognizing the child of God in everyone, you realize that your community is really just family.

NOW I KNOW

He who comes to God must believe that He is,
and that He is a rewarder of those who diligently seek Him.
—HEBREWS 11:6 NKJV

WHAT IS THE DIFFERENCE BETWEEN THOSE who know the truth and those who don't? They look alike. They talk alike. They sit side by side in the same church, eat at the same table, sleep in the same house. But some know and some don't.

Why is it that the most beautiful songs come not from professionals with trained voices, but from the raspy throats of old men and women of God who have suffered for their faith? How is it that two people can say the same phrases, but one will be ignored while the other will transfix us with his words?

The secret is found in the storms of life. In our defining moments, what we really believe is laid on the table. Do we believe that God has abandoned us, that He doesn't care, that He is focused on our failures?

All of us carry around lies like these deep inside. But the difference between those who know the truth and those who don't is this: Those who know turn to God in their darkest moments. There they discover: "God really does care. He is here, and He is rebuilding my life into something beautiful."

February 21

THANK GOD—FOR EVERYTHING

At all times and for everything giving thanks in the name
of our Lord Jesus Christ to God the Father.
—Ephesians 5:20 amp

IT'S BEEN SAID THAT GRATITUDE IS our most direct line to God. At least in one sense, that's certainly true. Pouring out your gratitude to God will often bring you immediately into His presence; in fact, whenever you feel that there's some distance between you and God, begin thanking Him—genuinely, from your heart—and see how quickly that gap disappears.

But what about those times when your life isn't running so smoothly? How can you honestly express your gratitude to God when you can't find much to be thankful for? You could start by thanking Him for being there during the rough patches, for welcoming you into His presence so you can unload your burdens on Him, for the good that will ultimately come from life's difficulties. Once you start thanking Him in that way, you're likely to find even more reasons to be grateful.

When you cultivate a grateful attitude during the good times, thanking God during the not-so-good times will come much more easily. Many people have found it helpful to keep a gratitude journal, a place where they keep a running account of everything they have to be thankful for. During hard times, your list of blessings can become your prayer of thanksgiving.

GIVING A SHOUT OUT

As Pharaoh approached, the Israelites looked up,
and there were the Egyptians, marching after them.
They were terrified and cried out to the LORD.
—EXODUS 14:10 NIV

INDIANA JONES, THAT INTREPID ADVENTURER IN the 1980s blockbuster *Raiders of the Lost Ark*, sneers as he's forced to turn over his hard-won treasure, the golden idol head, to his arch nemesis…then runs for his life! With tribesmen pursuing and poisoned darts whistling around him, Indiana hollers to his pilot to start their plane. Just when he's about to be overcome, Indiana scrambles aboard and is victoriously whisked away.

After all, there is a time to be independent and a time to yell for help.

Independence is a hard habit to break. It's deeply rooted in our beings. It makes us stand on our feet as toddlers and fight our battles as adults. But it can also be a weakness. It can blind us and keep us cocooned in our pride.

As His child, you're connected to God, the Almighty, who can do anything and who loves you just as you are. You have someone to turn to for help in your crisis times and even in your everyday routines—and He will never criticize you when you ask for help. You don't have to go it alone anymore.

When you find yourself in a crisis, cry out to God. He's there, waiting to help.

February 23

WISDOM AND REVELATION

*I keep asking that the God of our Lord Jesus Christ,
the glorious Father, may give you the Spirit of wisdom
and revelation, so that you may know him better.*

—**EPHESIANS 1:17** NIV

YOU CAN KNOW A LOT ABOUT your next-door neighbor without ever really knowing your neighbor at all. Similarly, we may assume that knowing God is merely a matter of knowing about Him.

An encounter with God cannot be reduced to the facts and historical data that fill the pages of books—even if that book is the Bible. The revelation of God is a relational encounter that occurs when you engage both your heart and mind in time spent with Him. He desires to capture your attention and your affections as you discover who He is in relation to mankind. He longs to reach your intellect and your emotions as He speaks to you through various interactions with people just like you in the Scriptures.

There are two questions to ask yourself as you read the Bible that will facilitate this encounter. The first is specific to what God is revealing in the Scriptures: *What is He really saying?* Revelation comes by understanding His message in its correct context.

The second question is concerned with your relationship with God: *Why is He saying this to me?* Having determined the message within its context, you are ready to take His message personally. Both are essential to really knowing God.

February 24

CONVERSATION STARTERS

The angel of the LORD found her.
—GENESIS 16:7 NASB

WHAT IS GOING ON IN YOUR life right now? What's most important to you? What do you care about? What do you want? What are your secret desires? What are your hidden dreams? What are you afraid of? What are you angry about? What are you most excited about? What are you thinking about? What messages are playing in your head?

God knows where you live. When God meets with you, He meets you where you are. He's interested in what you are interested in. He cares about what you care about. All of these things are conversation starters with God. Even when we desire something we know He doesn't want us to have, it opens up a door to conversation with Him. "This is what I want. I know You don't want me to want this, but I'm not sure how to stop wanting it. Can You help me?"

Pleasing God doesn't mean choosing a set of religious activities. Instead, it comes down to inviting Him into life as you really live it. Sunday morning is important to God. But so is Monday morning or Friday night or Thursday afternoon. God is inviting you into a 24/7 relationship with Him.

SURPRISED BY GOD

Look among the nations! Observe! Be astonished!
Wonder! Because I am doing something in your days—
You would not believe if you were told.
—**HABAKKUK 1:5** NASB

ARE YOU LOOKING TO ADD A little spice to your life—a bit more adventure than you're experiencing now? Not sure exactly what you want to do or even how to go about discovering what you want to do? There's good news! You can rest assured that your life with God can be one wild ride if you turn the reins over to Him.

God doesn't want His people to live a life that falls short of the one He has for them. People often assume that because they're "settled"—married, kids, steady job, mortgage—they have to settle for a less-than-exciting life. But when God is in control, when you reach the point where you want His best for you no matter what, you may be stunned by what He has in store for you—things you never thought were possible in your current situation.

A satisfying, full, rich life is yours for the taking, as long as you are willing to become completely abandoned to God and the life He wants you to experience. Following Him will put you on a path that's custom-designed for you—one that will offer you a better future than you could ever imagine for yourself.

PASSIONATE PURSUIT

*[My determined purpose is] that I may know him
[that I may progressively become more deeply
and intimately acquainted with him].*
—**PHILIPPIANS 3:10 AMP**

DATING: THAT MAGICAL DANCE WHERE TWO people have eyes only for each other, inviting each other into their hearts, minds, and emotions. Ahh, the passion of attraction. It absorbs us completely.

Jesus once said the most important thing you can ever do with your heart, your energy, and your mind is to love the Lord your God with all your being, above all else. That means you love God more than you love shopping, work, your kids, your spouse, your entertainment. Everything.

But how do we love the unseen God like that? How about pursuing a relationship with God as a great romance? Think about Him. Ponder what kind of love drives an all-powerful being to surrender to a cruel death…for you. Look forward to being in His presence, sharing your life with Him. Set aside priority time like you would for a date—and refuse to let anything get in the way of meeting with Him. Use your energy to discover what God loves and hates, what makes Him smile or cry. Regard Him as the passionate pursuit of a lifetime.

GLASSES OR NO GLASSES

May you have the power to understand, as all God's people should, how wide, how long, how high, and how deep his love is.

—Ephesians 3:18 nlt

HAVING JUST WATCHED A 3-D SCIENCE-FICTION thriller, the young woman struck up a conversation with her friend as they exited the theater.

"How disappointing it would have been had we seen the movie in just two dimensions!" she exclaimed.

"Yeah, I'm glad we put on the glasses," he agreed.

"Without the glasses, we would have missed that thrilling sensation that we were actually living the drama."

The love of Jesus is like that. More than simply a truth that you may observe and acknowledge, His love reaches into your very being, grips you with its intensity, embraces you in its diversity, pulls you into its depths, and lifts you to its loftiest peaks.

It takes courage to "put on the glasses" with Jesus: to enter into the drama where His love is experienced in its fullest dimension. Be sure to prepare yourself—it will stretch you, mold you, bend you, and compel you to become more than you ever dreamed of being. More real, more motivated, more in touch with the needs of others, more giving, more caring, more diligent, and more human than those who don't risk getting involved.

Glasses or no glasses…which will you choose?

February 28

THE UNEXPECTED

A Man wrestled with him.
—GENESIS 32:24 AMP

TWO BROTHERS, AGES EIGHT AND ELEVEN, were fighting one day. There were angry words and tears and more angry words. Both came to their dad expecting him to punish the other for his transgressions. *Surely*, each thought, *if Dad knew the real story, he would see how my brother was in the wrong.*

But this time the dad didn't listen to their elaborate explanations of why each was right and the other was wrong. Instead, he wrestled with them. Then he plopped them both down on the couch and sat down between them. Opening a book on navy aircraft, he started paging through it with them. At first they were pretty glum, but after a while they got lost with their dad in the world of Harriers and Tomcats. After twenty minutes, the dad asked them, "If I let you two go, can you find a way to be nice to each other?" The younger stood up and hugged the older. The older hugged the younger. Then they stepped back into their world as friends.

The point? We meet with God. But He doesn't always do what we expect. Each person is different. Each situation is new. And God is forever creative.

ACTIVATE YOUR FAITH

*The fundamental fact of existence is that this trust in God,
this faith, is the firm foundation under everything that makes
life worth living. It's our handle on what we can't see.*
—HEBREWS 11:1 MSG

TO SOME PEOPLE, THE WORD "FAITH" means little more than adherence to a particular set of truths. They may describe themselves as being of the Christian faith, the Jewish faith, or the like. But genuine faith is much more than ascribing to certain beliefs. It's abiding in the understanding that there's more to life than we can see—and trusting God with all that is unseeable.

Faith in God should also be a dynamic, active force in your life. It's one thing to rest in the knowledge that God is trustworthy, but that knowledge, that trust, becomes enlivened when you activate your faith. And you do that by living as if the things God has said and promised are *true*. That may seem like a tall order, but as God makes good on His word time and time again, your faith can't help but be strengthened, and living as if His words are true may soon become second nature to you.

When the things you *can* see begin to look bleak—when money is tight, your health begins to fail, your friends have gone AWOL—remember, there's an unseen reality all around you. And God is working on your behalf within that reality.

March 2

SUPERHEROES NEED NOT APPLY

You're going to wear yourself out—and the people, too. This job is too heavy a burden for you to handle all by yourself.
—**EXODUS 18:18 NLT**

THE LONE WOLF. YOU KNOW, THE type who goes out into the world with the attitude, *I can handle it myself. I don't need anyone else.* We see stalwart individuals everywhere, from roles in great action movies to the actions of corporate CEOs. But to God's way of thinking, this independent mindset is all backward. Nobody wants to burn out. God doesn't want people to burn out either.

That's why He recruits us to be team players. He wants us to share the load with each other. No grandstanding. No more superheroes. No more excluding other people and going it alone.

When everybody does a little, no one gets burned out. Everything is easier with a team. Think of television's celebrity interior designers who would flop without their electricians, carpenters, and assistants behind the scenes. Or imagine a professional sports team that only relied on one star player instead of a full cadre of multi-talented teammates.

The lifework God created you to do will require other people to complete the job. Jesus had the disciples. The president has his advisors. Who has God put around you to help you? Who are you around that God wants you to help?

LIFE AFTER GRIEF

How long will you mourn?
—1 Samuel 16:1 NIV

THERE IS A TIME TO MOURN and a time to move on. Sometimes we can get confused about that. Sometimes we run away from our feelings, deny the pain that's inside, and pretend that all is fine when it isn't. This, of course, isn't healthy. Jesus wept. He is called a man of sorrows and acquainted with grief. Sharing our sorrows with God and with others is an important part of life.

But sometimes we get stuck in our grief. We lose our moorings in a sea of sorrow. We've experienced a loss. Our dreams failed. Our hopes died. The one we love is no longer with us. Depending on the size of our loss, our grief may appropriately extend for days, weeks, months, or beyond. But there always comes a point when God is ready for us to move on. It's a new day, and God has more life for us to experience.

How do we get there? Bring our sorrows to Jesus and ask Him to carry them. Is there anything preventing you from doing that? If there is, bring that to Jesus as well. He will help you. There is life after grief, waiting for you in God's presence.

March 4

YOUR THOUGHTS OR GOD'S?

Trust in the LORD with all your heart and do not lean on your own understanding. In all your ways acknowledge Him, and He will make your paths straight.

—**PROVERBS 3:5-6** NASB

TRUSTING IN GOD DOESN'T SEEM LIKE such a difficult task—until you encounter a problem in which your own solution appears to make more sense or will solve the problem more quickly. In those situations, it's especially important to remember that God sees the whole picture, including the future. By contrast, you are able to see only a minute fragment of the picture.

Let's say your car is giving you fits. You've spent enough money on repairs already, and you just want to trade it in for a newer one. But every time you pray about it, God tells you to wait. That doesn't make sense; you can afford a better car. Why not get one and eliminate the hassle? But you acknowledge that little prod inside and wait. Two weeks later, you are laid off from work. You didn't see that one coming, but God did. He knew those car payments would soon become a burden to you.

Your perspective on a particular situation can seem so right and so logical, but it will always be limited. God's perspective, however, is infinite—and the trade-in value of your finite understanding for His eternal understanding is immeasurable. It's always a trade-up.

THE LITTLE THINGS DO MATTER

*If you are faithful in little things,
you will be faithful in large ones.*
—LUKE 16:10 NLT

SOME SAY IT'S THE LITTLE THINGS in life that matter most. The way you let another driver merge in front of you, the words of appreciation you share with someone, the sips of pretend tea from a child's plastic tea set. Little things on earth magnify into big things in heaven.

God doesn't miss the minute gestures you do for others, which actually you are doing for Him. The beloved Mother Teresa often spoke of doing a small bit for others as a reflection of serving Jesus. A smile. A hug. A shared tear. All these seemingly modest and minor actions carry eternal significance.

This is why when you reserve time to sit alone with God and read your Bible, it matters. When you talk to Him throughout your busy days and thank Him "just because," it matters. Every time you turn your thoughts toward inviting God into your minutes and hours, it matters.

In a world obsessed with gaining attention and admiring more visible possessions and more vocal people, it is wise at times to pursue the opposite. Instead of bigger, stronger, faster, higher, why not aspire to the little, often unseen gestures of love? Even if others do not notice, God certainly will.

CONSOLED TO CONSOLE

All praise to the God...of all healing counsel!
He comes alongside us when we go through hard times,
and...he brings us alongside someone else.
—2 CORINTHIANS 1:3-4 MSG

"I T TAKES ONE TO KNOW ONE." The old adage we associate with the identification of character holds true for empathy in suffering as well. You can't understand the grief of a widow until you've suffered the loss of a spouse. You can't grasp the pain of being terminated from your job until you've been fired. You really won't be able to empathize with the fear and dread of terminal cancer unless you are diagnosed with it.

But when you have suffered—really suffered—you gain the capacity to be a true source of understanding to those who are currently suffering. You are now equipped to become one of God's greatest resources for those who are in distress, sharing the comfort and consolation you have received from your times alone with Him.

Anyone can be empathetic toward people who are hurting, but not just anyone can actually walk with another person through the pain. Take notice of people in distress and ask God whether you are the one through whom He might bring consolation. If you are willing to be His partner, God can use you to make the world a little less painful for those whose lives you touch.

THE ADVENTURE OF PRAYER

Pray in the Spirit at all times and on every occasion.
Stay alert and be persistent in your prayers for all
believers everywhere.

—**EPHESIANS 6:18** NLT

MATURING IN YOUR RELATIONSHIP WITH GOD—sure of your destiny in Christ—you will find yourself more interested in what He is doing in the lives of others than you were before. Now the real adventure begins.

You'll discover that the Spirit of the Lord is capable of connecting you—in prayer—to places you could not go otherwise. God's Spirit may have you praying for people all the way across the world who are in difficult and dangerous circumstances. He can move you into the private pain of those who are suffering, as well as to the joyous heights of those who have overcome great trials. Through prayer, the Spirit of God can take you to the impoverished Third World where you may powerfully intercede on behalf of those who are hungry and malnourished. He can even usher you into the most secured quarters of the highest officials of any nation anywhere on the globe, with the authority to pray for them to pursue peace on earth.

Perhaps most amazing, the Spirit has the authority to give you a glimpse of the deep heavens—right up to the throne of God—where you enter into a powerful conversation concerning the mission God is bringing to completion: the salvation of the world.

WISDOM IN THE INFORMATION AGE

Wisdom is the most important thing; so get wisdom.
If it costs everything you have, get understanding.
—**PROVERBS 4:7** NCV

THINK FOR A MOMENT ABOUT ALL the ways you take in pieces of information throughout the day. You may acquire information through traditional media like TV, radio, and newspapers, through your interactions with others, through documents and reports at work, through the Internet or podcasts on your MP3 player, and in many other ways. In fact, you often hear people passing along bits of information that they say they "picked up somewhere," as if those bits were infection-spreading bacteria.

While some of that information may prove to be meaningful, much of it is useful only if you examine it through the lens of God's wisdom. For example, when you apply God's wisdom to seemingly disconnected news items from around the world, you may gain a deeper understanding of His global activity and how He wants you to participate in it through prayer, giving, or even mission work.

The random knowledge you acquire in an information-saturated society can become meaningful and even profound when you sit in the wisdom-saturated presence of God. The more time you spend with Him—not even thinking about all that knowledge you've accumulated—the better prepared you'll be to apply His wisdom to whatever you encounter throughout the day.

LIGHTEN UP

*Let us lay aside every weight, and the sin which so easily
ensnares us, and let us run with endurance
the race that is set before us.*
—HEBREWS 12:1 NKJV

WE CRAM WAY TOO MANY "ESSENTIALS" into our purses, computer bags, and backpacks. An on-the-street survey of handbags and the women who love them reveals that the average purse stash includes lipstick, wallet, checkbook, cell phone, gum, mints, hair accessories, sunglasses, and nail file—just for starters. Some women add in a calendar book, candy, diapers, eating utensils, mini flashlight, a change of clothes for the kids…you get the picture. Many of our handbags can moonlight as carry-ons, if not full-sized luggage.

Medical professionals warn us that lugging around hefty totes can cause long-term damage to our bodies, stressing nerves that can lead to permanent arm numbness. God warns us of a similar damage to our spiritual life when we schlep around wrong attitudes that encumber our hearts and numb our spirits.

What excess baggage are you dragging around these days? A growing grudge? A shaky self-image? A habit or two that you try to conceal from God and others? Perhaps it's time to lighten your load and place your weighty matters at the feet of Jesus. He wants to carry anything that prevents you from freely running the race called life.

March 10

THE GIFT OF CONSCIENCE

*The kind of sorrow God wants makes people change their
hearts and lives. This leads to salvation,
and you cannot be sorry for that.*
—2 CORINTHIANS 7:10 NCV

DID YOU EVER "GET CAUGHT WITH your hand in the cookie jar" when you were a child? The sorrow you experienced in your youth probably had more to do with the consequences of getting caught than with genuine regret over your disobedience. As you grew into adulthood, your conscience should have grown with you.

Conscience is one of the most amazing gifts that God gave man in creation. No other created being has one. He gave it to you as the principal catalyst through which you would become truly human. Your conscience not only sensitizes you to what is right as opposed to what is wrong, but serves as the guide to fulfilling your role as the image-bearer of God on the earth.

In an authentic relationship with God, your conscience is regenerated and refined. God teaches you through the counsel of His Word how to think about life, how to discern good and evil within your own motives, how to feel about people, what to value in this world, and how to apply all of these things to your life. Spending time with God in worship further develops your conscience as you discover that your heart is being conformed to His.

NEVER BORING

He has given me a new song to sing.

—PSALM 40:3 NLT

A FAVORITE LIE OF THE ENEMY is this: Life with God is boring. Don't you believe it! Every day with God is brand new. While God never changes, His methods do. He is wonderfully creative. Don't expect God to do the same thing twice. Sometimes people get stuck in ruts and fail to experience the full adventure of faith because of their fear of change. But God has no such fear. He is constantly looking for partners who will—with Him—pioneer new endeavors, break open new ground, try something a different way.

Any good educator or coach understands this. Consider a fitness trainer, for example. Helping people get in shape could be a boring, repetitive job. But a good personal trainer knows how to vary the exercises, come up with new routines, add a touch of creativity, and make training fun. God is the same way. He likes to have fun with His kids.

How do you experience this? Begin by letting God out of the box you may be keeping Him in. Come to Him and say, "I invite You into my life as You really are—even if it's wildly beyond all that I can imagine."

March 12

LIGHT FOR YOUR LIFE

Your word is a lamp to my feet and a light for my path.
—PSALM 119:105 NIV

POWER OUTAGES CAN HAPPEN ANY TIME, any place, and for a variety of reasons: storms, system overloads, traffic accidents, mistakenly cut power lines. They can cause inconvenience, misery, and even dangerous circumstances during the day, but at night, the ramifications of a power loss are intensified. Even though you think you know your way around your house, it is rare for people not to bump into something even in the most familiar surroundings while trying to find their way when it's pitch black.

God knows how risky it is for us to stumble around in darkness in a metaphorical sense as well, and He provided His Word, the Bible, to provide the light we need when darkness seems to surround us. That metaphor applies to every area of life and every level of difficulty. You don't have to be immersed in a gloomy situation to benefit from reading the Bible; whatever light you have on the problem areas of your life, God's Word will make it shine brighter.

When you spend time with God, ask Him to show you Bible passages that will shed light on the challenges you're facing—and expect those passages to help you find your way through the darkness.

March 13

YOUR ALLEGIANCE

If we are thrown into the blazing furnace,
the God we serve is able to save us from it,
and he will rescue us from your hand, O king.
—**DANIEL 3:17** NIV

MOST OF US HAVE READ ALOUD bylaws of a group we associate with or we've recited a pledge respecting our country. Even if we don't voice an oath very often, we still avow our loyalty to something or someone every day.

You may be surprised by the activities and priorities that captivate your allegiance. Maybe it's the way you look or your success at work. Or perhaps you're devoted to a certain parenting style or volunteering through your church.

These things can be benign in themselves, but what if you hold them a little too tightly, giving them the place in your life that belongs only to God? What if you unwittingly serve programs and people more than your Provider? What if you're subtly worshiping power and prestige instead of God?

At the risk of being thrown into a den of lions, Daniel from ancient Babylon held fast to his faith loyalties. He refused to bow down to an egotistical king and his golden idol. Even though the spiritual opposition you face today may not feel as obvious, it is just as deadly to your faith. Start fresh today with pledging your allegiance to your Creator. He loves to hear your voice and see your heart.

GOD'S STRENGTH FOR YOUR WEAKNESS

"My grace is…all you need. My strength comes into its own in your weakness." Once I heard that…I quit focusing on the handicap and began appreciating the gift.
—2 CORINTHIANS 12:9 MSG

WHAT DO YOU CONSIDER YOUR GREATEST strength? How does this strength of character correspond to your most obvious weakness? Typically, your most glaring insufficiency bears a direct and inverse relationship to your greatest strength. For instance, someone who has an uncommon sensitivity to justice will sometimes come up short on mercy, even lean toward being legalistic. On the other hand, someone with deep compassion might lack discernment about how compassion can turn into an unhealthy form of coddling.

The good news is that God's strength supplies what you are lacking. The key to accessing His strength is consistent prayer. Your relationship with God must be kept in good repair in order to fall back on His strength when yours fails.

How does it work? It happens as you learn what it means to rely upon God in your daily walk. That is simply another way of saying that you carry His principles for living into your life—into the work place, into your home life, and into your relationships. It works when you stay in conversation with God throughout the day, so that when you need to call upon His counsel in your weakness, you may.

God's sufficiency will complete whatever is insufficient in you.

WINNING

There is no wisdom, no insight,
no plan that can succeed against the LORD.
—**PROVERBS 21:30** NIV

ON OCTOBER 17, 1956, THIRTEEN-YEAR-OLD BOBBY Fischer startled the chess-playing world by sacrificing his most powerful playing piece in a game against twenty-six-year-old grandmaster Donald Byrne. Even though Byrne was considered one of the strongest players in the United States, Fischer went on to win in what has been called the "Game of the Century." For more than fifty years, chess analysts have studied this game, concluding that from the moment Fischer sacrificed his queen, there was no way his opponent could win.

The crowd gasped when Fischer gave up his most powerful piece. But they were soon cheering when he announced, "Checkmate." In the same way, sometimes God's actions make no sense to us until later. The disciples had no room in their minds for the reality that Jesus would be crucified. Only later, after He rose from the dead, did they understand that God was engaged in a battle He could not and would not lose.

What's happening in your life? Does it look like the Enemy is winning? Does it look like God has made a mistake? Give Him a chance. He has the pieces exactly where He needs them. With Him, you cannot lose.

SEEING IN THE NIGHT

My eyes anticipate the night watches,
that I may meditate on Your word.
—PSALM 119:148 NASB

IN A 24/7 WORLD, NIGHTTIME DOESN'T always offer the break from the day's routine the way it did in the past. With the arrival of electric lights, people began the process of tricking their minds into thinking that there was little distinction between night and day; that process intensified with the advent of around-the-clock factories and, later, twenty-four-hour television and stores. It has become more difficult to settle in for the night along with the setting of the sun.

Nighttime, though, is a precious gift from God, an opportunity to quiet down, slow down, and settle down so your body, mind, and spirit can recharge before the following day. It also provides an opportunity to spend precious time with God. Whatever you've stored up through-out the day—all the concerns, frustrations, joys, questions—you can talk over with God before you fall into a peaceful and restful sleep, knowing that you've placed everything in His loving care.

Recognizing nighttime for the gift it is can also help allay your fears. Even for adults who no longer believe in imaginary monsters, fears return as night falls. Meditating on God and His attributes, especially His role as your protector, can help dispel those fears.

GETTING OUT OF A PICKLE

Your God, to whom you are so loyal,
is going to get you out of this.
—DANIEL 6:16 MSG

THE BELOVED MOVIE AND TELEVISION CHARACTERS The Three Stooges and Lucy Ricardo have a lot in common. They all found themselves in one zany jam after another.

Some of us are just as prone to end up in a pickle. We innocently go about our business and the next thing we know, we are in over our heads and have some *'splainin'* to do. But unlike Lucy and Ethel or Larry, Moe, and Curly, we can turn to God to get us out of our rough spots.

In fact, we're much better off involving Him in our everyday choices and plans long before we're stuck. God is far more than just a button to push in an emergency—He's your friend, your Counselor, your Shepherd, your King. He waits for you with the longing of a loving parent, eager to hear about your day and ready to steer you clear of pitfalls. Keep your communication with Him open and spontaneous throughout each day. And next time you're in a pickle, you'll quickly know to turn to God and let Him direct your steps. His wisdom will become part of your thinking, creating straight paths for your feet.

A HEART PREPARED FOR WORSHIP

Praise the LORD! Let all that I am praise the LORD.
I will praise the LORD as long as I live.
I will sing praises to my God with my dying breath.
—PSALM 146:1-2 NLT

WHEN LOOKING FOR WAYS TO DEEPEN your devotions in your time alone with God, you might want to begin with worship. Worship quickens the spirit, awakening all of your senses to God. It realigns your heart in relation to the Lord and prepares your mind to receive Him, focusing all of your energies on Him.

One of the best ways to worship alone with God is through the Psalter. The Psalms of the Bible are unique among Scripture because they are inspired expressions of the heart offered up to God in poetic verse. By allowing one of the psalms to lift your heart to the Lord, you can actually sing your way into worship with your spirit instead of with music. And the song itself strokes the heartstrings of God.

Bringing a psalm into your prayer time will enrich your conversation with God, as well. It tunes your heart to God's frequency and sets your mind aright in a context of genuine devotion. Some find inspiration in reciting the verses out loud before the Lord, while others prefer their silence unbroken. You might experiment with the Psalms—getting creative with your expression of praise—and find great joy in discovering a delightful way to bless the heart of God.

GUIDANCE IN THE FOG

A person's steps are directed by the LORD,
and the LORD delights in his way.

—PSALM 37:23 GWT

L IVING OUT GOD'S GOOD PLAN FOR our lives is a process, not a download. Most of us who want to follow God would love to have a sit-down meeting with Him where we could learn exactly what His plan is for us and how to move forward with it. But it doesn't work that way. God doesn't lead us by removing all the fog from our lives. Instead, He gives us just enough direction to take the next step. Like a child learning to walk, we take His hand and make a step. Then we look upward.

Why does God do this? Why doesn't He just mark out a path so you know in advance exactly what to do and how to do it? Very simply this: God likes hanging out with you. If you knew everything in advance, there would be no adventure, no discovery, no shared experience with God. You would marry the right person, get the right job, live in the right place—in short, do everything right—but miss the most important part of the equation: the life-giving presence of God.

DEALING WITH DEPRESSION

*Why are you cast down, O my soul? And why are you
disquieted within me? Hope in God,
for I shall yet praise Him for the help of His countenance.*

—PSALM 42:5 NKJV

ONE SURPRISING DISCOVERY IN RECENT YEARS has been the evidence that depression affects followers of God as much as it does the general population. There are lots of theories, both medical and theological, for why this is so, but the fact remains that we as Christians can and do suffer from depression. While mental health professionals can provide medical and psychological treatment, God's treatment on a spiritual level is critical to recovery.

If you are depressed, spending time in God's presence is essential—the more time, the better. Often, though, when we feel depressed we are hesitant to face God, believing that we are unworthy to be in His presence. But Jesus' death on the cross—the only reason *anyone* is worthy to stand before God—wasn't conditional. It grants everyone access to the presence of God, including those of us who think we've let Him down because we've fallen into a state of depression.

God wants *everyone* to come to Him. Entering His presence when you're depressed may seem difficult, even impossible, but those first few faltering steps can bring you closer than you think—because God will come to you, and His steps never falter.

March 21

GUARD MY LIPS

Don't let any evil talk come out of your mouths.
Say only what will help to build others up and meet their needs.
Then what you say will help those who listen.

—**Ephesians 4:29 NIrV**

YOU'VE NO DOUBT EXPERIENCED BOTH THE upside and the downside of what comes out of people's mouths…even your own mouth. Maybe you've listened to a parent explode over a child's mistake. Maybe you were that parent. Perhaps you've experienced having a friend hurl insults at you. Maybe you were the one who launched the insults.

Speaking unkind words to another person only leads to hurt and regret. Instead, God directs us to better word choices. He asks us to guard our lips and choose words carefully to build others up and not tear them down. God wants us to stay in tune with the verbal messages we send throughout each day. He wants us to slow down and think about our reactions and responses to circumstances and people instead of just letting our words fly off our tongue.

God designed you with communication skills. Your words can also soothe and restore and inspire hope. He loves it when you uplift others verbally. "Great job!…You look fantastic!…I love you so much" are just a few of the life-giving words you can speak. Before you open your mouth each day, remember that what you say, and what you don't, reverberates into eternity.

BEYOND THE VEIL

Elisha prayed, "O Lord, open his eyes and let him see!"
The Lord opened the young man's eyes, and...he saw that
the hillside...was filled with horses and chariots of fire.
—2 Kings 6:17 NLT

OUR WESTERNIZED WORLD EMBRACES A HIGHLY analytical way of reasoning. We grow up believing that what we are able to perceive with the naked eye, the telescopic lens, or a microscope comprises all there is to see. The problem is, we fail to view the deeper mysteries of life through the eyes of faith, when that is exactly what we need.

Throughout history, people have encountered the inexplicable dimension of the heavens, usually when straining to reconcile difficult circumstances through the lens of faith. After a near fatal car accident, a woman told how a stranger pulled her from the burning wreckage and sat on the blistering pavement holding her head in his lap, comforting her, until an emergency vehicle arrived. Her mother verified that a "stranger" facilitated a long-distance phone call between them during the wait, but medics couldn't recall anyone on site when they rushed onto the scene.

What benefit is there in acknowledging a dimension of reality that is just beyond the veil of sight when we can't experience it at will? Perhaps the value is for faith itself. Maintaining a meaningful relationship with God postures you to cooperate with what happens in the deep heavens, whether you can see it or not.

THE POWER OF LISTENING

Everyone should be quick to listen.

—JAMES 1:19 NIV

D O YOU WANT TO CHANGE YOUR world? Start by listening.

In 1863 a young pastor named Abraham Kuyper began his ministry. He was disturbed because so many members of his church never attended services. So he began to visit them. Rather than lecture them for their absence, he listened. What would need to change in order for them to attend, he wanted to know. He soon discovered that his church was disconnected from its people. He began to champion the issues that mattered to them. In an effort to give the people a voice, he started first a newspaper, and later a political movement. In the end, he was elected prime minister of the Netherlands…all because he listened.

Everyone has a story to tell, and nearly everyone is eager to tell it—if he or she can find a listening ear. When you become that listening ear, your influence in that person's life is multiplied, and you're put into a position to make a difference.

Keep in mind that listening does not necessarily mean agreeing. Rather, we listen to validate the importance of another human being. Then we take what we've heard back to God and process it in our time alone with Him.

CREATED FOR WORSHIP

Come, let us worship and bow down. Let us kneel
before the LORD our maker, for he is our God.
—PSALM 95:6 NLT

WHAT IS YOUR UNDERSTANDING OF THE word *worship*? Do you think of it as something that happens only within the confines of a church or cathedral? Or have you learned that what you do in the course of an ordinary day also constitutes worship of God? It's exciting to worship Him, not only as the powerful King of the universe, but also as our personal God.

In its earliest use, the word *worship* implied ascribing honor and worth to someone. Later, it came to mean paying reverence to God. That means that any time you honor and reverence God, you are worshiping Him, no matter where you are or what day of the week it is. Whenever you pray, meditate, read the Scriptures, sing, obey, even work or play, in an attitude of honor and reverence toward God, you are worshiping Him.

If you want to worship God verbally but aren't sure where to start, think of an aspect of His nature that is particularly significant to you at that moment. If you're facing surgery or a frightening diagnosis, worship Him as your Creator and healer. If you're feeling afraid, worship Him as your protector. No matter what your circumstances, you'll never exhaust the ways you can worship God.

MODELING MERCY

Be kind and merciful, and forgive others,
just as God forgave you because of Christ.
—EPHESIANS 4:32 CEV

OUR WORLD APPLAUDS THE PEOPLE WE call role models. We have sports figures creating foundations for troubled youth, Hollywood celebs traveling the globe speaking out for the underprivileged, and everyday citizens doing their part to better their communities.

Would others consider you a role model and look up to you for the way you treat those around you? Sure, you've got your weaknesses, but overall do you reflect Jesus' kindness and mercy? Or when someone pushes your buttons, do you tend to respond with unkind words or simmer inside, even with vengeful thoughts? Maybe it's the coworker who makes you look incompetent or the fan who bashes your kids' sports team. Or perhaps it's your forgetful spouse, your disobedient children, or a thoughtless friend.

Spending time alone with Jesus is the best preparation to model His gentle and gracious character to the world around you. Getting to know God's temperament and reading how Jesus interacted with others will encourage you to extend compassion and forgiveness, especially to those with whom you'd rather even the score. Jesus' graceful words, "Father, forgive them," may well be the three most important words to guide you in upholding your reputation as a merciful God-follower.

CONSTRUCTIVE SORROW

*When you heard my words...you became sorry for what
you had done and humbled yourself...and you cried in my
presence. This is why I have heard you, says the LORD.*
—2 KINGS 22:19 NCV

THERE IS A TIME TO BE sorry. Likewise, there is an appropriate
way to let your sorrow be known. No one gets through this life
without needing to humble themselves and admit to wrongdoing
once in a while. This is true in human relationships and in your
relationship with God.

With God, you will find that honest confession concerning your
missteps is one of the most positive and productive conversations you
can have. God never holds grudges, and you will discover that the
patience of God is without limits for those who earnestly seek to do
His will. Not only is He patient, but He rushes to relieve the feelings
of guilt that often weigh on your heart. Furthermore, His mercy is so
lavish He more than compensates for your sorrow, seeking to fill your
heart with immediate peace, joy, and hope.

In addition, the Spirit of God will give you counsel for the
healing of human relationships where needed. Seeking guidance
from God's Word, consulting with friends who walk with God, and
gleaning insight from spiritual counselors will provide invaluable
wisdom concerning how to ask for forgiveness and work toward
reconciliation with others.

There is much to be gained through genuine sorrow.

GOD'S PLAN

What do you want?

—MATTHEW 20:32 NKJV

HOW DO YOU DISCOVER GOD'S PLAN for your life? How do you find God's plan for today? Is it really a matter of sacrificing all your own plans, giving up your own desires, canceling your own identity?

Usually not.

Yes, it is true that we submit to God. It is true that when God's desires and our desires conflict, we must yield to Him, knowing that He is wiser than we are. But, as a rule, God works through our desires to move us in the direction of the plan He has for us. God is a dance partner, not a puppet master.

Your dreams matter to God. You bring your questions to Him: "Whom should I marry?" "Where should I live?" "What job should I choose?" "How should I spend the weekend?" "What should I buy?" But, in return, He asks: "What do you want?" That becomes the starting point for a conversation with God that may include counsel from others, searching the Bible, and the quiet voice of God's Spirit within you.

What do you want? In your time alone with Him, this is one of the things that He wants you to share with Him.

THE GLORY TO COME

I consider that the sufferings of this present time
are not worthy to be compared with the glory
that is to be revealed to us.

—**ROMANS 8:18** NASB

THE FULLNESS OF GOD'S GLORY, WHICH we will one day see, is far greater than the most majestic scene you've ever witnessed on earth—brighter than the sun, even. The glory of God is one of the few things that can truly be described as awesome. It's so far beyond our human comprehension that our feeble attempts to envision it fall ridiculously short. We simply can't imagine it. We'll have to wait until we can experience it.

When we enter into the glory of God, we will also enter a dimension in which we will receive everything that God has for us—our eternal inheritance of healing, joy, peace, transformation, righteousness, and so much more. In the presence of God's glory, there will be no more suffering, pain, mourning, tears, or death. We'll be so transformed that even if we couldn't sing a note on earth, we'll sing praises to God right along with a choir of angels.

Each time you praise God in the midst of suffering or hardship of any kind, you're preparing for that day when every painful experience will disappear in the brilliant light of God's glory—and you'll receive your inheritance.

HELP IS ON THE WAY

*This is no afternoon athletic contest that we'll walk away
from and forget about in a couple of hours.
This is for keeps, a life-or-death fight to the finish
against the Devil and all his angels.*

—EPHESIANS 6:12 MSG

GOOD VS. EVIL. A FIGHT TO the finish. A sinister villain (usually
with a jagged facial scar and grungy teeth) wants to take over
the world. Sounds like a movie plot or a classic theme in literature.
Something deep within us rises up to cheer wildly when the seemingly
outwitted good guy thwarts the evil master plan.

In life, as in fiction, there are times when we feel like there's an
insurmountable force against us, blocking our progress. We can't
exactly see our opponent, but we see the obstacles he hurls in our
path. It's not always the big boulders, like a serious illness or a job
loss, but it's the everyday sand in our shoes that can wear us down—
the whining kids, the lack of sleep, the tiff with a neighbor.

Fortunately, you don't have to wait until you're in the heat of
spiritual battle to call for some backup. God is your strong champion.
He is eager to help you find a way to overcome your challenges. He is
ready to listen, ready to advise, and ready to help you conquer. All you
need to do is ask, and help is on the way.

FAITHFUL AND TRUE

O Lord GOD, you are God, and your words are true,
and you have promised this good thing to your servant.
—2 SAMUEL 7:28 ESV

RELATIONSHIPS WITH PEOPLE CAN BE DIFFICULT and disappointing. Friends can be fickle, siblings sometimes seem distant, parents can be frustrating, and marriages go through conflict. Is there anyone who always keeps their word?

Though you can't see Him with your eyes, touch Him with your hands, or hear Him with your ears, being in a relationship with God is the most consistent and fulfilling bond imaginable. But how does a person go about developing that kind of trust in God?

First, recognize that He is God. Though you can't see Him with your eyes, you learn to see Him in all of creation. You discover His flair for beauty in the variety and the detail of the flowers in your garden. You discover His lavish generosity in the way He cares for even the tiniest sparrow.

Then you begin to realize that His Word is absolutely true. Though you can't hear Him with your ears, you learn to listen for His personal message to you while reading Scripture. His voice becomes familiar, His words become life.

Finally, you find that He keeps His promises. Though you can't touch Him with your hands, you will find your own heart is deeply touched by His faithfulness.

March 31

FREE FROM THE FEAR OF FAILURE

Don't condemn those who are down; that hardness can
boomerang. Be easy on people; you'll find life a lot easier.
—LUKE 6:37 MSG

ONE OF THE MAIN REASONS WE become critical of others is our own paralyzing fear of failure. By focusing on others' failures, we hope that our own will shrink in size and importance. Not only does that make for some serious problems with other people, it also keeps some of us from ever getting past the failures that haunt us throughout our lives.

What we may not realize is that failure can be a friend by teaching us what doesn't work. Each time we discover what doesn't work, we move that much closer to discovering what does work. And even though some public failures can be embarrassing, they are never so humiliating that God can't turn them around. When we take our failures to God, admitting our defeat and our own contribution to the problem, we place ourselves in a humbled position before Him—which is always a place of victory. Like so many other paradoxes of a life with God, genuine victory can result from a blistering defeat in the transforming power of God's presence.

Don't hesitate to talk to God about your fear of failure. He's had great success with transforming failures ever since He set the first human beings on earth.

JESUS CALLS YOUR NAME

The sheep know their shepherd's voice.
He calls each of them by name and leads them out.
—JOHN 10:3 CEV

ONE OF THE STUNNING CHARACTERISTICS OF Jesus' ministry on earth is how personal it was. That was unusual at the time, especially when the focus of His ministry turned toward a woman, since it was a social taboo for a man to speak to a woman publicly. The magnitude of His impact on the people around Him— or, in all likelihood, the disdain the religious leaders of the day felt toward Him—was greater than we can fathom from a distance of two thousand years.

Today, Jesus continues His personal ministry by calling out to you, asking you to follow Him out of your ordinary life and into a life of restoration, transformation, and renewal. He wants *you* to be restored to the person He intended you to be all along, transformed into someone who lives above life's circumstances, and renewed to youthful energy by the Spirit who lives within you.

Listen for the voice of Jesus. You may hear Him calling to you as you read the Bible attentively, expecting Him to speak to you. You may hear His voice as you're praying, or even through someone else who speaks the words Jesus wants you to hear. You'll know it's Him— because Jesus will make it personal.

IT IS WELL

This hope is a strong and trustworthy anchor for our souls.
—**HEBREWS 6:19** NLT

THE GREAT CHICAGO FIRE OF OCTOBER 1871 raged for more than a day, killing three hundred people and stranding one hundred thousand more as homeless. The horrendous fire also destroyed the financial stability of many, including lawyer and real estate investor Horatio Gates Spafford. Spafford soon suffered another devastating blow—the loss of his only son.

Despite their own losses, the Spafford family assisted those impoverished by the fire. After two years of relief work, the family planned a vacation in England. Delayed by business, Spafford sent his wife, Anna, and four daughters on ahead. But tragedy struck again. The vacationers' ship collided with another vessel and all the Spafford girls died. Only Anna survived. Out of the harrowing grief, Spafford penned his now classic hymn, "It Is Well with My Soul."

How would you describe the condition of your soul right now? If the waves of daily stress and undertow of discouragement threaten to drag you under, don't abandon ship. Reach out to take hold of God's extended hand, "a strong and trustworthy anchor." He is the only one who can assuredly make it well with your soul.

April 3

BENEFITS OF SOLITUDE

I reflect at night on who you are, O LORD, therefore,
I obey your instructions. This is how I spend my life:
obeying your commandments.
—PSALM 119:55-56 NLT

WHAT IS IT THAT SOLITUDE WITH God provides? Once we begin, the answer becomes immediately obvious in the form of spiritual benefits. To start, time with God in the privacy of our devotions purifies our hearts. Making ourselves vulnerable to Him, we participate in loving and constructive self-evaluation, using the Word as a mirror through which we see our true reflection.

Naturally, as we reflect on His image, the counsel of God's Word begins the transformation of our minds as well. We discover a deep desire to become like Him, realizing that it's an inside job.

Amazingly, time spent in contemplative interaction with God over all that we've learned causes our will to bend in humility toward obedience. We are surprised at the delight we discover in pleasing the Lord.

And last, though not least, our prayers and petitions draw help from heaven, empowering us to fulfill the will of God moment by moment. The strength provided by the Spirit of the Lord invigorates and inspires us to persist in living in His presence every day and in every circumstance.

Your time alone with God fuels the fires of your faith, equipping you to live powerfully and joyfully in His will.

UNEXPECTED

They have taken the Lord's body out of the tomb,
and we don't know where they have put him!

—JOHN 20:2 NLT

JESUS DIED ON THE CROSS. HE was buried. He rose from the dead. This is the central teaching of Christianity. Nearly everyone knows the story. But few appreciate how totally unexpected these events were. His disciples believed that Jesus was God's Messiah. They expected Him to overthrow their Roman oppressors and establish Jerusalem as the central power in the world. The last thing on their minds was that He would die as a criminal on a Roman cross at age thirty-three. It was more than they could comprehend. Everything they believed in and hoped for was shattered.

Then, while they were still reeling, the message came that His tomb was empty. More bad news! It never once occurred to them that Jesus could grab death by the collar and toss it aside. In the end, Jesus appeared to them and invited them to feel the scars in His hands and feet to verify that He was and is forever alive.

Sooner or later, God will take us out of our comfort zone. Events will come that we didn't expect. Let's sort it out in God's presence. Let Jesus tell us the truth. We are forever alive with Him.

THE NEARNESS OF GOD

Draw near to God and He will draw near to you.
—JAMES 4:8 NKJV

DO YOU LONG TO DRAW NEAR to God and sense His presence? If so, you'll be glad to know that it's easier than you may think, though it does take intentional effort on your part.

Sensing the presence of God requires sharpening your spiritual senses. In part, that means focusing on God to the exclusion of everything else, asking God to help you quiet your spirit, be open to whatever He has for you, and avoid as many distractions as possible. It also means recalling everything you know about God's nature and being aware of those characteristics as He reveals them to you—His love, His forgiveness, His mercy, His majesty, and so forth.

Also, think about those times when you *did* sense God's presence. What were you doing? For some people, praying the prayers in the Bible, including entire Psalms or portions of Psalms, immediately brings them into the presence of God. Reading Bible passages that are especially significant to you can also help you draw near to Him.

Throughout the Bible, God promises to welcome His people into His presence. It's there that you will find peace, healing, and victory over everything that threatens to keep you from God.

April 6

NOTICING YOU

The slave girl gave a name to the Lord who spoke to her:
"You are 'God who sees me,'" because she said to herself,
"Have I really seen God who sees me?"
—**GENESIS 16:13** NCV

HAVE YOU EVER PLAYED PEEK-A-BOO WITH a baby? As you cover your eyes with your hands, the baby's eyes open wide in anticipation. Then that quick pulling away of your hands, "Peek-a-boo! I see you!" sparks giggles, wiggles, and laughter, and the baby glows with joy as he looks into the eyes of someone special.

Do you ever wonder if God sees you? Most of us have questioned that. Deep down, everyone has a hunger for love and an intense, seemingly insatiable need to be noticed. Centuries ago a teenage servant girl wondered if anyone noticed her. She became a surrogate mom for her wealthy employers, but turned a bit uppity. The wife retaliated by mistreating the girl. So the maid escaped and ended up lost in the wilderness—alone, pregnant, friendless, destitute, and desperate. Suddenly God spoke her name. She became visible and life spun an about-face.

God sees you. He knows you. He loves you. He sees you in your messes and draws close. He sees you in your triumphs and cheers. He knows your name and counts every hair on your head. And He adores you. He'll look you in the eye, if you let Him.

WHY ARE YOU HERE?

Who knows if perhaps you were made queen
for just such a time as this?
—ESTHER 4:14 NLT

A MISSIONARY COUPLE, TRAINED IN LINGUISTICS, spent more than twenty years in a remote village of Papua, New Guinea, first learning to speak the language of the tribe, then developing a written language into which they could translate the Bible. Finally the Scriptures were translated and sent away for printing. Unfortunately, the man suddenly died of a heart attack, leaving his wife and children behind, as well as his life's work in its final stages of completion.

Upon reception of the Scriptures in book form, all the villagers—though deeply grieved by the missionary's death—turned out for the celebration he had planned. Touched by the selfless love that inspired this man to devote his entire life to them, the whole village abandoned their pagan practices and turned to God.

No one knows if the man's life might have been extended if he had lived someplace where better medical care is available. But his wife is certain he would not have chosen to extend his life by living near modern medical facilities if it meant their beloved tribe failed to receive God's Word in their own language.

How thrilling to discover your life's purpose and spend yourself fulfilling it. Go to God and begin a conversation with Him about the purpose He has for you.

THE END OF THE STORY

God was behind it.

—GENESIS 45:5 MSG

THERE ARE DARK MOMENTS IN EVERY adventure. The best novels contain chapters where it looks like all hope is lost, the main character doesn't stand a chance, doom is certain. But we keep reading, don't we? We know, deep inside, that something isn't right. The picture isn't complete. Resolution will come. The hero will be okay in the end.

Reading these stories teaches us something: We can't judge the author by a single chapter. We cannot believe that the writer is a terrible person simply because the hero goes through terrible times. On the contrary, we believe that a good author won't leave the hero in despair. A good author will provide a way out.

In the same way, when we come to God, heavy with our own problems and burdened with the woes of others, we must understand that the story isn't over. We cannot take too thin a slice of life or history and try to judge God's character by it. God is ready to write the best possible ending to each person's life. If you are willing to make Him the Author of your life, He will bring you there no matter how dark your path may be in the process.

HEARING THE VOICE OF GOD

Your ears will hear a word behind you, "This is the way, walk in it," whenever you turn to the right or to the left.
—ISAIAH 30:21 NASB

HAVE YOU EVER HEARD THE VOICE of God? While some people say they've actually heard the audible voice of God, most often people "hear" God's voice in a different way. When they say they hear God's voice, what they mean is that they sense something deep in their spirit, and they believe God is the one who placed it there to give them direction for their lives or wisdom for a certain situation.

One thing you can be sure of is that those who have genuinely heard a word from God are people who pray and read the Bible. It's through your times of prayer and Bible reading that you begin to sense what God is saying to you. He will most certainly give you direction and wisdom at other times, but you learn to distinguish His voice and discern His will when you spend time praying and reading His Word.

You may never hear the audible voice of God here on earth, but you can have the confidence of knowing that He will "speak" to you in many different ways throughout your life. His "voice" can be heard as He gives you wisdom, guidance, instruction, and even warnings through the Bible, through prayer, and even through the most unlikely people.

REMEMBER ME

*God remembered Rachel. God answered her prayer
and made it possible for her to have children.*
—GENESIS 30:22 GWT

ARCHIMEDES IS CONSIDERED ONE OF THE greatest scientists
and mathematicians in world history. But apparently the scholar
from Greece was also an absentminded genius. When the Romans
invaded Greece, a Roman soldier was ordered to bring Archimedes
before the emperor. Lost in deep thought, Archimedes kept tracing an
important problem in the dust while the soldier kept tapping on the
intellect's shoulder. He didn't pay attention even after the frustrated
soldier drew his sword.

Sometimes in the more pressing moments of life, it can feel as if
God is absentminded. You keep tapping on His shoulder, but He seems
distracted by some other problem. Sometimes it can feel as if God has
passed you over and moved on to more urgent affairs of the universe.

But the truth is, the Creator, who knows the complexities of every
individual who has ever lived, always remembers you. Although He's
truly ancient, He is never forgetful. He recalls and cares about every
detail in your days, right down to that scratch on your arm and the
words you'll speak today. He will not overlook a single second of your
day. Nothing fades from God's memory—especially a beloved child
like you.

April 11

PEOPLE OVER PRINCIPLE

*The midwives, however, feared God and did not do what
the king of Egypt had told them to do; they let the boys live.*
—EXODUS 1:17 TNIV

I HAD TO DECIDE WHETHER TO break your rule or break the old woman's heart, and I couldn't live with the latter!"

An experienced security guard was being reprimanded for having stepped away from his post to rescue an elderly woman's small dog that had slipped under the fence where a fierce fleet of Dobermans were kept on watch.

Have you ever found yourself at risk of breaking a rule for the benefit of others?

There have always been courageous men and women throughout history who have such a clear vision of what it means to be human that they would sooner break the law—even at risk of their lives—than stand by and watch people suffer.

During World War II, a young Polish nurse smuggled hundreds of children out of a holding area where Jewish prisoners were waiting to be transported to death camps. In deliberate defiance of the law, she persisted in order to save the children's lives.

You may never face the dilemma of breaking the law for the sake of saving lives, but you will likely find yourself in a situation where people must be considered over principle. Walking intimately with God, you will find that mercy often trumps judgment.

FINDING THE ABILITY TO BLESS

David returned to bless his household.

—2 Samuel 6:20 amp

WHERE DO WE FIND THE CAPACITY to bless those closest to us? How do we find the ability to speak life-giving words of hope and encouragement to those around us? What needs to happen in us so that our actions nurture those in our circle of influence?

In a sense, the answer is simple: You can't pour water from an empty pitcher. We need to find "the blessing" ourselves. We need to be filled up to overflowing inside before we can pour affirming love out on others.

Some of us are fortunate enough to have real or surrogate parents who communicated to us, "I love you just as you are. I believe in you. You matter." Some of us are not that fortunate. But, ultimately, for all of us, our "blessing" and affirmation come from God Himself. This is why it is so important that you let yourself be loved by God. Linger in His presence and let Him share with you the joy He feels that you are you. Drink in the love of God. From that place, you will be empowered to go into your world and touch people with the life-changing presence and love of Christ.

IS HOLINESS FOR TODAY?

A highway will be there; it will be called the Way of Holiness.
The unclean will not journey on it;
it will be for those who walk in that Way.
—ISAIAH 35:8 NIV

HOLINESS—THAT SOUNDS LIKE SUCH AN ANTIQUATED concept. The very word conjures up images of late-nineteenth-century women in high-necked, long-sleeved, full-length dresses and men in stiff, starched white shirts under their funereal black suits—and not a smile to be found on the women or the men.

But God does call His people to a life of holiness. What do you make of that? How can that possibly resonate with people in the twenty-first century? It helps if you break down the word "holiness" into some of its essential components, such as prayer, devotion, obedience, and humility, which have nothing to do with dress codes or a grim countenance. Quite the opposite: true holiness produces freedom and joy.

At its core, holiness is a natural result of a right attitude toward God. Are you devoted to God? When you pray, do you approach Him in an attitude of obedience and humility, and do you live out those qualities in your everyday life? Then yours is very likely a life characterized by holiness—although you'd probably object to that, since your humility wouldn't allow you to claim that description for yourself. That's fine; God sees your holiness, and His opinion is the one that counts.

CLOSER THAN YOU THINK

GOD was still with Joseph: He reached out in kindness to him; he put him on good terms with the head jailer.

—GENESIS 39:21 MSG

SOME OF THE LONELIEST PEOPLE ON earth are the millions of prisoners in detention centers, jails, and prisons across the globe. Correctional facility inmates are isolated from the rest of society and can certainly feel abandoned by those of us on the outside. Most must feel particularly abandoned by God.

Even if we never spend a second behind prison bars, we can be locked up in holding cells of wrong perceptions about God. When things don't go our way, we may think God has skipped over us. When we pray and pray and don't see our requests fulfilled, we may believe God is unable to answer.

Yet all these conclusions are based on our limited human viewpoint. Although our feelings may indicate that we are isolated from Him at times, He is still with us. God is ever-present and ever-mindful. He knows our every moral failing and yet He remains loyally steadfast in relationship with us.

If today is one of those days when God seems distant to you, pause right now and ask Him to reach out in kindness and show His presence in ways you cannot miss. He is closer than you think.

NOT JUST TALK

*The Good News we brought to you came not only
with words, but with power, with the Holy Spirit,
and with sure knowledge that it is true.*

—1 Thessalonians 1:5 ncv

HAVE YOU HEARD THE GOSPEL REFERRED to as "good news"? What makes it so good and for whom?

The good news about Jesus is good, first of all, because it comes from God. All that is good originates with God. It is worthy of your attention primarily because of who sent you the message in the first place.

The good news about Jesus is truly good news for all who receive it, not merely for those who proclaim it. It is an announcement regarding your secure status as a citizen in the heavenly city. It is a proclamation from God that peace, joy, and freedom are now available to you to the fullest possible extent. And it is the declaration from on high that when you pray, the Creator and Ruler of the cosmos will bend His ear to listen.

The good news about Jesus is also powerful. A profound sense of awe grips the hearts of those who grasp this message. It is capable of changing your perspective and empowering you to make a difference. Life with God is not just new words you speak, it brings new definition, purpose, and power.

Spend time alone with God and get a good look at the good news.

FORGIVING OTHERS

*Forgive us our sins, for we also forgive everyone
who sins against us.*

—LUKE 11:4 NIV

MOST OF US UNDERSTAND THAT WE need to forgive others. But how do we do it? How do we forgive someone who doesn't "deserve" to be forgiven?

We must begin by understanding what forgiveness is not. Forgiveness is not inviting an abusive person back into our lives. Forgiveness is not minimizing the sin of those who hurt us. Forgiveness is not something that happens when we grit our teeth and say, "I forgive you."

True forgiveness takes place when we look honestly at the ways in which we have been hurt, hand our anger over to Jesus, and let it rest with Him. How do we do that? We figure out all the reasons why we don't want to forgive the offense and hand our anger to Jesus. Then we lift those reasons up to Him and allow Him to change our hearts. Soon our hurt and anger is turned to peace and joy as we find freedom in Him.

Forgiving someone requires supernatural grace from God. We cannot do it on our own. But when Jesus gently empowers us to see from His perspective, then forgiving others becomes possible.

YOUR NEW SELF

You were taught, with regard to your former way of life, to put off your old self...and to put on the new self, created to be like God in true righteousness and holiness.

—EPHESIANS 4:22, 24 NIV

WHEN YOU CAME INTO A RIGHT relationship with God, He gave you a new "self"—a new you. It can take years, even a lifetime, to fully grasp that concept. *If I have a new self,* you may wonder, *why am I plagued by the same old temptations? Why don't I feel transformed?*

If you are among those struggling to live as a new creation in Christ, ask God to show you what it is that prevents you from living victoriously. While you're at it, ask Him to renew your mind, erasing any doubt that His promises are true, that they're meant for you, and that they will result in transforming you into the person He intended you to be from the very beginning.

Your new self is not some person you have to work the rest of your life to become, striving for perfection and making yourself miserable in the process. Your new self is the person who will emerge once you begin living in closeness to Him. Trust God to transform you into His image—and that begins with your next breath.

FOR YOUR OWN GOOD

You intended to harm me, but God intended it for good to
accomplish what is now being done, the saving of many lives.
—GENESIS 50:20 NIV

ENEMIES COME IN MANY FORMS: VINDICTIVE people, addictions, debilitating illnesses—even your own self-limiting beliefs. At one time, you might have despaired, sought revenge, even given up.

But with God in your life, you are able to start viewing your enemies and your circumstances through a different lens. God's Word has given you a window into His mind and His ways. He reveals not only how He's dealt with enemies in the past but how He's working in the present and the future to right wrongs, ease human suffering, and restore hope. He's promised to protect, strengthen, and prosper you; He's "got your back." More importantly, He wants to use *you* to show others that they too can overcome.

It's been said that knowledge is power. God's Word is like a protein shake for the soul. Read it regularly and know that the Enemy will not get the best of you! Ponder what you read, and choose to follow God's guidelines, which are intended for your good.

Today, ask yourself who and what are the enemies in your life. How can you bring your attitudes in sync with God's promise to bless you and not to harm you?

WHEN STILLNESS IS GOOD STRATEGY

The LORD will fight for you; you need only to be still.

—EXODUS 14:14 TNIV

WHEN CONFLICT COMES, YOUR NATURAL INCLINATION is to choose either fight or flight. However, those who walk with God are challenged to choose another alternative—stillness.

What does being still have to do with facing conflict? Stillness has several implications, all of which are helpful.

First, stillness is a state of calm. The most common mistake people make when facing adversity is to react impulsively and rashly. When you feel anger or panic washing over you like a tidal wave, run to God in prayer. Nothing brings calm like prayer, nor will anything restore your peace like the quietness of conversation with God.

Second, stillness is a form of waiting. There is so much wisdom in waiting for some time to pass so you can gain a clearer and more objective perspective.

Third, stillness is faith in the peace that is coming. Those who trust in the Lord find their security in what they believe rather than in what they see. Learn to trust the Lord's counsel and provision, even when it looks as if things may not pan out the way you prefer.

When everything around you is in chaos, being still gives God a chance to do His best work.

April 20

ARMED AND DANGEROUS

Elijah was a human being just like us. He prayed that it would not rain, and it did not rain on the land for three and a half years! Then Elijah prayed again, and the rain came down.
—JAMES 5:17-18 NIV

THE WORLD HAS ALWAYS UNDERESTIMATED THE power of the children of God.

Eva Barker was a soft-spoken, four-foot-ten-inch woman who lived in rural southwestern Wisconsin not far from the Mississippi River. Born in 1896, she was seventeen before she saw her first automobile. In her later years, with her long, white hair in a bun, she looked the part of a grandma. She liked to set "a little lunch" in front of whoever came into her tiny cottage, and then disappear into the background, invisible, like the angels, while her guest took center stage.

She wasn't sophisticated. Most of her life she wasn't even allowed to attend church. But whenever she thought no one was listening, you could hear her praying in Norwegian, her mother tongue. She was powerfully connected to her God, and drew her sustenance from His presence.

She lived to be 102. She saw the rise and fall of Nazi Germany and the Soviet Empire. Hitler, Lenin, Stalin—she outlasted them all. True, she was unknown except to a few. But only God knows how much damage this small, harmless woman did to the domain of evil through her many prayers. To the forces of evil, she was armed and dangerous. You can be too!

April 21

EXPERIENCING PURE JOY

You'll go out in joy, you'll be led into a whole and complete
life. The mountains and hills will lead the parade,
bursting with song. All the trees of the forest will join
the procession, exuberant with applause.

—ISAIAH 55:12 MSG

DO YOU KNOW THAT YOU CAN experience true joy even when things aren't going your way? Some people don't understand the difference between happiness and joy, so when circumstances rob them of their happiness, they think joy automatically disappears too. But you can still have a deep, abiding joy even when happiness eludes you, because, while happiness is tied to your circumstances, joy is closely linked to your relationship with God.

Joy sees the world through the eyes of faith. Here's one example of what that means: Your physical eyes may look in the mirror and see someone who's aging much too quickly, and that doesn't make you very happy. But your eyes of faith see a person whom God has blessed with many years, and you joyfully determine that you are going to make the best of the years that are left no matter what happens, blessing Him in return.

Your eyes of faith help you to see that the things that so often bring people down are of little consequence in comparison to the joy that comes from knowing God—and knowing that there's nothing on earth that can rob you of that joy.

AVOIDING SPIRITUAL NECK STRAIN

Do not fear, for I am with you; do not anxiously look about you, for I am your God. I will strengthen you, surely I will help you.

—ISAIAH 41:10 NASB

RUBBERNECKING" MAY BE ONE OF THE greatest words ever coined. It refers to a person craning his or her neck to get a better view, stretching the neck to gawk at something of interest. Often rubbernecking is associated with drivers trying to get a peek at the damage from a car accident.

Today many of us are spiritual rubberneckers. When we encounter a rough road or a fearful situation, we tend to waggle our neck from left to right in search of more solid footing. We distend and reach, looking for any way out of our struggles.

Our anxious search for our own way out of tight spots doesn't please God. Instead of elastic necks straining to get the scoop on our surroundings, God wants us to have pliable hearts and flexible minds. He wants us to let go of our rigid rules that do not align with His truth. He longs for us to stay open to His working in our lives, even in ways we least expect. Instead of focusing on daily distractions, God directs us to fix our eyes on Him as the one who will steady us, strengthen us, and support us.

FALSE GODS OR TRUE GOD

*I am GOD, your God, who brought you out of the land
of Egypt, out of a life of slavery. No other gods, only me.*
—EXODUS 20:2-3 MSG

HOW MANY POTENTIAL GODS ARE THERE within a typical household? There is the god of the corporation, the god of wealth, the god of education, and the god of good health. There is body worship and the worship of celebrities, athletes, and icons in the music industry. There are expensive-car gods, designer-fashion gods, gourmet-food gods, and the worship of our elaborate houses. Some people even place good things on a pedestal, such as a spouse or the idea of marriage and family.

Whatever claims your first priority—your deepest devotion—can become a rival to the true God. So how do you go about putting God first when many of these things are essential and important?

The key to worshiping the God of all gods requires a simple change in perspective. Committing your employment to God's will is radically different from being enslaved to your job and amassing your own empire. Exercising to stay healthy and strong in order to fulfill your purpose in life is far from an obsession with a certain body type.

God risked everything to deliver you from the tyranny of false gods. Worship only Him—don't let anyone or anything else into your moments alone with Him.

LEARNING TO COUNT

The LORD replied, "My Presence will go with you,
and I will give you rest."
—EXODUS 33:14 NIV

SOMETIMES WE COUNT THE WRONG THINGS, like how much money is in the bank or how many bills are on the table. Don't misunderstand. We should be responsible and manage our money well. But all of us go through seasons in life where our best plans, our best efforts, our best intentions fall short. That shortfall might be felt in our wallets, in our health, in our relationships.

Jesus counted five loaves and two small fish and judged that He had enough to feed five thousand. Maybe you have been the recipient of a miracle of faith. You know there are some things that simply cannot be explained. On paper, it looked like it would never work. But it did. Money showed up in the mailbox. The phone call you didn't expect came. The doctor's report came back, and the tumor was gone. You don't know how these things happened, but they did—they do!

When your assets grow thin and your troubles are adding up, it's time to run to the One who counts a little differently than you do. It's time to shelter yourself in His presence and let Him do the math. Let Him teach you that one plus God is much more than enough.

THE SPIRIT WITHIN YOU

*God can do anything, you know—far more than you could
ever imagine or guess or request in your wildest dreams!
He does it not by pushing us around but by working within
us, his Spirit deeply and gently within us.*

—EPHESIANS 3:20 MSG

THINK FOR A MOMENT ABOUT SOME of your wildest dreams.
How could you make those dreams come true? It would be
impossible, right? That's why they are so wild; they are beyond your
ability to fulfill. The Spirit of God, however, would have no problem
making them a reality. It's just that there's a very good chance that the
Spirit's dreams for you are so much better than you can imagine, and
those are the dreams God wants to make come true.

That's why God has placed His Spirit within you—to make God's
dreams *your* dreams. He won't force anything on you that you don't
want; He'll work on your heart until you catch the vision that God has
for you. By then, you'll likely be so fired up with a passion for what
God has shown you that the vision will have become your very own.

When you follow God's dreams for your life rather than those you
imagined for yourself before you knew Him, you may not end up
where you once thought you would. But wherever the Spirit of God
leads you, you can be certain it will be a far better place.

CELEBRATE ANYWAY

Fig trees may no longer bloom, or vineyards produce grapes;
olive trees may be fruitless...and cattle stalls vacant—but I
will still celebrate because the LORD God saves me.

—HABAKKUK 3:17-18 CEV

FAIR-WEATHER FRIENDS ARE A PAIN. EVER have one? You know, the kind that stick with you when everything is even-keeled, but when trouble comes into your life they seem to fade into the next dimension.

God's not keen on us being fickle either. When we take a second and think about His unfailing love, why would He like it? After all He did to rescue us, God wants friends that are in it for the long haul. He wants friends who believe in Him at all times.

No matter how much we wish it weren't so, troubling times can stir up feelings of being abandoned by God. And the Devil will milk that feeling by hissing into our thoughts: *God doesn't actually love me, because if He did, wouldn't I have more money / a better boss / a better marriage / a spouse?*

When everything seems to turn sour, don't ditch your faith. Hang on to that part of you that knows God is good, that His love is the best thing that's ever happened to you. Build your faith and your friendship with God by celebrating His extraordinary presence in your dark times. When you sense life is drying up around you, God will always be your steady source of joy.

KNOWING GOD UP CLOSE

They stayed at a distance and said to Moses,
"Speak to us yourself and we will listen.
But do not have God speak to us or we will die."

—EXODUS 20:18-19 TNIV

MOST PEOPLE MAINTAIN A COMFORTABLY SAFE distance from God. Even Christians sometimes prefer to sit safely in their pews, hearing about God from clerical "professionals" rather than interacting with Him themselves. Why? Because being a friend of God is dangerous business. His story bears witness to the fact that living in close proximity to Him can be extremely risky.

Consider the plight of some of His closest friends: Jonah, who found himself in the dark, slimy stomach of a fish; Jeremiah, who was thrown into a dark, slimy pit; John the Baptist, who lost his head in a dark, slimy dungeon; or Peter, who awoke one night in a dark, slimy cell. God's friends often find themselves living anything but a normal, routine existence.

Is it any wonder that many people hold God at a distance? The fear of what He will say—or worse, demand—drives many from closeness with Him.

But what about the end of the story? Those who choose to live out their days in an intimate relationship with God are those who experience great power in prayer, amazing adventures in faith, and the intense and abundant affection of the Almighty.

Do you dare miss it?

TOUGH QUESTIONS

*When I tried to figure it out, all I got was a splitting
headache...until I entered the sanctuary of God.
Then I saw the whole picture.*
—PSALM 73:16-17 MSG

THROUGHOUT LIFE WE WILL BE TEMPTED to question God's
motives. When prayers go unanswered, troubles linger, and
hopes fade, we come face to face with the question: Why? If God really
loves us, why does He allow such things? We read terrible accounts of
suffering, talk to survivors of horrendous abuse, ponder the punishment
of the wicked, and our minds are left spinning. Is God aloof?
Is He vindictive? Is He petty? What version of God fits the reality of
our circumstances?

These are tough questions. If they were easy to answer, someone
would have already given the definitive answer for them. But they have
puzzled people almost since time began.

In the process of grappling with these questions, some lose their
way. But others become stronger than ever in their faith. What's
the difference?

The secret is to bring these questions into the presence of God,
to share with Him in complete honesty our doubts and fears about
Him, to give Him opportunity to show us the truth. The answer that
satisfies will be a little different for each person, but God knows what
that answer is. And He will share it with you.

ALWAYS BE READY

Be ready to speak up and tell anyone who asks why you're living the way you are, and always with the utmost courtesy.

—1 PETER 3:15 MSG

READINESS" HAS BECOME A BUZZWORD IN recent years, particularly in the contexts of military strategy, national security, and disaster preparedness. There's a sense in which "readiness" applies to your faith as well. One way is that which Jesus spoke about: the need to be on guard and prepared for the attacks on your faith that are sure to come.

In another context, followers of God are advised to always be ready to explain to others the reasons why they have faith in the God of the Bible and why they have a steadfast hope in a better world to come. Preparing to answer questions of that kind isn't like cramming for a test. Even though the answers are found in the Bible, until they become your own—until you can demonstrate through your life that your faith and hope have substance to you personally—your answers won't have the ring of truth that others need to hear.

Spend some time thinking deeply about what you really believe and talk over any doubts you have with God. He'll give you the assurance you need to respond to any questions or challenges to your faith that others may pose.

STAR LIGHT, STAR BRIGHT

Look up and see: who created these? He brings out the starry host by number; He calls all of them by name. Because of His great power and strength, not one of them is missing.
—Isaiah 40:26 hcsb

G RAND SPACES IN NATURE MAKE THE spirit and soul breathe. A million glittering stars overhead viewed from a quiet mountain meadow still the mind and make the soul feel its place in the universe. Why is that?

Our souls are drawn to God's greatness. Our innermost being longs to restore its equilibrium. We were fashioned by the Creator, who is so incomparable that no mind can grasp His magnitude or His majesty. Yet in His immensity there is rest and joy. He designed, named, and tracks each of the billions of stars. We find solace in that kind of power.

Time spent in nature, whether a simple walk during lunch break or a weekend camping trip, connects you to the vastness of the invincible God. Surrounded by displays of His glorious strength, you will discover more of His immeasurable character.

Remember watching the clouds as a kid, trying to see animals and ships in the sky? Take time today to experience that childlike joy again. Spend time outside this week and be refreshed by the unrivaled works of your God. Ponder anew how you are even more cherished by Him than any specially named gleaming star.

May 1

PRAISEWORTHY PRIORITIES

*Because your greatest desire is to help your people,
and you did not ask for wealth, riches, [or] fame...I will
certainly give you the wisdom and knowledge you requested.*
—2 CHRONICLES 1:11–12 NLT

IF YOU DISCOVERED THAT YOU HAD a personal genie and could make one wish—anything you wanted—what would it be? A million bucks? A racy sports car? A trip around the world or a mansion? Most of us would be immediately consumed with possibilities for ourselves.

But what if, on the other hand, you discovered that there is a God in heaven who generously gives to those who make requests of Him concerning the healing of humanity, the mending of the world? What then?

Power in prayer is much more frequently experienced when we get beyond our own desires, our own interests, and our own needs. Not that those are unimportant, rather that those who see the bigger picture and seek the welfare of others tend to align themselves more objectively with God's motives and intentions.

Your heart begins to bend to the higher will of God when you earnestly pray for the welfare of other people. It changes you. It makes of you a person that God can entrust with vast wisdom and deep insight. Interestingly enough, such valuable commodities will answer most of your own concerns in life, but they will also equip you to faithfully handle wealth and power should it come your way.

MORE THAN MEETS THE EYE

I don't have a nickel to my name, but what I do have,
I give you: In the name of Jesus Christ of Nazareth, walk!
—ACTS 3:6 MSG

WHEN IT COMES TO THE CHILDREN of God, we are more than meets the eye. On the surface, who are we? Mainly a bunch of average Joes and Janes, not exceptionally powerful, rich, or strong. But underneath it all, we have an incredible identity. Much of our time alone with God is spent in exploring and discovering what it means to be a member of God's family. The life-changing power of God flows in our veins. As children of God, our words and our actions bring healing. Our acts of kindness touch and transform lives. We are empowered to sweep aside evil and build up good in the lives of people God has put in our paths. Our prayers register in heaven and change the face of things on earth. We can speak to "mountains" and they will move.

How and why can you do these things? Because of who you are! In Christ, you are a member of the supreme royal family in the universe. You are God's ambassador to your world, and He will not send you out without fully equipping you to carry His life-changing presence with you.

May 3

GOD'S ABUNDANCE

*Why do you spend money for what is not bread, and your
wages for what does not satisfy? Listen carefully to Me,
and eat what is good, and delight yourself in abundance.*

—ISAIAH 55:2 NASB

IF YOU'RE LIKE MOST PEOPLE IN the world, you're not living in
the lap of luxury. And abundance? What's that? All you ever seem to
see an abundance of is bills.

The reality is that you can experience abundance—and may
already be experiencing it—though it may not be the kind of
abundance that comes to mind immediately. Look at the people in your
life; are you rich in friends, relatives, people who care about you? Look
at your possessions; do you have anything beyond what is necessary to
sustain life? Look at your environment; do you see evidence of God's
goodness anywhere in your immediate surroundings? Look at what is
stored inside of you; are you rich in the treasures you've discovered as
you've spent time with God and His Word?

You may never have an abundance of wealth in this lifetime. That's
all right. Accumulating wealth is not a godly goal in and of itself
anyway. But you can still enjoy God's abundance—in the people
He has placed in your life, in His promise of provision, in the world
He created for you to enjoy, and in the wisdom He has given you as a
guide for your life.

May 4

FRESH STRENGTH

Those who trust in the LORD will find new strength.... They will run and not grow weary. They will walk and not faint.
—ISAIAH 40:31 NLT

ON THE SOCCER FIELD, THE LOPSIDED loss tastes bitter to the six-year-old. He didn't mean to score one for the other team. Dejected by the final outcome and by his own performance, the boy trudges off the field. But suddenly, he spots his dad waiting at the edge of the field. The father gently reaches for his son's hand. Hope quietly resurges in the youngster as he clenches his father's sure grip.

Your heavenly Father is reaching for your hand too. He knows you work hard. He knows you give your all but sometimes come up short. He knows when you're worn out by life and feel faint in your faith. God understands when you feel like crawling into a hole or plopping down in defeat. When you feel like you've endured one too many lopsided losses, God wants you to simply put your hand in His— and trust. He promises to exchange His strength for your weariness.

So what are you holding on to these days? Are your fingers wrapped around your relationships, your work, your social calendar? What or whom are you trusting in for hope, renewal, and vitality? Put your trust in the One who longs to revive you with fresh strength.

GOD WITH SKIN ON

The LORD passed in front of Moses, calling out, "Yahweh!
The LORD! The God of compassion and mercy! I am slow to
anger and filled with unfailing love and faithfulness."
—EXODUS 34:6 NLT

HAVE YOU EVER HEARD OF THE song "The All-Seeing Eye"? It conjures up images of God as a foreboding giant—a Cyclops, no less—standing with His arms folded across His heaving chest just waiting for us to slip up so that He can take us down. That image has haunted people throughout the ages, frightening them away from the truth about God.

On the contrary, the Scriptures teach that God's character can be seen in Jesus—the exact image of God. In other words, Jesus interpreted God to His contemporary world and is still doing so.

In the Scriptures, you'll find Jesus spending His days caring for sick people. You'll track Him through a barren wilderness where He serves up a banquet to several thousand souls because of a heart full of compassion. You'll discover Jesus offering a gift of acceptance and abundance to a woman who had failed at marriage so many times she hadn't bothered to marry the man with whom she was currently living. You'll discover His reputation for hanging out with the rowdies and hanging on to rejects.

Who is this God? He is the ultimate expression of goodness, gentleness, and grace. Go to Jesus and get acquainted with God.

May 6

AN INTIMATE INVITATION

*In six days I made the heavens and the earth. I made the
oceans and everything in them. But I rested on the seventh
day. So I blessed the Sabbath day and made it holy.*
—**EXODUS 20:11 NIRV**

AFTER SEPARATING LIGHT AND DARKNESS, SKY and earth,
oceans and continents; after planting trees and flowers, molding
finches and zebras; after breathing into humanity the breath of life,
the Bible says God rested. He paused. He stopped, not to catch His
breath, but to survey, celebrate, and enjoy all His accomplishments.
He wanted to watch black-eyed Susans bloom, hawks soar, and the
first man and woman explore their new home. He wanted to listen
to coyotes yip and howl, to the starling's song, and to the thunder of
waves crashing on the shore. He wanted to walk around and feel the
grass under His feet.

It's a very intimate invitation that God extends to us, His children,
to join Him in this cycle of work and rest. Once a week, we pause and
set our work down next to His and look at our combined accomplishments together. Whether we dug wells or wrote poems, mopped floors
or stopped crimes, He grabs us by the hand and dances around with
us. We did it! He did it! And it's all worth celebrating.

"It's good," He says. "It's very good." In that moment, we begin to
understand on a whole new level how much we matter to Him.

WHY FAST?

*Is this not the fast that I have chosen: to loose the bonds
of wickedness, to undo the heavy burdens, to let the
oppressed go free, and that you break every yoke?*
—ISAIAH 58:6 NKJV

FASTING—GENERALLY UNDERSTOOD AS ABSTAINING FROM
food for a particular period of time—isn't usually at the top of
anyone's to-do list. The practice is even rare among people who follow
God and understand that fasting was commonplace among the Jews as
well as the early followers of Christ. Many consider it to be an ancient
ritual that isn't required today.

But those who do practice fasting today will likely be quick to tell
you why they do it and what the benefits are. Instead of focusing on
food, they spend their mealtimes in God's presence. As a result, they
learn a great deal about themselves and their priorities, and they learn
to become more grateful for all that God has provided for them. The
health benefits are also well-documented. What they've learned is that
when they deny themselves something they depend on or even love—
whether food or something else—they're much more likely to see God
as the source of their energy and life itself.

As you fast, keep your focus on hungering and thirsting after
righteousness—wanting more of God and His transforming power in
your life. That focus will help feed your spirit and satisfy your longing
for a closer relationship with Him.

BIGGER THAN BIG BROTHER

I will also hold you by the hand and watch over you.
—ISAIAH 42:6 NASB

FAMED AUTHOR GEORGE ORWELL PENNED THE social science fiction novel *1984*, in which the Big Brother character wields power over the people through persistent government surveillance and public mind control. Orwell's novel was published in 1949, and fifty years later the reality television show *Big Brother* was launched. The popular program features about a dozen people all living together in a spacious house—without contact with the outside world—and all continually observed by television cameras.

There's just something a bit creepy and confining knowing that someone is recording your every move via cameras and microphones. Gratefully, you have someone bigger than a Big Brother fixed on your daily activities. God does more than just watch you; He watches over you with a protecting eye and a concerned heart.

Whether you're sitting still in His presence or zipping around in crowded traffic, God is keenly attentive to how you're doing in every aspect of your life, from the physical and emotional to the relational and spiritual. What a comfort to meditate on His vigilant observation, knowing that He's not poised to record your blunders or eager to hold your words against you. God is more than a hawk-eyed Big Brother—He's your loving, watchful Father.

IT SHOWS ON YOUR FACE

As he came down from the mountain with the two tablets of the covenant in his hand, Moses did not know that the skin of his face shone because he had been talking with God.
—EXODUS 34:29 NRSV

YOU ARRIVE EARLY TO PURCHASE YOUR tickets and line up inside the theater, worried that you won't get the seat you really prefer. Suddenly, the doors fling open and the ticket-holders of the previous showing file out of the theater. Everyone's countenance is stained with the same gut-wrenching sorrow. What did they just experience in there? Should you back out while you are still smiling?

Your face is the barometer of your heart. It gives others a read on what you are feeling. If you slam on your brakes to avoid hitting a child who darted out in front of your car, the fear on your face won't fade for a while. If you've just come from the championship football game where your team took state after a long, fierce battle, the glow of victory remains for hours.

Those who live in close proximity to God—who walk with Him minute by minute, who speak with Him in intimate conversation—are easy to spot. Resonating peace, their faces are radiant with joy, particularly when they emerge from their prayer time, causing you to wonder, *What did they just experience in there?*

Doesn't it make you want to get in line?

NO LONGER ALONE

GOD said, "It's not good for the Man to be alone."
—GENESIS 2:18 MSG

HOW DO YOU CURE LONELINESS? RESEARCH tells us that one out of four adults feels friendless on a regular basis. Most of us know this painful feeling of isolation. What do we do when it strikes?

First and foremost, remember that God is in the business of bringing us out of isolation into friendship. God puts the lonely into families. He created us for relationship, and He has in mind people who are right for us—people who will be good friends or lifelong companions.

But often we need to take an intermediate step before we start meeting new people. We need to take our loneliness to Jesus and let Him bring healing comfort into our lives. He will tell us the truth: We aren't alone; we do matter; we do have a place in His heart. The more we soak in these truths from God Himself, the more we can enter new or renewed relationships from a position of strength. Conversely, the more desperate we are to have friends, the more friendship will elude us. But as God meets our deepest needs, we can find good friends and build relationships that will endure.

May 11

THE GOD WHO LISTENS

It shall be that before they call I will answer;
and while they are yet speaking I will hear.
—ISAIAH 65:24 AMP

ONE OF THE GREAT DISTINCTIONS OF both Judaism and Christianity is the idea of a personal God. Even in their earliest history, the Israelites, later known as the Jews, had a close relationship with God, as have Christians for the last two millennia. The Judeo-Christian God is one who listens to the prayers of His people and responds to them as a loving father would—a far cry from the gods of other cultures whose people quaked in fear at the retribution they often expected from the gods they worshiped.

Isn't that astonishing? You have the ear of the Creator of the universe and He doesn't ever feel as if you're bothering Him. He *wants* you to talk to Him—to ask Him questions, to tell Him what you need and what you want, to unload all your burdens on Him. Not only that, He also wants to talk to you—to answer your questions and requests, to comfort you in the difficult times, to express His love to you.

You serve a God who listens and responds to you—and who rejoices when you respond to Him. Go to Him often and open your heart. He's waiting for you.

BLIND, BUT NOW I SEE

*I will lead the blind on unfamiliar roads. I will lead them
on unfamiliar paths. I will turn darkness into light in front
of them. I will make rough places smooth.*
—ISAIAH 42:16 GWT

THE EXACT ILLNESS IS UNKNOWN, BUT many today conclude scarlet fever or meningitis robbed nineteen-month-old Helen Keller of her eyesight and hearing back in 1882. Fortunately, at the age of six Helen became a pupil of Anne Sullivan, a young woman visually impaired herself. Helen's breakthrough in communication came within a month as Anne was pouring cool water over Helen's hand and making motions for the word *water* in Helen's other hand.

In a literal sense, the almost-blind was leading the blind into an incredible adventure of language and knowledge. Through Miss Sullivan's continued guidance, Helen became the first deaf-blind person to earn a bachelor of arts degree.

Although we may not be physically blind, we sometimes stumble in the darkness of the unfamiliar. We sense God nudging us forward, but without a clue of the road ahead, we feel hesitant, awkwardly fumbling for sure footing.

The Bible encourages you to walk by faith, turning your eyes toward God and not depending solely on what you can see in this world. God promises to lead you through the unknown and shine light on the dark pathways. With Him as your faithful guide, your eyes will be opened to incredible adventures ahead.

May 13

BEYOND BELIEVING

*Ezra had committed himself to studying the Revelation
of GOD, to living it, and to teaching Israel
to live its truths and ways.*
—**EZRA 7:10** MSG

IT IS ONE THING TO GAIN understanding. It is quite another thing to live as if you have understanding. And it is something else altogether to help others understand.

Gaining insight into God—His ways and His will—may come through various means: study of His Word, listening to sermons, reading books on relevant topics, or even observing God's amazing creation. Your mind gets stretched out of its previous paradigm and expanded to receive the vast revelation of the incredible God that He is.

Taking the next step—putting your understanding into action—requires more than merely an intellectual exercise. Your heart and your will become engaged in the motivation and determination to conform your life to what you have learned. This moves you from the arena of academia into the realm of authentic experience where character is forged, decisions are made, and people are deeply impacted.

But even more—getting beyond yourself—you discover, at last, that helping someone else to know the Lord brings with it a joy and a measure of fulfillment unlike anything you've experienced yet. That joy multiplies—within the community of faith and within the heart of God.

Don't settle for mere understanding. Go beyond belief.

May 14

TEMPTATION

*Because [Jesus] himself suffered when he was tempted,
he is able to help those who are being tempted.*
—HEBREWS 2:18 NIV

WHAT WILL YOU FIND AT THE center of every temptation you face? A lie! "God doesn't care about you. God wants to deprive you. God is not good. You are all alone. No one will ever care about you. You aren't good enough for God to help you. God can't rescue you. God wants to hurt you." And the list goes on. These are all lies.

All of us face temptations. As we do, however, we have the choice of bringing the temptation to Jesus. "Jesus, this is what I'm tempted to do. What do I need from You? What am I not understanding? What have I failed to experience in You?" Sometimes we can do this on our own; sometimes we need help from a skilled counselor or prayer minister. But if we make a habit of inviting Jesus to handle our temptations, if we let Him answer the door when temptation knocks, we will find that temptations lose much of their power.

We don't go looking for temptations. On the contrary, we ask God to remove them from our path. But when they come, they can be an opportunity for us to experience God on a whole new level.

May 15

INTENDED TO INFLUENCE

This is how the LORD responds: "If you return to me,
I will restore you so you can continue to serve me.
If you speak good words rather than worthless ones,
you will be my spokesman. You must influence them;
do not let them influence you!"
—JEREMIAH 15:19 NLT

D O YOU THINK OF YOURSELF AS an influencer? If not, why not? No matter how small your world is, unless you live in isolation, you very likely influence a fair number of people in your everyday life. You may not give much thought to the number of people you have contact with each day, but if you spend a few moments thinking back on a typical day, you may be surprised at the amount of human contact you had—at work, running errands, in the neighborhood, even at home.

Now consider the kind of influence you have on those people and they have on you. Who's doing the most influencing? And what kind of influence is it? God doesn't expect you to bring up His name in every conversation, but He does want you to love others on His behalf. Your daily acts of kindness and compassion, your willingness to listen, encourage, and help out, your ability to express hope in difficult situations and make people feel that their lives matter, and your offer to pray for others can have far-reaching effects. You can be a major influence on a person's life—without even realizing it.

OVER YOUR HEAD

When you're in over your head, I'll be there with you.
When you're in rough waters, you will not go down.
When you're between a rock and a hard place,
it won't be a dead end.

—ISAIAH 43:2 MSG

YOU'VE PROBABLY HEARD OR USED THE words "in over your head." This idiom is essentially an analogy of an inexpert swimmer who has encountered water that is too deep. You may be in this precarious state right now.

You invested heavily in stocks that soured and now you're sinking financially. You promised the committee you could find plenty of volunteers, but only one person has stepped up. You promised you'd help with your son's homework, but you are clueless about differential equations.

Getting "in over your head" is common to all of us. The Bible has its share of troubled swimmers too. Eve didn't bargain for marring the world when she demurely talked to the serpent. Joseph didn't expect to be hurled into a pit when he related his dreams to his brothers. Peter didn't anticipate bailing on Jesus even in that darkened courtyard.

None of us really plans to take on more than we can handle or promise more than we can deliver. Sometimes our performance tendencies and even our pride keep us from getting an accurate view of a situation. Thankfully, even if we miscalculate and get in too deep, God is right there with us holding His secure lifeline.

May 17

PRAY TO PAPA

*You can tell for sure that you are now fully adopted
as his own children because God sent the Spirit of his Son
into our lives crying out, "Papa! Father!"*
—GALATIANS 4:6 MSG

DID YOU GROW UP HEARING PEOPLE pray? The many forms of prayer reveal a wide spectrum of experience and proximity to God. There are those whose formal approach to God reflects a perception of an authoritative and demanding God. There are some who seem intimidated, as if they've barely made His acquaintance and are unsure of His audience. There are people who speak as if they are instructing God about who He is and what He needs to do. There are many who go to God only to present a long wish list, prioritized for His convenience. Some pray out of desperation, often bargaining for what they need. Some resort to confessional prayer because they can't live with their guilt any longer. And many perform their prayers as if scripted.

But those who cry, "Abba…! Papa…! Daddy…!"—whose passionate expressions seize upon your heart with an authenticity and intimacy that causes you to gasp—those are the people who have been completely immersed in relationship with God. They are children of the Almighty who know where they stand.

If you long to be a true child of God, run into His embrace, jump up in His lap, look into His face, and say, "Abba."

FROM THE PLACE OF EMPTINESS

*The earth was formless and empty, and darkness
covered the deep waters. And the Spirit of God was
hovering over the surface of the waters.*
—GENESIS 1:2 NLT

THERE WILL BE TIMES IN LIFE when nothing makes any sense. All is dark. Confusion reigns. We hoped for something great and came up empty. There we stand with nothing in our hands—no plans, no dreams, no hopes—nothing but desolation.

But be assured that even in this place of darkness, God is present. This can be the prologue to a great story. This can be the backdrop to a great adventure. Throughout history, every great work of God started in this exact place of emptiness. This is the kind of situation that causes Him to roll up His sleeves and rub His hands together in anticipation.

God gives shape to those things that do not yet have any form. Just as Michelangelo "saw" the sculpture inside the stone, so also God sees what we cannot see. What is now hidden from our sight will someday be revealed. God fills those things that are empty. His light easily overcomes the darkness in our lives. When Jesus enters the place of darkness, it will never be the same. Laughter will return. What is dead will be brought to life.

Here in this unlikely place, God's Spirit is hovering, waiting, ready to do the impossible.

A PERSON OF WORTH

Live a life worthy of the calling you have received.
Be completely humble and gentle.
—**EPHESIANS 4:1-2** NIV

WISDOM AND KINDNESS COMPLEMENT EACH OTHER, especially in the words you speak. Saying the right thing at the right time and saying it with gentleness, grace, and compassion is more than a gift, it's a skill acquired with practice over time.

Are you ready to discover the person of worth in you? It starts with how you talk to yourself. When you speak to yourself with words of kindness and truth, the purity and glow of your heart will spill over onto all those around you. Your own family will probably be the first to notice. After that will come neighbors, coworkers, and friends. In time, your words will bless even strangers.

Ask God to give you the right words to say and show you the right time to say them. Avoid lofty words that make others feel small and preachy words that make them feel judged. Instead speak the words you would want to hear—loving words that impart life.

You are precious to God, so precious that He has placed the gift of His Spirit in you. He will be there to teach you as you learn to speak words of life to those around you and to do so with kindness.

THE GIFT OF COMPASSION

All of you be of one mind,
having compassion for one another.
—1 PETER 3:8 NKJV

EVERYONE WANTS TO MAKE A DIFFERENCE in the world. Some express great aspirations like finding a cure for cancer, eliminating poverty, putting a stop to human trafficking, cleaning up the environment. While we admire those lofty goals, we may wonder how we could tackle the problems of the world when we have so many of our own to deal with.

But making a difference may not be as overwhelming and difficult as you think. You don't need great aspirations or unattainable goals; you just need to act on the empathy you feel for others when you sense a deep need in their lives. Sometimes the only thing people need is your willingness to listen to their heart's cry, or sit with them in silence if that's what they want, or stand in the gap for them and believe God.

Remember, too, that though their needs may not be as easy to spot, people who live relatively comfortable lives have deep needs as well. Having compassion for them—having compassion for *anyone*—simply involves asking God to reveal what that person needs and how you can share His love. Compassion is a gift you can give every day.

YOUR GPS

Thus says the LORD, your Redeemer, the Holy One of Israel,
"I am the LORD your God, who teaches you to profit,
who leads you in the way you should go."
—ISAIAH 48:17 NASB

YOU'RE AT A STANDSTILL. THINGS DIDN'T turn out the way you expected and a situation you thought you could handle just imploded. It was so unexpected. Things were getting a little tricky, but you were so confident you could pull it off. Just one more deal, one more moment, one more around-the-next-corner and you'd have it made. Now you feel stuck in the dark, dizzy and disoriented.

What now?

Tell God every one of your concerns. Let Him know you feel lost and unsure of your next steps. There's no need to panic, but you'd be wise to pray. God is the original GPS: Guidance and Protection Service. He is acutely aware of all the details—your details. As King of the universe, He has the bird's-eye view of your best route. Ask Him to guide your steps. He will teach you what you need to know. He will lead you forward inch by inch, protecting you every step of the way.

It's always bewildering when you're uncertain about which course to follow. That's okay. God always knows the best path for each day of your life. And He will never fault you for asking for directions.

May 22

FREE TO BE

*Christ has truly set us free. Now make sure that you stay
free, and don't get tied up again in slavery to the law.*
—**GALATIANS 5:1 NLT**

RELIGION WAS DESIGNED TO SIZE YOU up, fix you up, and
bind you up. Relationship with God, on the other hand, lifts you
up and sets you free.

First, there's freedom *from* something. Initially, we think of freedom
in terms of deliverance. Christ has come to set you free from the
guilt that hunts you down and holds you hostage to your burdened
conscience. It is freedom from the self-imposed pain that plagues your
memories in the quiet of the night and troubles your sleep. It includes
freedom from the wreckage and ruin that darkens your days. Jesus
fought for—and won—your deliverance from the Enemy of your soul.
Furthermore, He has declared liberty on your behalf from the tyranny
of self—the cruelest tyrant of all.

But there is more to freedom than deliverance from things that
oppress and enslave you. There is the other side of freedom that sets
you free to *be*. The freedom that Christ claimed for you opens vast
possibilities for you to explore. You have been liberated to become all
that you were created to be—free to fulfill your potential in relationship with God rather than a codified religion. Free to discover the
abundance of His lavish love.

May 23

GOD'S FEELINGS

The Lord was very sad...His heart was filled with pain.
—GENESIS 6:6 NIRV

GOD HAS FEELINGS. HE EXPERIENCES HAPPINESS, anger, sadness, contentment, and so on. One of the invitations He extends to us when we spend time alone with Him is to feel what He feels. If God had no emotions, then much of life would be unexplainable. Many people lose their way because they don't understand how angry God is over injustice or how much He rejoices over His children or how He weeps with those who have been hurt.

Allowing God to share His feelings with us empowers us to grow. Sometimes feeling God's anger over an injustice will spur us into action, advocating for those who cannot stand up for themselves. Sometimes sensing God's contentment will help move us to a place of peace and maturity. Sometimes sharing His sorrow will motivate us to pray and to act with compassion. Experiencing His joy can fill our hearts with gratitude.

How can you begin to feel what God feels? Two things will help. First, immerse yourself in the biblical narrative in order to understand God's heart. Second, ask Him how He feels about what you are experiencing. He will find a way to let you know.

May 24

KEEP IT SIMPLE

*There is no time to waste, so don't complicate your lives
unnecessarily. Keep it simple—in marriage, grief, joy,
whatever. Even in ordinary things—your daily routines
of shopping, and so on.*
—1 Corinthians 7:29-30 MSG

HAVE YOU EVER HEARD OTHERS REGRET the fact that their lives are uncomplicated? It's unlikely that you have. Most people instead regret that their lives are becoming increasingly complex. What's worse, they have no idea how to stop the momentum toward even greater complexity, let alone reverse it.

One way to simplify your life is to spend time—yes, you'll have to *make* time to do this!—reflecting on what is truly important to you and to God, and then start eliminating those things that don't line up with what you discover. Don't, however, make the mistake of thinking that "important" means serious. Jesus apparently considered it important to spend much of His time socializing and creating deep relationships with His earthly friends.

The next time you find yourself on autopilot—running out to the store, for example, for something you really don't need *now*—stop and consider what important thing you could do instead. Do you know someone who is going through a rough patch and needs a listening ear? Or maybe *you're* going through a rough patch, and you need to cry out to God's listening ear. Take a deep breath, ask God to calm your spirit, and focus on what's important.

May 25

SHAKEN BUT LOVED

*"Though the mountains be shaken and the hills be removed,
yet my unfailing love for you will not be shaken nor my
covenant of peace be removed," says the LORD,
who has compassion on you.*
—ISAIAH 54:10 TNIV

BEN FRANKLIN IS CREDITED WITH POINTING out that nothing is ever constant but death and taxes. Change is certainly inevitable. Sometimes it sneaks up on you and takes you unaware in a happy way, like an inheritance. Sometimes change looms far out on the horizon. Sometimes it's in your face. There are upbeat changes like new babies and new cars and sad changes like job loss and poor health. Change seeps into our lives constantly and can rattle our personal stability.

As you stop to reflect today, consider what bolsters your security. Is it relationships? Love? Accomplishments? Your job title? Your investment portfolio? Imagine that the things that make you feel rock solid suddenly shift. Friends drift, investments tank, companies downsize. What can you count on to make it when life spins off kilter?

Count on God's personal love for you. He won't leave, won't walk out, won't betray. He isn't a human capable of erratic tendencies. His promise to stand by you is bankable. So when life circumstances are unsettled, you can have perfect peace because the one who steadily sustains you doesn't shift, slip, warp, crack, disappear, or…change.

When the only constant in life is change, rely on the unchangeable One.

May 26

CONFIDANTS AND COMMITMENTS

The LORD said, "Shall I hide from Abraham
what I am about to do?"

—GENESIS 18:17 NIV

AS YOUR CHILDREN MATURE, BECOMING MORE and more responsible for their role in the family, you feel more inclined to share with them your goals and plans for the future. You delight to discover that they may even make viable contributions to your plans at times, even entering into respectful debate when appropriate.

Believe it or not, the same thing can happen with God and His children. Throughout His history with mankind, God has revealed His desires, His motives, and His plan of action to those whom He trusts. He makes Himself and His plans vulnerable to His children, listening to their responses, taking their words and their reasoning into consideration as He moves forward.

There were even times when God altered His plan of action due to the persistence of men who had proven themselves worthy of His trust because of their love for His people.

Can you imagine being one of those trusted friends of God?

No one becomes the confidant of another without demonstrating the love and loyalty that confidentiality requires. There is a certain selflessness that communicates trustworthiness. The key to having that kind of relationship with God is a selfless and relentless pursuit of His will, no matter the cost.

May 27

DEALING WITH ANNOYANCES

The anger of man does not produce the righteousness of God.
—JAMES 1:20 ESV

WHAT DO YOU DO WITH PEOPLE who annoy you? Sometimes people just irritate us. Perhaps they haven't committed an offense that we could classify as a sin or a character defect, but they bug us nonetheless. They talk too fast or sneeze too loudly. They drive too slow or smile at odd times. Or maybe we don't even know what it is about them that bothers us.

The solution begins when we understand that our annoyance is rooted somewhere else. That person isn't "making us mad." Rather, that person is reminding us of an unresolved issue inside. Deep within, we aren't at peace about something, and that person "triggers" those disagreeable feelings. For example, that person might remind us of a childhood bully or an embarrassing personal fault. Once we've re-framed the problem, we can bring the real issue(s) to Jesus in our time alone with Him.

Ask Him to give you the courage to see what this annoyance is really connected to. Then bring those matters before Him to see what healing He brings into your soul. The results are amazing. The very things that used to exasperate us no longer even show up on our radar screen.

TRAINING FOR RIGHTEOUSNESS

For the moment all discipline seems painful rather than
pleasant, but later it yields the peaceful fruit of righteousness
to those who have been trained by it.

—HEBREWS 12:11 ESV

IF YOU'VE EVER TRAINED FOR AN athletic competition, you
know how painful the required discipline can be. Not only is there
physical pain, there's also the mental stress of constantly striving to
be better than the other competitors. When you become a follower
of God, you also enter into training, but thankfully, you're not
being trained to compete against others. You're being trained for
victorious living.

Like a loving parent, God must sometimes discipline His children
in order to teach them the lessons they need to learn to become
mature in their faith. Never resist that discipline; it's intended for
your benefit. When you were a child, your parents likely disciplined
you for your protection, to help you make wise choices, and to teach
you responsibility. That discipline wasn't fun, but as an adult you
realize how critical it was. God's love is even stronger than the love your
parents had for you. His discipline is perfect. It is always constructive
and administered with love.

As you mature in faith, you'll look back on God's discipline with
gratitude, realizing how many mistakes it helped you avoid. Open
your heart to the lessons He wants to teach you.

GOD OF ALL COMFORT

I will turn their mourning into joy and will comfort them
and make them rejoice after their sorrow.

—**JEREMIAH 31:13 AMP**

AT SOME POINT IN LIFE, DEATH'S finality will cover each of our hearts and wrestle with our deepest emotions—we'll lose a grandparent, a parent, a spouse, a child, a friend, a pet.

Perhaps you are walking the meandering path of grief right now. Your bruised heart pleads silently for someone to hear your inner agony, "Will this pain ever end?" In your sorrow, you long for the comfort and safety of expressing your tattered emotions without camouflaging how you *really* feel. As much as others care, they cannot fully soothe the depth of your pain.

How reassuring to know that God is that ever-present, safe someone who longs to listen to your pain and alleviate the agony of your loss. He is your trusted traveling companion throughout each step of your journey. Over the coming weeks, months, and years, He will, bit by bit, replace your mourning with joy.

Gladness of heart and a rejoicing spirit may seem impossible right now, but lighter times will eventually lift your heaviness. For the present, simply rest in knowing God empathizes with you because He also lost someone dear to His own heart—His only Son. And through His loss, we receive hope and eternal life.

WORDS OF LIFE

*The word of God is alive and powerful. It is sharper than
the sharpest two-edged sword, cutting between soul
and spirit, between joint and marrow.
It exposes our innermost thoughts and desires.*

—HEBREWS 4:12 NLT

SOME PEOPLE HAVE THE PERCEPTION THAT God's Word is a
book of rules for the religious, something similar to an employee
handbook at a corporation. Others perceive it to be a compilation of
wise sayings and timely truths, comparable to the works of ancient
Greek philosophers. And still others believe it to be a storybook full of
charming fairy tales and whimsical anecdotes.

As a whole, the Scriptures are comprised of a variety of literary
genres, composed over a vast span of history by a diverse group of
writers. But the most amazing thing about the Word of God is its
unique capacity to reach deeply into the hearts of its readers with
profound relevance. It is the *living* Word.

The words of this book are not merely stored in your brain as data
ready to be retrieved. They are words that enter into your mind and
heart with the power to transform your perceptions, your decisions,
your principles, your relationships, and your will. These words can
search out and reveal your hidden motives. They find their way into
the secret places of your heart, giving counsel in wisdom, bringing
healing to your wounds, whispering hope in your despair, and lending
courage in the face of your fears.

May 31

MAKE ROOM

Get as many as you can.

—2 KINGS 4:3 NIrV

WHAT ARE YOU EXPECTING FROM GOD?

Long ago there was a widow whose sons were about to be sold into slavery to pay for her late husband's debts. Desperate, she turned to a prophet who showed her the way out: "Go to all your neighbors and ask for empty jars. Ask for many jars." Why? Because God intended to miraculously fill those jars with oil, giving her a product she could sell at the town market to provide the funds, not only to pay off the debts, but to give her money to live on.

God looks for us to make room for the miracle. Think about things from God's point of view. Here He is, limitless in love, wanting to pour Himself out into our lives. There's only one catch: our limited capacity to receive. So what does God want to do? He wants to increase our capacity to receive. Why? He wants to give us more.

A few years ago someone created a cartoon that showed two people ice fishing. One was standing over a small hole in the ice. The second person was standing over a hole the size and shape of a whale. Two people—two different expectations.

June 1

STAY IN THE RACE

*Since we are surrounded by such a great cloud of witnesses,
let us throw off everything that hinders
and the sin that so easily entangles, and let us run
with perseverance the race marked out for us.*

—HEBREWS 12:1 NIV

QUIETNESS, CONTEMPLATION, AND STILLNESS ARE ALL components of your devotional relationship with God. Even so, you may be walking while you're praying, running on a treadmill as you read the Bible, or jogging around the neighborhood as you listen to a Christian podcast on your MP3 player. But running for your life? Not many people think of that as a faith-related activity.

There's a sense in which a life of faith is exactly that. It's a run for your life—but not out of fear or terror. It's an active, heart-pumping, adrenaline-infused race in which you throw off everything that is weighing you down. You're not running away from anything; you're running toward everything God has for you.

You have this one incredible, thrilling, amazing life. You can slog your way through it, or you can run the course that God has set before you, taking advantage of every good and perfect gift He has placed in your path. The best part is that you can choose the life you want to live. If you run toward an exhilarating life of faith in the God who loves you and wants the best for you, you'll never regret it.

DOCTOR'S ORDERS

I will refresh the weary and satisfy the faint.

—JEREMIAH 31:25 NIV

WE TYPICALLY HEED THE DIRECTIVES OF doctors, especially when we're in pain and want immediate treatment to get us back on track physically. But some ongoing ailments in our lives arise from stress and the weariness of responsibilities and demands. If we're not watchful about the use of our daily time and energy, we'll deplete not just our physical reserves, but our spiritual and emotional well-being also.

The positive news is you were not designed to live out of balance, wobbling to the point of exhaustion. God didn't create you as an automaton programmed to overcome limits of the human mind and body. He created you in His image and instilled in you the power of His Spirit. With the Almighty on your side, you can make wise choices about not just your physical health, but your spiritual health too.

Start with reserving regular times for refreshment before God. As you meet with Him, He wants to lift the cares that weigh you down and give you a fresh boost of energizing truth to keep you balanced and strong no matter what circumstances arise in your life. Getting a daily spiritual checkup is just what the Great Physician ordered.

GOD KNOWS YOUR GOODNESS

God doesn't miss anything. He knows perfectly well all the love you've shown him by helping needy Christians, and that you keep at it.

—HEBREWS 6:10 MSG

IS THERE A LIST OF GOOD deeds that Christians are required to check off in order to please God? If so, where is it, and what quotas must be met?

Many people do have that perception and are driven by guilt and intimidation concerning their salvation and reward. But the truth is, there is no such list; neither is there a merit system by which you can earn your way into the abundant life. That isn't to say that God is unconcerned or unaware of your acts of kindness and compassion.

One of the most peculiar things about God is that His memory is very short when it comes to the things you do wrong. Provided you remain honest and humble before the Lord, He forgives and forgets with remarkable speed. However, when it comes to things you do right, He never gets over it, nor does He ever neglect to reward you. This is particularly the case when, out of the goodness of your heart, you help His people. And most thrilling to Him of all is when you've done that—and keep doing that—without anyone knowing or applauding you. Why? Because your secrets tell the truth about what's in your heart.

June 4

THE PATH TO HONOR

Honor your father and your mother.

—EXODUS 20:12 NKJV

HOW DO WE HONOR A PARENT who has been less than honorable? The first step is clear: We need to get free of any lies we may have believed while growing up. All of us carry around messages in our heads, many of which can be destructive: "You'll never amount to anything." "You're ugly." "It's all your fault." "You're not as good as your sister." And so on. The more we can receive from Jesus the healing, transforming truth about who we really are, the more we can look objectively at our parents and our growing-up years.

The second step is to forgive. Every parent makes mistakes. Some parents commit atrocities. Finding grace from God to forgive puts us solidly back on our own two feet, so we can approach this from a position of strength. While some of us can process this on our own before God, it's a sign of health to reach out for help when we need it.

From this position of strength, we can see our parents through the eyes of Christ and discover those things that are redemptive. With honest gratitude, we are now free to honor our parents as God tells us to do.

June 5

EVIDENCE OF A GENEROUS GOD

If any of you needs wisdom, you should ask God for it.
He is generous to everyone and will give you wisdom
without criticizing you.

—JAMES 1:5 NCV

WHEN YOU THINK OF GOD'S GENEROSITY, what's the first thing that comes to your mind? Many consider it to be His material blessings—the nicer house than you ever thought you'd be living in, a car that runs smoothly, or maybe a totally unexpected raise. But God's generosity extends beyond the material world. The evidence of His generosity lies in the essence of who you are.

Through your relationship with God, you acquire unseen traits, character qualities, and values that become evident to others through your actions. Every wise decision you make in difficult circumstances reveals how generous God has been with His wisdom. Every time you forgive someone who in reality deserves your scorn and revenge, it shows how generous God has been in giving you the ability to extend forgiveness and mercy—undeserved kindness.

But those attributes don't come to you as if by magic. They become integrated into your character and your spirit as you spend intentional, purposeful time with God. You can get to know *about* God's attributes through personal study and the teaching of others, but to make them your own, you need to spend time alone with Him, allowing Him to lavish on you the qualities that come from Him alone.

June 6

STRONG ARMS

He tends his flock like a shepherd: He gathers the lambs in his arms and carries them close to his heart; he gently leads those that have young.
—ISAIAH 40:11 NIV

IF YOU'VE EVER COMFORTED A CRYING baby or young child, you know how little ones love to snuggle in close to you. The longer the infant or toddler remains in your arms, the more the sobs lessen and the child's previously tense and squirming body relaxes. There's just something soothing about being held by someone you trust.

The same can be said of your relationship with God. He knows just when to let your tears fall and when to let you have your own tantrum. He also knows just when to draw near and enfold you in a comforting embrace. When you feel like you're limping and crawling, He knows just when to pick you up and carry you until you've regained your footing.

Do you need God to point you in the right direction or come alongside you with a calming hug? He longs to reassure you and sustain you no matter what unfolds in your life. There's no need to wait until you're surprised by tough news or overjoyed with unexpected blessings before you lean upon God. The more you get to know God each new day, the more you will entrust yourself to His all-powerful arms and His loving heart.

June 7

AWAKE AND ATTENTIVE

Morning by morning he wakens me and opens my understanding to his will.

—Isaiah 50:4 NLT

L IVING IN GOD'S PRESENCE RESULTS IN an awakening of your senses to everything around you that pertains to His will. You begin to see people from a new perspective, looking at circumstances differently. You become aware of the constant conversation available in prayer, finding God's vast store of wisdom readily available to you for the sake of helping others through their struggles.

Living in closer proximity to God means adjusting your sights to His instead of requesting that He narrow His vision for you. You catch a glimpse of God's perspective on the world and let it open your mind to possibilities that you hadn't considered. You see not only the possibilities but ways in which you can "flesh them out."

Being in God's will means taking notice of what He is doing and how He is equipping you to join Him in His mission. It means becoming aware of where you fit into His plan and helping others to realize their role as well.

Learning to listen for the voice of God throughout the day requires that you not only seek Him but that you anticipate Him. Tune yourself to His frequency by being attentive and aware.

June 8

FRAGILE DREAMS

Don't tease me with false hopes.
—2 KINGS 4:28 MSG

WHAT DO YOU DO WITH SECRET dreams that are quietly dying inside? Most of us will come into seasons when it seems like God has taken away our dreams, robbed us of the good life that we were meant to have, and left in its place an existence we never would have wished on anyone. It may seem like God has pulled the rug out from beneath us. There will be times in our lives when God seems cruel, when our experience seems to contradict all we have learned about His goodness.

If you are in such a place right now, know this: Whether your circumstances change or not, God is preparing you for the most important discovery of your lifetime. But first He asks this question: Will you dance with Me, holding on to Me with an embrace of trust? Will you take the plunge? Will you open up your heart so wide that you lose part of yourself to Me?

Heaven holds its breath while you decide. Will you say "yes"? Will you hope for the dawn even though all you can see is darkness? When you choose Him, you open the door to discovering the truth: your most fragile and precious dreams are eternally safe with God.

June 9

SUFFERING INJUSTICE

The LORD is a God of justice.
Blessed are all who wait for him!
—ISAIAH 30:18 NIV

HAVE YOU EVER BEEN FALSELY ACCUSED? Blamed for something you didn't do? Suffering the consequences for an unwise action is one thing, but suffering when you are innocent? Imagine how that might feel. Around the world, there have been many who have suffered this fate—some for their faith, others for their politics, and still others as the result of flawed justice systems.

Jesus suffered the penalty of death for crimes He didn't commit. He did so to pay for our transgressions. Nevertheless, He stood silently while those He had come to rescue spit on Him, accused Him of making false claims and subverting the nation with His teachings, and even refusing to pay taxes. Through it all, it was Jesus' relationship with His Father that sustained Him. During the quiet moments in the garden before His arrest, He asked for strength. Even as He was dying, He committed His spirit to God.

You may never languish inside a prison, but you are certain to feel the sting of injustice at some point. When you do, remember that there is One who knows and understands what is happening to you. Quiet yourself before Him, knowing that He sees the truth, even if no one else ever does.

June 10

PERSPECTIVE

One day Kish's donkeys strayed away.
—1 SAMUEL 9:3 NLT

SOMETIMES WE SEE OURSELVES AS HAVING so very little, while God is looking at us, shaking His head and saying, "If she only knew."

Long ago, a seemingly insignificant farm boy was sent by his father to track down some missing donkeys. After he embarked on his errand, things went from bad to worse. Not only did he fail to find the missing animals, but he ended up miles and miles away from home, on foot, with no food and no money. He didn't know where to turn.

But unknown to this farm boy, a bigger drama was playing out, one that would change an entire nation. As he stumbled on, hot, tired, hungry, and discouraged, he came across a prophet who told him what was really going on. "Your donkeys have been found. We have a feast prepared for you. Everything about your life is going to change because God has chosen you to be the king of our entire nation."

What do we have? While we are rummaging through our empty lunch sacks, God is arranging a feast. Just when we think our mission has failed, God is planning a coronation ceremony.

THE JOURNEY TO WISDOM

*Real wisdom, God's wisdom, begins with a holy life
and is characterized by getting along with others.*
—JAMES 3:17 MSG

WE OFTEN PRAY FOR WISDOM WITHOUT taking pause to consider what it will look like when it arrives. Most of us expect it will come as an answer to a specific question, holding forth a remedy for whatever dilemma we face. Some expect that it will come as a profound moment of insight into a situation they are facing.

Though it does include both answers and insight, wisdom is more specifically a way of *being* in this world, a way of processing our reality. In fact, if you boil it down to its barest essence, wisdom is all about relationships because wisdom exists for the sake of right relationships with God, with others, and with ourselves.

Having asked God for wisdom, you can expect that He will begin answering your request by revealing to you things about yourself that you need to know. If there is any inadequacy in your thinking, He will gently expose it to you for your growth. He will also lead you to be more open and approachable, more compassionate and understanding, full of peace and joy.

The way to wisdom is a journey with God through character development and genuine love for others.

June 12

GOD LIKES YOU

Look, God's home is now among his people!
He will live with them, and they will be his people.
God himself will be with them.
—REVELATION 21:3 NLT

GOD LIKES YOU. STOP AND THINK about it. Yes, God is well aware of all your imperfections, but He likes you nonetheless. He likes you a lot. If you could make a list of God's favorite activities, hanging out with you would be first on the list. He likes your personality. He likes to laugh with you. He likes to hang out with you and your friends. He is excited about the things you are excited about.

Jesus came to earth because God wanted to be with us. All of history is headed toward one inescapable conclusion: God is moving in with us. He is going to live right here in our home. Why? He wants to be with us. That's how He wants to spend His eternity…with us.

This is one of the reasons why prayer doesn't need to be a fancy ritual, but rather an open conversation between you and your Father in heaven. This is why Sunday morning worship is only a small part of our experience with God. God is into much more than stained-glass windows or worship choruses. He's into experiencing life with you. If it's on your calendar, it's on His too, because He wants to be with you.

TAKE GOOD CARE OF GOD'S GRACE

As each one has received a special gift, employ it in serving one another as good stewards of the manifold grace of God.

—1 PETER 4:10 NASB

DO YOU REALIZE THAT GOD HAS placed His grace in your care? It's true. He has made you a guardian of the grace—the favor and kindness—He extends to His people even though they do not deserve it. He wants you to not only treasure His gift of grace but also extend it to others.

Think about someone who has wronged you. It's only natural that you would be inclined to seek revenge on the one who hurt you rather than bestowing grace on that person. But if you have the Spirit of God within you, there's no need for your responses to be "only natural," because you have access to a *supernatural* power that transcends natural human emotions and actions. Once you have drawn on that power to show undeserved kindness to someone, you will likely experience a measure of joy that can only come from a supernatural source— God Himself.

You already have everything you need to share God's grace with those who deserve much worse. In fact, God gives you the grace to actually *lavish* grace on others. And doing so makes you the best kind of caretaker of this precious gift.

June 14

COUNTING ON GOD

Trust in the LORD with all your heart,
and lean not on your own understanding.

—PROVERBS 3:5 NKJV

PERHAPS YOUR PARENTS OR A FAMILY member helped you learn to swim as a child. Or maybe they paid for you to take swimming lessons. Do you remember learning to float on your back and that hesitant feeling the first time your instructor completely let go and there was no supportive arm to steady you? After a number of reassuring words, you eventually dared to float a few seconds on your own. Over time you graduated to solo swimming and even diving off the board. But your confidence in the swimming pool all started with knowing you could count on the one instructing you.

The same is true of counting on God. God is 100 percent reliable, 100 percent of the time. He is fully aware of your surroundings. When you're in rough waters, His arm is either snugly around you or just inches away, ready to bolster you against the waves. Even when life is smooth sailing, God remains always nearby, ready to advise and support and rescue you if need be. He loves to see you stretch and attempt new challenges. He also loves your gaining faith in His trustworthiness as you continue to know Him more.

CHARACTER AND SPIRIT

The life-giving Spirit of GOD will hover over him,
the Spirit that brings wisdom and understanding, the Spirit
that gives direction and builds strength, the Spirit that
instills knowledge and Fear-of-GOD.

—ISAIAH 11:2 MSG

HE'S JUST LIKE HIS FATHER." YOU'VE heard people say those words about sons. Whether they are referring to physical attributes or character, you trust the observation is intended as a compliment.

In the case of Jesus, it was. The Scriptures indicate that Jesus was not an imitation of God, but God incarnate. He was "God among us." In this case, it is specifically His character to which those words would apply. In fact, God filled Jesus with His own Spirit, manifested in specific ways: deep insight, good judgment, wisdom, strength of character, intuitive understanding, true knowledge, authentic love, relentless mercy, and genuine joy. Is it any wonder that Jesus' presence on the earth had an unparalleled impact on the history of mankind?

Here's the really exciting news: after Jesus was resurrected with power, He did the very thing that His Father had done for Him—He sent His Spirit to take up residence within the hearts of His devoted followers. Like Him, we can be filled with insight, wisdom, understanding, love, mercy, and joy.

June 16

GOD'S SILENCE

I will look down from heaven, where I live.
I will be as quiet as summer heat in the sunshine.

—Isaiah 18:4 NIrv

WHY IS GOD SOMETIMES SILENT? GOD speaks to His children in many ways, but sometimes we go through a period of silence when we want answers that don't seem to come.

God's silence usually means one of three things. First, it may mean that we are doing just fine and don't need any input from Him at this time. Maybe the choices we've made and the direction we are going is okay, and He is content to quietly listen to whatever is on our hearts.

Second, it may mean that we have rejected some clear instruction from Him, and He is not willing to speak to us further until we obey what we already know to do. This requires some soul searching on our part.

Third, God may have something to share with us but is waiting for something to happen first. He might be waiting for a circumstance to change. He might be teaching us to be persistent in prayer. He might need us to be honest with ourselves. Meanwhile, we keep on meeting with Him, reading His story in the Bible, sharing our lives with Him. At the right time, His answer will come.

YOU, A CONQUEROR

Every God-begotten person conquers the world's ways.
The conquering power that brings
the world to its knees is our faith.
—1 JOHN 5:4 MSG

WHAT'S YOUR IMAGE OF A CONQUEROR? History buffs may think of someone like Alexander the Great, who conquered much of the known world of his time, or Attila the Hun, who subdued most of Europe in the fifth century AD. But you too can be a conqueror—not by ruthlessly taking over a geographical area, but by relentlessly warring against the spiritual forces that try to bring you down.

Those forces take many forms: the devastating effects of a drug culture that continually tries to entice your children to join in its addictions, the hidden habits of your own heart that tempt you to deny your marriage vows, the unforgiveness that prevents you from living a joyful life in God's presence. The good news, however, is that God has given you everything you need to overcome whatever the world throws your way. That "everything" is Jesus Christ and your faith in Him.

The faith that conquers the world—those spiritual forces that oppose you—is simply an abiding trust that God will do what He has said He will do. Take God at His word. His power working in and through you is all you need to become the conqueror He said you can be.

June 18

WINNING WARRIOR

You give us victory over our enemies,
you put our adversaries to shame.
—PSALM 44:7 NIV

THERE IS A WINNER'S DNA INSIDE you. Even when you've endured awful things, there is a spark within you that resists giving in to defeat. It's the thing that makes you get up again after being knocked down. It's the inner warrior that refuses to quit and puts on the gear for one more go-round.

God salutes that. He is cheering you on, inspiring you to stand up. Defeating something big in your life that's been hounding you is God's line of work. Take a minute and think about your picture of God. In that view, has He ever lost? Are the forces against Him ever bigger or greater than He is? Have you heard any stories about that time God almost made it but went down in the last round? No! Those stories don't exist. God is the most decorated warrior in history.

So, does God care about your battles? Emphatically, yes. God cares and is on your side for your success. Your God is a God who saves. He is a tide-turner and a game-changer. When you're up against it, ask Him how to respond like the winner He's making you to be. Then be alert for His encouragement.

June 19

HONESTY AND HONOR

Honor your father.

—Exodus 20:12 nlt

G OD GIVES FATHERS THE SACRED TASK of preparing their children to be fathered by God Himself. That's a tall order! Most dads try their best but understand their own limitations. Most dads look back at their fathering years with a mixture of satisfaction and regret.

Your own experience with the one you called "dad" can run the gamut. Some of us had fathers who were wise and wonderful. Some of us had fathers who were abusive. For some of us, dad was absent altogether. Your response to the fathering you received (or missed) might be gratitude or anger, laughter or sorrow, or a mixture of all this and more.

This provides us with a great opportunity to process with God an important part of our lives. As you take time with your heavenly Father, your relationship with your earthly father is an important topic to discuss. What are your real feelings toward your dad? Share them with God. Let Him inside that protected place in your heart. Share with Him your fond memories and your disappointments. Ask Him for His perspective. As you do, you will gain new insights into your relationship with your dad and forge a deeper relationship with God.

June 20

THE HEART OF THE MESSAGE

I will put my law in their minds and write it on their hearts.
I will be their God, and they will be my people.
—JEREMIAH 31:33 TNIV

IF YOU'VE READ THE OLD TESTAMENT, you're aware of the history of Israel: how God led His people out of slavery and then handed down regulatory guidelines by which they were to live. His intention was that the people would learn what it meant to be truly wise and compassionate human beings, conforming to His original plan for creation. Unfortunately, the Israelites let God's intentions fall into obscurity over time, and the regulations were unintentionally reduced to a long list of legalistic dos and don'ts.

The good news is that Jesus came to restore the meaning of the law by His interpretation, which was full of grace and truth. Breathing new life into the original covenant through His relationship with the Father, Jesus eventually brought it to its fulfillment through His love for mankind. As a result of His insightful interpretation, the teaching was transformed into the most incredible love story ever told. And that's the story—the story of sacrificial love—that grips you when you spend time with God in His Word, engraving itself upon your heart with incredible inspiration. Now, instead of discovering a legal document when you go to God, you discover that you've become part of the story.

June 21

THE MEANING OF YOUR LIFE

I know the thoughts that I think toward you,
says the LORD, thoughts of peace and not of evil,
to give you a future and a hope.
—JEREMIAH 29:11 NKJV

WHAT'S THE MEANING OF LIFE? THAT question will never go away, no matter how many answers are given. How do you answer that question? As important as it is, you have an even more critical question to answer: what's the meaning of *your* life?

Though you may not realize it, God has infused your life with purpose and meaning. Reflect on that thought and its ramifications. What if your life has a purpose beyond what you can see? Even if your life's work is filled with purpose—if you spend the day training young minds to acquire knowledge and learn to navigate the adult world, or if you help save the lives of critically wounded people who are rushed into the emergency room—consider the possibility that God wants even more for your life. Not *from* you, but *for* you.

Take that possibility to God in prayer. Ask Him what more He has for you. Maybe it's imparting His wisdom to the next generation or restoring souls, not just bodies, to a healthy condition. Listen for the answers He gives you. When you discover the meaning of *your* life, the answer to the larger question tends to fall in place.

June 22

BOOKMARKED GOD

Let the wise listen and add to their learning,
and let the discerning get guidance.
—**PROVERBS 1:5** NIV

THESE DAYS YOU CAN GATHER ADVICE from a variety of sources. Financial planners, investment brokers, and money management gurus eagerly dish out statistics and trends to point you to greater wealth. Nutritionists and health-food consultants warn you of body-depleting foods and how to jump-start your metabolism. Auto-care technicians expertly note when your tires and transmission are heading for trouble.

But have you ever stopped to consider that God knows what's best for you in all these areas and more? He knows exactly how many pennies are in your bank account right now and how many you'll have in the future. He created your body and the precise nutrients you need for healthy living. He keeps track of millions of vehicles and their drivers every day.

With God's vast databank of knowledge, He is by far the number-one lifeline to call upon 24/7. Sure, Google.com and Ask.com are readily available, but when you start your day, make sure you ask God for His input and direction. It's helpful to turn to other resources for counsel, but keep God on speed dial and bookmarked. His advice is free and always guaranteed to be the right answer.

GIVING UP MEASURING UP

Man looks at the outward appearance,
but the LORD looks at the heart.
—I SAMUEL 16:7 NKJV

WHEN YOU CONSIDER WHETHER YOU HAVE anything to offer God, you may conclude—like many people—that you come up short. In fact, if you are anywhere near normal, you think things need fixing before you can make any significant contribution.

It might surprise you to discover that being useful to God's purposes is not about your ability, it's about your heart. What God longs to put to work in His Kingdom is who you are, not who you aren't—what you have, not what you don't have. Amazingly, He can take your willing heart and do extraordinary things. In fact, that is what He does best. And that makes sense when you consider that when God created the cosmos, He made the visible universe out of invisible properties.

Start the adventure: go to God in prayerful conversation and dedicate all that you are to Him and to His use. Give voice to what you have to offer, and entrust it to Him, not only for His care and keeping, but for His service. Then watch what happens. Be alert, awake, and attentive to His response, and be ready to spring into action.

PROCESSING BAD NEWS

*Then he went into the sanctuary of God
and spread the letter out before God.*

—ISAIAH 37:14 MSG

WHAT DO CHILDREN DO WHEN THEY'RE in pain? Their first response is to cry out for their parents. They do this automatically, naturally, because there is an established bond between parent and child. They won't cry out to a stranger, because they don't trust a stranger to care for them.

In the same way, when we as children of God receive bad news, our natural response is to cry out to Him. If we weren't His children, most likely we wouldn't think to go to Him. But we do. What kind of prayers are appropriate when we're in trouble? Honest ones.

A man came to a young minister and asked him to pray for his wife, who had just been diagnosed with cancer. The minister prayed the best prayer he could and then asked the husband if he wanted to pray. The husband could find no words to express what was in his heart, so he simply wept in God's presence. Soon after, the cancer was surgically removed and his wife fully recovered. But the young minister never forgot the lesson of the prayer. It isn't the words that count. It's the honesty.

A PICTURE OF GOD

The Word became flesh and made his dwelling among us.
We have seen his glory, the glory of the One and Only,
who came from the Father, full of grace and truth.

—JOHN 1:14 NIV

MANY PEOPLE CARRY AROUND PICTURES IN their mind of what God looks like, no matter how much they try not to. Even those who understand that God is spirit often admit that they think of God as an old man with a long, white beard sitting on an enormous throne—an image they've carried around with them since childhood.

Having an image of God is so important to some people that they say they can't pray without a visual image of Him in their heads, and they struggle to find an image that fits. Well, they need look no further than the image of Jesus, because He is the perfect representation of God the Father. In everything that He said and did, Jesus reflected the glory of the Father. His love, compassion, tenderness, grace, even His rebuke of hypocritical religious leaders showed us who God is. And the greatest picture of God is the image of Jesus' sacrifice on the cross.

Think about the picture of God you carry around in your head. Is it a holdover from your childhood? Does that picture need to change to better reflect your adult understanding of God? Ask God for some help—He'll show you who He is.

June 26

CLEARING CHAOS

*Step out of the traffic! Take a long, loving look at me,
your High God, above politics, above everything.*
—PSALM 46:10 MSG

THERE ARE HEAPS OF BOOKS WRITTEN and seminars taught on organizing. Magazines inspire with new ways to sort clutter and store belongings. Online stores and big concrete buildings are devoted to the boxes and bins and sorters that will end your mess and create a peaceful environment.

But what about internal chaos? Chaos can begin in your heart and mind and then spread to your environment. If your thoughts are cluttered with schedules, assignments, due dates, and other anxieties, you can't see how to get through the maze. The mayhem piles higher and higher inside, making so much noise you can't hear yourself think. Your spirit cannot find rest. Pretty soon your life overwhelms you with pressures that God never intended for you to bear. That's a signal that you've lost your center.

Taking a break creates inner space to see beyond the urgent and live within the important. Keeping an eye on your inside view brings clarity. Getting away from the demands that pull at you and concentrating on your immovable God balances you from the inside out.

Step off the treadmill daily. And in these moments, lift your eyes heavenward to Someone greater than yourself whose name is the Prince of Peace.

June 27

A LOVE LEGACY

We loved you dearly. Not content to just pass on the Message, we wanted to give you our hearts. And we did.
—1 THESSALONIANS 2:8 MSG

SUPPOSE YOU DISCOVERED THAT YOU HAVE only three years left to live…three years to make a difference. What kind of person would you want to become for the sake of those you love? What would you want to leave behind to benefit them? Wouldn't you want to leave a legacy of the heart?

But how would you go about leaving such a legacy? What would it look like and where would you begin?

This is precisely what Jesus did. He knew His time was short and He made the most of it, entrusting His heart to those He loved. Since His story is such a reliable point of reference, why not take the time to go with God into the story of Jesus and get a good look at His priorities? Observe the way He deals with people. Then ask yourself: *How would Jesus' ways change the look on my face, the tone in my voice, the way I use my time?*

Taking every discovery to God in prayer, ask Him to transform your heart as He leads you through the day—remembering the words of Jesus, putting into practice the things you learn from Him. Seek to imitate His love as your legacy.

June 28

RHYTHM OF RELATIONSHIP

Seven times a day I praise you.
—PSALM 119:164 NIV

GOD LOVES TO BE WITH YOU, but He doesn't smother you. He gives you room to think, to explore, to create, to relax, to be yourself. There is a rhythm in a relationship with God. Yes, He is always here to sustain you, to protect you, to provide for you. But He doesn't expect intense worship and attention from you 24/7. He knows you need time to work, read books, pay bills, buy groceries, have coffee with a friend, tuck the children into bed, or whatever.

Even in Eden, unspoiled perfection, God gave us our space. He walked with Adam and Eve in the cool part of the day.

Many of us have chosen a certain part of the day for spending time alone with God. For some it works well to make it first thing in the morning. Others prefer a different time. Some people take shorter times to meet with God several times throughout the day. You may find that one system works well in one season of your life but needs to be adjusted in another. We are always available to God, and He is always available to us. But our focused time together follows a pattern or a rhythm. That is exactly what He intended.

JESUS, YOUR FRIEND

No longer do I call you servants, for a servant does not know what his master is doing; but I have called you friends.
—JOHN 15:15 NKJV

IN A CULTURE IN WHICH THE word "friend" can be used as a verb and defined to include the complete strangers who follow you on Facebook, it's no wonder that the concept of friendship has been diluted. But when tragedy, grief, or adverse circumstances strike your life, you know full well who will be there to offer a comforting hug and a helping hand. It will be the flesh-and-blood people who enhance the quality of your life through their genuine friendship.

In one of the many great paradoxes of your life with God, the closest friend you have isn't one of those flesh-and-blood people, nor is it one of your online buddies. It's Jesus Himself. He's the most faithful and trustworthy friend you'll ever have, and what's more, He's always with you. He will never leave you.

No matter how impressive it may seem to have thousands of online friends, having Jesus as your friend is one fact of your life that can be accurately described as *awesome*. As with any friendship, your relationship with Jesus depends in part on commitment and communication. By spending time with Him and engaging in conversation with Him, listening to Him as well as talking to Him, you show Jesus your dedication to your friendship with Him.

June 30

GOD'S SPECIALTY

*God, be merciful to me because you are loving. Because you
are always ready to be merciful, wipe out all my wrongs.*

—**PSALM 51:1** NCV

WE ALL BLOW IT AND MAKE mistakes at times. Political leaders, celebrities, sports figures—all of us at times—incur lapses in judgment and find ourselves giving in to temptation. It's disappointing when we commit errors and disappoint ourselves, others, and God. When we slip up, we may respond in a number of ways: defend our innocence, blame someone else, cover up the evidence, or admit we were wrong and accept the consequences.

No person on this planet is an ideal role model in overcoming offenses and making things right. Dealing with human failures is God's specialty. Only He can grant redemptive forgiveness and true cleansing of the heart, soul, and mind. Next time you're feeling bogged down with guilt or regrets over a wrong attitude or action, take that heaviness straight to God. Don't hold back the truth. Tell Him everything. Then thank Him for a clean slate made possible by Jesus taking your punishment on Himself.

Finally, listen. Lean in to what your merciful God wants you to do next. Maybe make an apology. Or seek godly counsel. Or determine to give up a habit. As you move forward, be sure to stand strong in your grace-filled freedom.

July 1

THE WITNESS OF CREATION

The heavens declare the glory of God; the skies proclaim
the work of his hands. Day after day they pour forth speech;
night after night they display knowledge.
—PSALM 19:1-2 NIV

AS STRANGE AS IT SOUNDS, THE whole creation can speak. Stranger still, it speaks in unison about one thing: the glory of God.

It seems reasonable to say that humans speak about God, and by some stretch of the imagination we might say that some animals attempt to communicate. It pushes the limits of logic, however, to say that grass, clouds, trees, and starfish can tell us anything, considering that they all have in common the absence of a brain.

But the truth is there is no limit to what creation can tell us about God. Spending time alone with God in creation, you'll discover His appreciation for beauty, His flair for design, His supreme artistry in the blending of color and shapes.

By observation of trees alone, you'll grasp God's love of variety in the many types, shapes, and sizes on display. You'll thrill to discover His lavish generosity in the many delectable fruits with their delightful flavors and textures. You'll sense His power in the thunder, contrasted with His tender concern in the gently falling rain.

As you reflect on His creation, you'll come to realize that God is a glorious, multifaceted Being, full of imagination and brimming with intentional expression.

July 2

EMPOWERED BY FORGIVING OTHERS

Peter came and said to Him, "Lord, how often
shall my brother sin against me and I forgive him?
Up to seven times?"
—MATTHEW 18:21 NASB

IT'S EASY TO THINK THAT FORGIVING someone else benefits the culprit but taxes the victim. In reality, it works quite differently than that. Forgiving another person's violation empowers the offended.

What is forgiveness? It's simply turning over our unresolved anger to God. We were wronged. We probably had a right to be angry. But anger is like ice cream on a hot day. If we let it go too long, we have a mess on our hands. It may be okay to get angry, but it's not okay to stay angry. Unresolved anger turns into bitterness that rots us from the inside. That's why we need to turn the anger, the offense, the perpetrator over to God.

Forgiving someone does not require us to contact the offender or renew any kind of relationship with him. The level of friendship we have with someone is based on that person's track record of trustworthiness, not on whether we have forgiven him.

But forgiving someone does require us to process a transaction in the presence of God. We hand the offense, the anger, the wrongdoer over to Jesus. We can be sure that whatever we place in His hands will be well taken care of.

July 3

THE GOD WHO ASTONISHES

The Jews then were astonished, saying, "How has this man
become learned, having never been educated?"
—JOHN 7:15 NASB

WHEN WAS THE LAST TIME GOD left you speechless—
so astonished at something He did that you could hardly
believe it? Some of us think we have God all figured out; we decide that
this is what God will do in a given situation or that there's no way God
would ever do *that*. We're so unprepared for God to do the unimaginable
that we fail to recognize God's surprises when they come along.

The more time you spend in God's presence, the more you come
to realize that you can't possibly figure God out. While He will never
do anything or ask you to do anything that is contrary to the teachings
of the Bible, there's enough latitude in those teachings to allow for
some unpredictable actions on His part—maybe even revealing a sense
of humor that will catch you off guard. It's in your time alone with
Him that you discover a God who is never boring and can never be
restricted by the limitations of humanity's perceptions of Him.

When you dismantle the box you've placed God in, you'll finally be
able to recognize the surprises He has in store for you. Demolish the
box, and let Him astonish you.

July 4

MANY FREEDOMS

Wherever the Spirit of the Lord is, there is freedom.

—2 CORINTHIANS 3:17 NLT

IT'S NO COINCIDENCE THAT GOD'S FIRST word in the Bible is "Let." *Permit. Allow. Make room for. Open up.* In the New Testament, the first word spoken by Jesus was also "Let" (Matthew 3:15). *Allow things to unfold.*

God is not a micromanager who wants to rob us of all our choices. Not at all. Consider two of the central stories of the Bible: God opened up the Red Sea so that a nation of slaves could choose to march across dry land to freedom. Jesus died on the cross so that we could choose to be free from the curse of our own corruption.

The freedom to dream, to know the truth, to live in peace, to have fun, to seize opportunities and move forward, to enjoy rich friendships, to experience a personal relationship with the Creator of the universe—these are all freedoms God wants for us. For a son or daughter of God, restrictions are few, freedoms are many. Many are the possibilities that lie before us—so many in fact that it will take all eternity to explore them. One of God's biggest questions to you is: *What do you want?* God wants to know. He wants to discuss your dreams with you.

NEVER-ENDING DISCOVERY

Every day I will praise you and extol your name for ever and ever. Great is the LORD and most worthy of praise; his greatness no one can fathom.

—PSALM 145:2-3 NIV

THE MORE TIME YOU SPEND WITH God, the more aware you become that you will never reach the end of your discovery of Him. He exceeds the limits of human understanding.

Why? Because God is infinitely great and we are finite creatures. Just as is true with numbers, an infinite Being does not have limits where finite creatures do. There simply is no end to the wonders of God.

Take, for instance, His wisdom. No matter how many times you read His Word, you'll find that you will never plumb the depths of its meaning, you'll never reach the end of His understanding. God's wisdom is beyond fathoming because His mind is more vast than the universe.

Or consider His infinite power. Have you ever seen evidence that God's power has been overreached? Neither men nor angels have ever thwarted His ability to accomplish His will.

And how about His love? Have you ever reached the limits of God's love? If you search throughout Scripture, you'll find that no one has ever done so. There are those who reject His love and refuse to receive it. But there is never a case in which God's love has ever been exhausted. It endures forever. How thrilling to realize that the discovery will outlast you.

July 6

THE WORTH OF OUR PRAYERS

Each had a harp and each had a bowl, a gold bowl
filled with incense, the prayers of God's holy people.
—**REVELATION 5:8** MSG

ONE OF THE WOMEN WORKING WITH Mother Teresa came to her one day with a problem. She had miscalculated. As a result, there was no food to feed the three hundred people under their care. Expecting Mother Teresa to call one of her benefactors, she was surprised by the response: "Sister, you're in charge of the kitchen this week. Well then, go into the chapel and tell Jesus we have no food." A few minutes later someone came to the door. A man they had never seen before stood there with a clipboard in his hands. He explained that the teachers at the city schools were going on strike. Classes were dismissed, and they had seven thousand lunches they didn't know what to do with. Could Mother Teresa find a use for them?

It's easy to forget how powerful our prayers really are. How are our prayers treated in heaven? They are regarded as treasure. The Father never forgets the cry of His children. What have you asked God for in secret? Your prayers, your tears, your heart's cry—these things are never wasted with God. He does hear. He will answer. You will see God's goodness in the end.

LET GO OF FEAR

Have I not commanded you? Be strong and courageous.
Do not be terrified; do not be discouraged, for the LORD
your God will be with you wherever you go.
—JOSHUA 1:9 NIV

D O YOU BRISTLE WHEN A FRIEND says you shouldn't be afraid of something that is clearly about to wreak havoc on your life? *I can't help it!* you think. *You'd be afraid too if you were in my situation!* What's even more annoying is that your friend is right; you shouldn't be afraid. And more than that—you *can* help it.

Fear actually provides a measure of comfort by allowing you to dwell on a frightening situation rather than breaking out and challenging your circumstances by trusting that God really does have your back. To believe God on that level requires taking your eyes off the thing you fear and looking only to God. That can be a scary thing to do. As long as you have even one eye on the danger, you can deceive yourself into thinking that maybe, just maybe, you can control it— or at least hold it at bay.

But faith requires looking to God alone, trusting that He's in control of your life, the lives of your loved ones, and the threat itself. Only when you take your eyes off the danger will you have a clear-eyed view of the only one who can conquer it.

July 8

RISE AND SHINE

In God, whose word I praise, in God I trust;
I will not fear. What can man do to me?
—Psalm 56:4 HCSB

M ANY OF US GREET THE MORNING rehearsing a litany of to-dos and what-if scenarios for the day. Several of these concerns are laced with a dollop of dread. We stew over how to motivate a defiant teen, when to engage with a backbiting coworker, and what to do about our lagging finances. Before we're even out of bed, some of us have worried ourselves into a tizzy, wondering how we can face the people and problems of another day.

It's a good thing God has a remedy for these trepidation sessions—besides a nutritious breakfast and your favorite caffeinated beverage. Your calm, cool, and collected Wonderful Counselor already knows what your future holds. He knows how every millisecond of your day will unfold. He knows your thoughts and fears before you even put words to them. He also knows how to redirect your stewing and stressing with one word: trust.

God calls you to drop your load of worrisome details at His feet. His Word directs you to turn aside from your fretting and fidgeting and lock your faith on to His promises to be with you and uphold you and protect you. Trusting in Him is one reliable reason to rise and shine each morning.

July 9

CHERISHED GIFTS

*Do not neglect the gift that is in you, which was given
to you through the prophecy with the laying on of hands
by the council of elders.*
—1 TIMOTHY 4:14 NRSV

IN OUR CULTURE, ONE OF THE first questions we ask of each other is, "What do you do?" What if the defining question suddenly changed from one of status to one of service? That could happen if we were suddenly seized with the values that prevail in the heavens. We would ask, "What gifts have you been given that bring blessing to others?"

Gifts? Yes. We're talking about that amazing ability God gave you to make conversation meaningful. The talent you have for encouraging others to reach their goals. The intuitive impulse that sees beyond the surface and reaches behind synthetic smiles. The mercy you lavish on those who have lost heart. These are gifts from God in you that serve a specific purpose. He delights to see them in action.

When alone with God, ask Him to help you discern those abilities that He has cultivated so carefully. Be intentional and open to the truth about your giftedness. Resist the temptation to be critical of yourself, and try to see yourself from His tender perspective—in the same compassionate way that you would evaluate a child of your own.

Once you've gotten a glimpse of God's gift in you, pay Him the compliment of putting it to good use.

July 10

APOLOGIZING TO THE ALMIGHTY

God is faithful and fair. If we admit that we have sinned,
he will forgive us our sins. He will forgive every wrong thing
we have done. He will make us pure.

—1 JOHN 1:9 NIrV

HOW DO WE APOLOGIZE TO GOD? Must we *feel* a certain level of sorrow? Do we get "extra credit" for tears? The Bible teaches us that if we confess our sins, God will forgive those sins. What does that mean?

The Bible assures us that as we embrace Jesus as our connection to God, we have eternal life. God sets everything right between us. Our sins are blotted out. Our eternal place in God's presence is secured.

Part of the process of living out that relationship is confessing our sins. The idea is to come into agreement with God about what we have done. If we embrace Jesus, then we will see things from His point of view. Tears sometimes come, but God is more interested in the attitude of our hearts.

What if we don't feel sorry for what we've done? Here God stands ready to empower us. We can come to Him with a simple prayer: "Here is what I've done. Please bring me to the point of seeing myself and my choices through Your eyes." God will open our eyes to enable us to see as He sees. Our appetite for wrong will diminish. Our desire for God will grow.

July 11

THE GIFT OF MERCY

He arose and came to his father. But when he was still
a great way off, his father saw him and had compassion,
and ran and fell on his neck and kissed him.

—LUKE 15:20 NKJV

"MERCY" IS A WORD THAT ISN'T used much in ordinary conversation today. Maybe that's because there's something about it that sounds old-fashioned, conjuring up an image of a nineteenth-century woman crying "Mercy!" at the sight of an exposed ankle. But maybe the word isn't used much today because mercy—withholding punishment from someone who deserves it—is in such short supply. Wherever a wrong has been committed, you'll find people who want the perpetrator punished *beyond* the full extent of the law.

The problem with unmerciful thinking is that when we practice it, we probably don't realize how often we've been on the receiving end of mercy. As children, we likely received mercy from our parents, our teachers, or other people in authority when we did something deserving punishment. As adults, we may have received mercy from a boss without even realizing it.

Every person, no matter their age, has received mercy from God. Mercy is a gift He lavishes on His people despite our disobedience, our rebellion, and our disregard of His many blessings. You can be one of those who acknowledge that gift by expressing your gratitude to God for the many times—seen and unseen—that He has shown mercy to you.

TRUE SUMMITS

*From the end of the earth I will cry to You, when my heart
is overwhelmed; lead me to the rock that is higher than I.*
—**PSALM 61:2** NKJV

ACROSS THE GLOBE THOUSANDS OF MOUNTAINS await brave
and fit climbers. The United States alone is home to four primary
mountain chains: the Appalachians, the Ozarks, the Rockies, and the
Sierra Nevadas. Within these higher-altitude land masses are a series of
phenomena known as false summits. In hiking, a false summit is the
pinnacle you reach only to find that the actual mountaintop looms
behind this front summit. The true peak is farther in the distance and
always appears more daunting (especially if you've been hiking all day
and you're thirsty, hungry, and exhausted).

Life has its share of false summits. You lose five pounds only to
find the next week that you've gained back three. You pay your bills
only to find that a certain family member forgot to mail them. Or you
accomplish a long-awaited goal only to discover that the end point
changed. Fortunately, in the midst of false summits you can always
count on God to be a stable, secure, immovable rock. Each day, as
you spend time getting to know Him, rest assured that He will lead
you to true summits and rewarding destinations in your relationship
with Him.

HABITS OF THE HEART

We do not want you to become lazy, but to imitate those who through faith and patience inherit what has been promised.
—**HEBREWS 6:12** NIV

HABITS ARE HARD TO BREAK. THAT isn't such bad news, considering that good habits are as difficult to dispose of as undesirable ones. For instance, since you're in the habit of brushing your teeth regularly, you can't imagine going to bed without doing so. And because you have a habit of turning on the alarm at night, you don't lie awake worrying about how you'll wake up in the morning.

There is something to learn from the constructive habits of other people too. Particularly when it involves their relationship with God. Take, for example, the habit that Abraham had of "calling on the name of the Lord." It seems that everywhere he went—traveling all throughout the Promised Land for years and years—he built an altar and called upon the name of the Lord at regular intervals.

The really encouraging thing is, God responded to those habitual petitions, and Abraham ended up receiving what God had promised him—a son.

Now that's a habit you want to imitate. Marking your journey by days rather than by miles, you can build an altar of worship every day by calling on the name of the Lord in praise, in adoration, in thanksgiving, and in prayer.

July 14

WHEN WE STUMBLE

I have no greater joy than to hear that
my children are walking in the truth.
—3 JOHN 1:4 NIV

HOW DOES A CHILD LEARN TO walk? By falling down! In the same way, as we learn to walk with God, we will stumble. We will make mistakes. We will make bad choices that have undesirable consequences for ourselves and others.

What does a good coach do when players make mistakes? Does he rub their nose in it? Does he kick them off the team? Does he write the word "failure" over their lives? No! He meets the problems head on, turns them into lessons, and moves on.

This is one way to recognize the Spirit of God in our lives. When we blow it (and we will), there's always forward momentum in how God deals with it. He doesn't leave us in condemnation. He brings us to the place where we can face our wrongdoing squarely, do what's possible to make it right, learn from our error, and move on. If a voice inside your head is loading you with condemnation without giving you a way out, that is not the Spirit of God. God restores us.

Have you done wrong? Rush back into God's presence. God will receive you. He will repair you. You will be whole once again.

THE POWER OF YOUR WORDS

Words kill, words give life;
they're either poison or fruit—you choose.
—PROVERBS 18:21 MSG

NEVER UNDERESTIMATE THE POWER OF YOUR words.

One of the very first things we learn about God in the Bible is that He speaks. When He speaks, entire worlds are created. He spoke into existence oceans and continents, sunshine and forests, tigers and butterflies. His very words bring life. When Jesus speaks to the dead, they stand to their feet, alive!

We, as God's sons and daughters, created in His image, have a similar power to create—or destroy—with our words. We speak life into our children by assuring them that they belong, that they are loved, that they are capable, that they are beautiful. Our words honor or dishonor those around us. When we recognize good character in others and call it out with sincere and specific compliments, we are offering a nourishing meal for someone's soul.

Years from now, people will remember your words of kindness, spoken at a critical moment, changing the course of their lives. Where do these words of life come from? As you soak up the presence of God, He will give you a heart filled to overflowing with blessing and love. From that heart, the words will come.

SPIRITUAL SATISFACTION

You are my God. I worship you. In my heart, I long for you,
as I would long for a stream in a scorching desert.
—PSALM 63:1 CEV

SPIRITUAL HUNGER IS DEEPER THAN PHYSICAL hunger. The growl of emptiness in our souls is a feeling more than a sound. Its rumblings are dissatisfaction with life, yearning for something more, questioning God's goodness and fairness. Like a physical appetite, the pangs start small and grow to screaming proportions.

You know the feeling if you've ever felt empty after reaching a long-sought-after goal. You know the feeling if life feels flat even though you are doing all the things you thought would make you happy. You just want more.

That inner emptiness is your yellow warning light, cautioning you to turn around and get some food fast, but not fast food. Fast food for the soul is the morsels that fill your eyes—TV, romance novels, adventure movies—but leave your spirit empty. The quest ends as you turn your search to God.

Spiritual hunger can only be satisfied by time spent alone with God. Opening your Bible to learn about Jesus and do what He says will fill you up. Praise and worship are like a feast. God alone satisfies the hunger of your soul.

PRESENCE AND MEDITATION

*How I delight in your commands! How I love them! I honor
and love your commands. I meditate on your decrees.*
—PSALM 119:47-48 NLT

DAILY DEVOTIONS BEGIN WITH DECISION, CONTINUE with
determination, persist because of discipline, and eventually
become an integral part of your life out of sheer delight. Spending time
daily in the presence of God enriches your understanding of Him,
enlightens your perspective on your purpose in life, and helps you to
develop the character with which to fulfill it.

However, it's one thing to be in the presence of God in the quiet
of your devotional moments meditating on the goodness of God, but
it's another thing to carry His presence into the distractions of your
day and reflect His goodness in your actions and words. Longing to
fill your days with the fruit of your devotion, you ponder over how to
take the presence of God into the busyness of your day so that you can
experience Him then too.

Why not venture an experiment? Before leaving your quiet place,
try handing over to God something that you do not want back: give
up the need to control the hour you're currently living in. Surrender
it to Him and let Him know you mean it in earnest. Then every hour
on the hour, check your bearings to see if you're still letting Him hold
the wheel.

GIVING UP

When Jesus heard that, he said, "Then there's only one thing left to do: Sell everything you own and give it away to the poor. You will have riches in heaven. Then come, follow me."

—LUKE 18:22-23 MSG

WHAT DO YOU DO WHEN GOD asks you for something you don't want to give? Most of us understand that God owns everything. He owns all our possessions. He owns our time, our loved ones, our very lives. Technically, we don't "own" anything. We manage these things. God does have the right to demand anything from us. That does not mean that He necessarily will. Nor is He petty or mean or cruel. But, sometimes, for His eternal good purposes, He asks us to give up something that's hard to give up.

If that happens, what do we do? We bring the conversation into God's presence. Sometimes our possessions mean something more to us than they should. Sometimes they take God's place in our hearts. God knows that a new sofa, for example, can't bring lasting peace and joy. But God's Spirit can. So we ask ourselves, *What do I imagine that I will lose if I give God what He is asking for?* We bring the answer to that question to the Lord and ask for His perspective. When we know the truth, we will discover that what God gives us will far outweigh whatever He asks us to give up.

July 19

WHAT MATTERS MOST

Jesus replied, "The most important commandment is this:
'Listen, O Israel! The LORD our God
is the one and only LORD'"
—MARK 12:29 NLT

YOU'VE PROBABLY HEARD PEOPLE TALK ABOUT living a well-integrated life. No doubt that means different things to different people, but the fundamental idea is a healthy balance of one's physical, mental, emotional, and spiritual conditions—the body, mind, soul, and spirit.

For those of us who live in close relationship with God, a well-integrated life can be defined in even simpler terms: It's a life so encompassed by God that He is integrated into every aspect of it. God is not just first and foremost; He's everything to us. In practical terms regarding our everyday routine, God is so important to us that His Spirit permeates our every waking (and sleeping!) moment, whether we're brushing our teeth or fighting rush-hour traffic or deciding which cereal to buy. That doesn't mean we are conscious of His presence every single moment; it does mean that His presence is like the air we breathe—always there, whether or not we're thinking about Him.

Only one thing can have top priority in your life. When that one thing is God, He transcends "top priority" to become the all-embracing, comprehensive, inclusive, "be all and end all" of your life.

BETTER THAN PRINCE CHARMING

As for me, I am poor and needy;
please hurry to my aid, O God. You are my helper
and my savior; O LORD, do not delay.
—PSALM 70:5 NLT

YOUR KNIGHT IN SHINING ARMOR. YOU call, he comes. Not that he exists in the everyday world. This "knight" can fail to show up on time for the rescue, much like his "lady" can fail to ask for help. Oh, for a real-life fairy-tale romance!

In reality, there are times when each of us, male and female, long for someone bigger and stronger to come swooping down to help us. Cape and white horse intact, scattering our enemies, he would remove all distress and bring us safely to his kingdom where the sun always shines and the birds perpetually sing.

There is such a Savior. Although the best-hearted hero may fail, He will not fail you. Though your heart has been broken and your trust shattered by others, He will treat you gently. His name is Jesus Christ. He is the Prince of Peace, the King of all kings, and the Lover of your soul.

Quietly ponder who you would rather have as a rescuer—one you can see who will likely let you down? Or one you cannot see who is faithful and true? Calling to Him for help, even if it's no louder than a whisper, always results in a rescue. Now that's even better than Prince Charming.

HONEST TO GOD

*Do this in the fear of the Lord, faithfully,
with integrity and a blameless heart.*
—2 CHRONICLES 19:9 AMP

AN INTEGER IS A NATURAL NUMBER, a whole number. The integer is the root concept for the word *integrity*, a word that curiously interprets the character of a human being through a mathematical grid. What's the point? The point is that a condition of wholeness within the human heart is the most natural state of human existence, completing the equation of relational fulfillment.

If you were guessing, what would you suggest as the most accurate antonym for integrity? How about "duplicity"? Your heart is in its greatest dilemma when engaged in hypocrisy—a form of self-betrayal. A divided heart can destroy not just your reputation, but your spiritual, emotional, and mental health, not to mention your relationships.

How do you go about keeping your integrity intact? The key is prayer. A good exercise in intellectual honesty is to hold your motives and your actions up for examination in conversation with God on a daily basis. Since it is impossible to pull the wool over His eyes, talking things out with God forces the issue of honesty, turning up the fertile soil of integrity in the heart. Interestingly enough, being honest with yourself before God is one of the most cleansing and rejuvenating experiences possible.

THE LIGHTBULB PRINCIPLE

The written Law kills, but the Spirit gives life.

—2 CORINTHIANS 3:6 NIrV

MANY PEOPLE QUOTE THE BIBLE, BUT not everybody uses it for good. Cults quote it. Atheists quote it. In the account of the temptation of Jesus, the Devil himself quoted Scripture. Some use the Bible to corrupt the truth. Some use it as a weapon. But others use Scripture to obtain hope and guidance for their lives. What's the difference?

It helps if we understand that the Bible is like a lightbulb for our spiritual journey. Without light, most of us cannot function. We would trip over things, fall, and injure ourselves. That's why Scripture can illuminate the path of faith for us. God's Word tells us who He is, what He requires, and how we can be safe in Him.

But a lightbulb by itself does not produce light. It must be connected to a power source. Apart from an electrical socket, it's useless. And if a lightbulb is broken, the sharp edges can injure and harm.

In the same way, the Bible was never meant to be used apart from the Spirit of God. He is the Source of power and love. When we invite God to speak through His Word, the Bible brings life.

A QUIET PLACE WITH GOD

Because so many people were coming and going that they
did not even have a chance to eat, he said to them,
"Come with me by yourselves to a quiet place and get some rest."
—MARK 6:31 NIV

LIFE IN THE TWENTY-FIRST CENTURY CAN be so rushed, so busy, so filled with activity that it seems impossible to find the time or the place to be quiet and get alone with God. But do you know what? It's been difficult for people to find time for God for centuries—in fact, for millennia. In the early years of Christianity, monks took to the desert to live so they could get away from the busyness of life. Over the ensuing centuries, countless writers recorded their dismay over how hard it was to find time to be alone with God.

At the same time, however, other writers told of spending hours in prayer despite a busy schedule. Martin Luther famously spent more time in prayer when he was the busiest, because he saw prayer as even more important on those days.

But how can *you* do that? There are numerous ways, but one that many people find helpful is to designate a particular place to spend time with God. A "place" can be nothing more than a chair or a park bench or even your car. The place itself doesn't matter; what matters is that going to that place prompts you to spend time with God.

July 24

OUTSIDE SOURCE

*My flesh and my heart may fail, but God is the strength
of my heart and my portion forever.*
—**PSALM 73:26** NASB

ONE OF THE MOST TENUOUS PARTS of a computer system is its power supply. Cut off its power, and down it goes. Home users and tech-savvy professionals alike know the importance of having an uninterruptible power supply, allowing the computer to automatically switch to an alternate power source when normal power goes out. If you've ever been through a storm that knocked out your power in the middle of an important project, you can relate to how crucial that is.

In your personal life, having a power source outside yourself is equally important. When you hit the wall, drained of emotional, physical, or mental energy, you need a fresh power supply. You're going down and everyone around sees it.

That's the moment to plug into your main source—God. His energy never fails. He gives you an internal lift that powers your spirit, mind, and body. You go from using your own energy to relying on His strength. Prayer flips the switch. A simple, direct "Help! I need You" is all that's needed to effectively plug in to God's power.

In a quiet space, take stock of your power supply. Are you connected to an uninterruptible source?

July 25

DEVOTED IN WORK

In all the work you are doing, work the best you can.
Work as if you were doing it for the Lord, not for people.
—COLOSSIANS 3:23 NCV

A THLETES SPEND THE LAST FEW MOMENTS before the race or the big game preparing their minds for what lies ahead. Though they cannot know how the contest will play out, they train their minds to imagine various scenarios for which they have practiced. Most importantly, they envision themselves winning!

In a similar way, alone in the presence of God you can prepare your heart, mind, and spirit for your workday before it begins. You don't have to know precisely how the day will unfold. You simply need to meditate on the possibilities and commit them to the Lord ahead of time.

For example, you've been trained to use specific skills related to your work. How wise it would be to seek a blessing from God concerning the implementation of those skills. You have a certain allotment of time in which to do your work, and an expectation concerning your productivity. Why not ask the Lord to enter into your hours and to be present with you in strength as you work toward your goals.

Perhaps most importantly, there are people with whom you interact all day. Pray for the wisdom to be a blessing to others while you work. And remember to envision victory!

July 26

ENOUGH

For his anger lasts only a moment, but his favor lasts a lifetime;
weeping may remain for a night, but rejoicing comes in the morning.
—PSALM 30:5 NIV

HAVE YOU EVER CONSIDERED HOW COMFORTING it is that God gets angry? Suppose for a moment that God never got angry. Suppose He acted like an overly permissive parent and let His creation go wild without making any move to stop the chaos. Where would that leave us?

In reality, that would leave all of us in an extremely vulnerable and unsafe position. We would be at the mercy of whatever bully started picking on us, and there would be no recourse, no justice, no salvation. But our hope and comfort is this: Even though we live in a mixed-up world, God will eventually make everything right. God's anger at wrong is the first step toward putting things right. The result will be justice, wholeness, and heaven.

The time will come when God says, "Enough!" When that moment arrives, we will rejoice and all of creation will breathe a great sigh of relief.

Meanwhile, linger in God's presence. Become acquainted with what angers Him. In response, you can also say, "Enough!" to whatever God puts on your heart.

People who aligned themselves with God's justice brought an end to slavery, reformed child labor, and stopped a host of social ills. You too can make a difference for good.

THE VALUE OF ONE SOUL

*What do you benefit if you gain the whole world but lose
your own soul? Is anything worth more than your soul?*
—MARK 8:36-37 NLT

WHAT IS THE VALUE OF YOUR soul? Can anyone, even in
a consumer-oriented society, ever pin a price tag on a soul?
Of course not. Each human being is priceless, of such a great value
that our worth cannot be measured apart from the dimensions of the
cross. It's only in the context of Jesus' sacrificial death on the cross
that we can even begin to understand how much God values each and
every person.

Meanwhile, people strive to accumulate wealth and achieve great
success. But no matter what they acquire in material possessions,
no matter how much power and authority they wield on earth, no
matter how successful they are in the eyes of others, the value of all
of those trappings doesn't come close to the value of *your* soul. If that
doesn't leave you speechless, read that sentence again. Your worth to
God is immeasurable.

Meditate on how much you mean to God. Imagine Him brushing
aside all the diamonds and precious gems in the world just so He can
get to you. You! Now imagine yourself doing the same to get to Him.
Then you'll begin to comprehend your value to Him—and His value
to you.

TOUCHSTONE

*Remember, LORD, Your compassion and Your
faithful love for they [have existed] from antiquity.*
—PSALM 25:6 HCSB

WALKING A ROMAN ROAD IS STEPPING in the footsteps of
millions before you. Touching a pyramid is touching thousands of years of human history. How many winds and rains have swept the surfaces of these ruins? Yet touching something so old can still send tingles all through you. What a thrill to touch something that is in a sense unchangeable, even though it has kept only a fraction of its former glory.

God's steadfast mercy and kindness go back thousands of years too. Story after story is written—many in God's Word, the Bible—recording His intervention in people's lives. Some individuals were healed, some led by a cloud, some were delivered, but all were touched. Now you're writing your own story.

God touches your life as you talk with Him and invite Him into your world. He sends a perfect song on the radio, the lyrics saying exactly what you need to keep going. He sends groceries when your bank account is as empty as your refrigerator. He prompts a friend to call in a moment of loneliness.

God's personality is more dependable than the pyramids. He doesn't erode or diminish with time. Reserve time this week to consider what He's building in your world.

July 29

LISTENING WITH HEART

Are you listening to me? Really listening?
—MATTHEW 11:15 MSG

DO YOU RECALL YOUR MOM EVER saying: "Listen to me!" If you are a parent, you can identify with a common concern that children often hear the words but fail to take them to heart.

The prophets of old sometimes felt the same way about the children of God. They often warned people about having ears but not hearing. In other words, having the ability to hear but failing to listen.

What is the key to really listening? It's realizing that the focus is not on your ears but on your heart. Listening to the Lord requires hearing with your heart.

When alone with God, it is important to open your heart and mind to receive Him on His terms. In other words, allow the Scriptures to say what they mean to say rather than squeezing them into what you already believe. You'll be amazed by the fresh and invigorating revelation God extends through His Spirit. Then, thinking hard on the insight you receive, take it into your being—just like the body consumes the nutrients in food—allowing His words to nurture your faith, refine your character, and teach you obedience.

Finally, live like someone who listens. Live powerfully from your enlightened heart.

A UNIQUE RELATIONSHIP

Long, long ago he decided to adopt us into his family through Jesus Christ.

—EPHESIANS 1:5 MSG

YOUR RELATIONSHIP WITH GOD IS UNIQUE to you. God will parent you differently, coach you differently, befriend you differently than He will someone else. Jesus healed many people. But in each recorded instance, He healed a little differently. He gave a group of lepers an assignment; as they carried out their assignment, they were healed. He put mud in a blind man's eyes and told him to rinse it out. He spoke the word and a Roman officer's servant was healed. In the Old Testament, God sent a fish to swallow Jonah, but He sat down and had a meal with Abraham.

Parents of multiple children will tell you, often with amazement, that each of their children is radically different than the next. What works for one doesn't work for the other. Not only are each of us unique in temperament, but we are each at a different stage in our spiritual growth. And we each grow in different ways.

Here's the takeaway: There's no one formula for a time alone with God that works for everybody. God will use that time we spend with Him differently for each individual. Let Him deal with you in the way that's right for you.

LOVE GOD WITH YOUR MIND

Jesus said, "'Love the Lord your God
with all your passion and prayer and intelligence.'
This is the most important, the first on any list."
—MATTHEW 22:36-38 MSG

HAS IT OCCURRED TO YOU THAT *thinking* can be a way of loving God? Most of us have no problem with the concepts of loving God with our hearts or through our actions. But our minds? How can we love God with our minds?

Think of it this way: God gave you a brain for more than controlling your nervous system and superficial thinking. He made humanity capable of deep, critical thought—analyzing situations and information to make the best possible decision in every circumstance. That's true, not only on physical and mental levels, but also on a spiritual level. When you act on a spiritual impulse, for example, after thinking through what you know of God, the Bible, and the way God works in the world—coupled with prayer—you are loving God with your mind. You're using all the faculties He has given you to make informed decisions and live life responsibly.

Using the intelligence God has given you leads you onto the path of wisdom. The brain acquires knowledge—such as biblical information—which your spirit transforms into wisdom. When you love God with your mind, He turns your intelligence into a powerful tool designed to equip you to live wisely.

NO MORE EGGSHELLS

You, O Lord, are a God of compassion and mercy,
slow to get angry and filled with unfailing love and faithfulness.
—PSALM 86:15 NLT

THE "EGGSHELL WALK." EVER TRY IT? Alice did it with the Red Queen in *Alice in Wonderland*, and the Queen yelled, "Off with her head!" The eggshell walk is tiptoeing around a sticky, prickly person with whom you must always be guarded because you never know what will set him or her off.

You can't approach this volatile individual without fear. Regular ways of relating to people don't work with this type of person because of their unpredictable and destructive responses. Their rash impulsiveness has a ripple effect on people all around these toxic individuals. You want to resolve the interpersonal conflict, but to do so could mean your job, your friendship, your marriage.

God is not like that. You can move toward Him anytime and He'll warmly welcome you. You can tell Him anything, even that you're really upset with His actions (or inaction), and He'll listen without an angry reaction. He's approachable because He truly loves you. He's simply available.

Draw near to His presence. Soak in His steadiness. Let yourself unwind, speaking the deepest truths of your heart to Him. Feel His acceptance and approval.

August 2

SAVING UP FOR THE FUTURE

Your laws are wonderful. No wonder I obey them!
The teaching of your word gives light;
so even the simple can understand.
—PSALM 119:129-130 NLT

IN ADDITION TO ABUNDANCE FOR YOUR own life, your quiet times with God alone hold something in store to benefit others as well.

Among the many blessings of being in God's presence, wisdom ranks very high. God's Word overflows with the kind of wisdom that makes you effective among people, prosperous in work, rich in relationships, humble in spirit, patient in trials, courageous in the face of fear, and insightful concerning the will of God.

Interestingly, this wisdom is not only a gift of God to you; it is a gift from God through you to the wider world. While you are accruing wisdom from God, you are also storing it up for the benefit of others to whom God will send you as His resource.

The same principle applies concerning comfort, hope, love, encouragement, mercy, knowledge, and even faith. God supplies these resources first to you for your own spiritual development and practical implementation; He then provides them through you for nurturing others and aiding them in their struggles.

And not least of all, your commitment to prayer becomes a great source of blessing and power on behalf of those who haven't truly encountered God yet.

STAGES IN OUR JOURNEY

All the stages of my life were spread out before you.
—PSALM 139:16 MSG

BEING A PARENT IS AN EDUCATION in itself. Just as we get comfortable with a certain stage in our children's development, they move on to a new stage. The game changes and we need to learn how to parent all over again. Teens require a very different approach than toddlers. Each stage presents its own challenges and its own rewards.

The same is true in our spiritual journey. As we grow spiritually, God begins to deal with us differently. The rules change. For example, if a certain spiritual experience was very meaningful to us early on, we may naturally assume that everyone should have that same exact experience the same exact way. But as we grow, we realize that God works differently with different people. That opens the door for us to appreciate others and to marvel at God's work in their lives.

We also grow in our time alone with God. A more structured approach usually works best early in our spiritual journey. Prayer may be a one-way monologue. But, as we grow, our time with God may become less structured, more meaningful, more of a two-way conversation. A beautiful relationship is unfolding and maturing.

August 4

THE ART OF ACCEPTING YOURSELF

You're blessed when you're content with just who you are—
no more, no less. That's the moment you find yourselves
proud owners of everything that can't be bought.
—**MATTHEW 5:5 MSG**

SEVERAL MOVIES AND TELEVISION SHOWS IN recent years have depicted a situation in which one character has the ability to hear what other people are thinking. Most often, this device is used in comedies, and the ability to hear others' thoughts is viewed at first as a gift. Its entertainment purposes aside, the fanciful "gift" of hearing thoughts might have one unexpected benefit: You could hear what other people *really* think of themselves, and you would realize others have as much difficulty accepting themselves as you do.

Accepting yourself requires recognizing that God made you to be exactly who you are even with that nose you may not like or those hips that are out of proportion to the rest of your body. If you don't like what you see, you may have a hard time thanking God, who gave you that appearance. Instead of fuming about it, talk to Him about it.

Tell God exactly what you think of His artistry. It's okay; this isn't anything new to Him. He wants to free you from the prison of self-loathing. He wants you to vent so that when you've run out of complaints He can wrap His arms around you, showing you His unconditional love and acceptance.

August 5

CRYING UNCLE

*I cry out to you for help, O LORD, and in the morning
my prayer will come into your presence.*
—PSALM 88:13 GWT

HAS SOMEONE EVER TICKLED YOU UNTIL you cried uncle?
"Crying uncle" means to admit defeat or surrender. Have you
ever cried uncle with God, finally confessing to Him that you've
had enough?

Often we zip through our daily routines and responsibilities
sensing we have a handle on our schedules and plans. Many of us
approach God only when we hit a major snag or have entirely
exhausted other reasonable options for help and input. Sometimes
we're a bit reluctant to be honest with God about our real needs.
Maybe we just don't quite trust Him to guide our way or intervene in
our predicaments. Perhaps deep down we figure we can keep the ship
upright and on course ourselves. But can we always?

The Bible is replete with stories of people who came to the end
of themselves and cried uncle before God. Fearless warriors. Affluent
kings. Captivating divas. Crying out to God is not a sign of defeat, but
a sign of deference or humble submission. When you candidly tell God
everything and stop squirming to be in control, you show that you
respect His character and are placing your needs in His trustworthy
hands. You'll wish you had cried uncle sooner.

August 6

GROWING UP INTO GOD

Jesus grew in wisdom and stature,
and in favor with God and men.
—LUKE 2:52 NIV

CONTEMPLATING THE LIFE AND WITNESS OF Jesus, we become curious about what it was that empowered Him to see the things He saw, to say the things He said, and to do the things He did. The gospels themselves tip us off by reporting that the Spirit of God had descended upon Him and taken up residence within Him.

What does that mean? It means, at the very least, that Jesus was living in the vivid and vibrant awareness of God's presence. In other words, Jesus never lost touch with the conscious awareness of and attentiveness to God's immediate proximity. Imagine that!

No wonder Jesus had such confidence that He was always in the will of God—He was right there with Him.

Part of the value of spending time in God's presence is the training that it provides for living fully aware that He is with us all the time. The momentum of your quiet time should carry over into your day. It takes some mental discipline to stay focused on God's nearness when the distractions of the day tempt you, but with training in diligence, you will progressively grow in that awareness. That is, after all, the way Jesus lived on earth. He grew up into God.

HELPING THOSE IN TROUBLE

Under the circumstances it's hard to keep quiet.

—JOB 4:2 MSG

HOW DO WE COMFORT THOSE IN TROUBLE?
First of all, it's hard to give what we haven't received. As we go through troubles of our own, we discover that, yes, good people have problems that sometimes don't go away. We discover that God always cares, always helps, always empowers us to move forward. None of us likes to have problems, but most of us can look back at our problems and see how God used them to make us into better, stronger people. Over the course of time, we learn what it is to be comforted and coached by God through our own troubles.

But none of that puts us in a position to completely understand why someone else is experiencing trouble or what that experience is like for them. We don't know how they feel, and often we will not have the answers for them—even when we think we do.

What we can do, though, is offer the comfort we have received, the hope we have found, the presence of God that we have experienced in our times of struggle. When we invite God into the lives of those who are struggling, we give them a gift greater than any advice we could offer.

THE MOST IMPORTANT THING

*Seek (aim at and strive after) first of all His kingdom
and His righteousness (His way of doing and being right),
and then all these things taken together will be given you besides.*
—MATTHEW 6:33 AMP

WHAT'S THE FIRST THING YOU THINK about when you wake up on a typical morning? Most likely, it's what you have to do that day—more specifically, what you have to do *first* that day, like taking the kids to school or going to work. In any event, your first thoughts are not likely to be on the righteousness of God—His goodness, His holiness, His "rightness."

So how can you make the righteousness of God the focus of your life? How can you give God His due when you need to make a living and care for your family and look out for others as well? You do that by bringing everything into harmony with God's purposes and into alignment with His goodness.

Are you having problems with a coworker? Let God's righteousness pervade that situation. Do your children need to be disciplined? Administer correction in the spirit of God's discipline of you. Are you concerned about a friend's excessive drinking? Allow God's goodness to flow through you into your friend's life.

When you make God and His way of doing things the most important thing in your life, His righteousness will permeate all you do. He's pretty clear about that. It's a promise worth believing.

August 9

STRAIGHT AHEAD

My eyes are ever toward the Lord,
for He will pluck my feet out of the net.
—Psalm 25:15 AMP

PERHAPS YOU'VE SEEN THOSE BLACK EYECUPS on the sides of a horse's bridle. If you've watched horse racing events or seen TV shows or movies with Amish buggies, you've probably seen these equestrian devices called blinders or winkers. As a crucial piece of horse tack, blinders keep a horse's eyes from wandering to what's behind and often prevent him from gazing off to the sides. Blinders are a safety precaution to stop horses from getting spooked in crowds and to avoid unnecessary distractions.

We humans could use a protective set of blinders too. Every day life presents a plethora of distractions and situations that can spook us. Recalls on tainted foods and malfunctioning vehicles. Roller-coaster stock markets. Alarming gang violence and insurgent retaliations. If we turned our eyes continually toward the world's commotion, we would bolt like a startled horse.

Instead of equipping us with cumbersome eyecups, God advises us to simply keep our focus on Him and the things of heaven. It's tempting to keep looking behind us or peering around for greater peripheral vision, but God tells us to steady our eyes straight ahead, locked on His.

REACHING THE DEWPOINT

I will be like the dew to Israel; he will blossom like a lily.
—HOSEA 14:5 NIV

IN THE STILLNESS OF THE NIGHT while you sleep, a mysterious thing happens. Provided that conditions are right, a curious condensation appears upon the surface of the ground and refreshes the earth. It bathes creation in nourishing and rejuvenating moisture. It can only occur when the temperature of the open surface drops to the *dewpoint*. In other words, when the earth is properly prepared to receive the moisture in the atmosphere, it materializes…into dew.

Even more curious is the fact that the Spirit of the Lord acts like dew—coming in the stillness of the soul to rejuvenate and renew the hearts of those who believe. He especially comes to those who are prepared to receive His refreshing presence. The Spirit is always there—in the atmosphere, so to speak—but does not presume to impose.

The quiet times you have with God prepare your heart to receive the Spirit's refreshing. You open your spiritual pores to the Lord to receive the lavish benefits of His grace. His Spirit bathes you in the witness of His power and peace. And as a result, you bear the fruit of God's own nature: patience, kindness, gentleness, faithfulness, and love.

A MARGIN OF SAFETY

Do not lead us into temptation.

—MATTHEW 6:13 NKJV

PROFESSIONAL DRIVERS WHO DRIVE FROM CITY to city on the freeway understand that traffic on the highway travels in "packs" of five to thirty cars. Inside those packs, if something goes wrong, the chances of being involved in a multiple car collision is very high. Between the packs, there's plenty of space to manage an emergency without endangering another motorist. The safest professionals avoid the packs, preferring to maintain as much space as possible between themselves and other vehicles.

Likewise, God wants us to build a margin of safety into our spiritual lives. Do we find ourselves negatively influenced by certain people? For a season, we decide to avoid them. Do certain television shows, websites, books, or magazines tempt us with thoughts that are not helpful to ourselves or pleasing to God? We choose other activities instead. Do we find ourselves getting stressed when we take on too many responsibilities? We learn to say no.

You can create a margin of safety by taking time in God's presence to gain the strength you need to say yes to your faith and no to temptation. God is always ready to help you stay safe.

WHO IS GOD TO YOU?

God is not a man, that he should lie, nor a son of man,
that he should change his mind. Does he speak
and then not act? Does he promise and not fulfill?
—NUMBERS 23:19 NIV

A MAJOR MISCONCEPTION ABOUT GOD, ESPECIALLY among those who don't know Him, is that He has human qualities. It's only natural; our frame of reference is the people in our lives. Since God is said to love and forgive—and hate and punish—then, without thinking it through, we attribute other human qualities to God.

But God is not like us. His love and forgiveness are so far beyond our understanding that it bears little resemblance to our own. The same is true for His hate and punishment. Our understanding of justice pales in comparison to His. The differences between God and man are incomprehensible—which is probably why so many of us have trouble trusting Him.

People lie, cheat, break their promises, fail to follow through on their commitments, disappoint us, let us down, and generally act the way people have acted since the first humans walked the earth. But God—well, He has been perfectly consistent as well, and for much longer. He has consistently dealt with His people faithfully, reliably fulfilled His promises, and continually loved us with an everlasting love.

If you don't see Him that way, it's time to strip Him of the human qualities you've laid on Him and enjoy Him for His true nature.

August 13

RAGS AND RICHES

Know that the LORD Himself is God;
it is He who has made us, and not we ourselves;
we are His people and the sheep of His pasture.
—PSALM 100:3 NASB

ALMOST TWO-THIRDS OF THE WORLD'S NEARLY 950 billionaires arrived at their fortunes by way of grit and tenacity, not a silver spoon and inherited wealth. At least fifty of these moguls are high-school and college dropouts, including Microsoft's Bill Gates and tycoon Li Ka-shing from Asia.

It's fascinating to hear the rags-to-riches stories of these self-made billionaires. Some have overcome dire poverty and lives locked in hopelessness. At least one was a welfare mother; another simply knitted sweaters at home that her brother peddled by bicycle. Something deep inside us rallies for the underdog and cheers the determination and sacrifice of brave bootstrappers. But truth be told, none of us are totally self-made and successful without the hand of God. We may think our persistence and keen decisions reward us with the security of money, notoriety, and conveniences, but in an instant all that can crumble—and often does.

God is the Creator of not just your body but also your life journey, including your finances and social status. In your time alone with Him, thank Him for crafting your life story and express sincere gratitude whether you've got rags, riches, or a blend of both.

KNOWING GOD'S SECRETS

Surely the Lord GOD does nothing unless He reveals
His secret counsel to His servants the prophets.

—AMOS 3:7 NASB

EVERYONE KNOWS THAT THERE ARE DIFFERENT levels of relationships. There are those who are mere acquaintances, and those with whom you work. There are friends you choose to spend time with socially, and those with whom you can even go on a vacation. There are people in whom you confide, and those whom you would even trust with your life. Most everyone desires to have at least one relationship that attains to the deep reaches of intimacy.

But what does this say about your relationship with God? Even God experiences different depths of commitment and interaction with people. There are those He considers His friends and those He calls enemies. There are even people He perceives as strangers.

To be an intimate friend of God is not so different from being intimate with anyone else. In order to be the kind of person with whom He can entrust His secrets, you will want to spend a considerable amount of time with Him—getting to know Him and making yourself known. It means learning to care deeply about His passions and desires and becoming invested in what He is doing in the world so He can share with you His plans and the secrets of His heart.

ESCAPE ROUTES

Deliver me in Your righteousness, and cause me to escape.

—PSALM 71:2 NKJV

A SAFE DRIVER ALWAYS HAS AN escape route in mind. If there's an emergency, he or she has a plan for steering around it if need be. In the same way, God, with our cooperation, creates escape routes in our lives. While evil may conspire to lead us into paths of self-destruction, God always has a way out for us.

What does this look like? When Jesus was tempted by the Devil in the wilderness, He answered each temptation with a quotation from the Bible. For example, knowing Jesus was hungry, Satan said, "If you are the Son of God, command these stones to become bread." In His reply, Jesus quoted a passage from the Bible that affirmed that dependence on God is the key to life, but acting independently from Him never works.

Truth and Scripture are powerful escape routes, but they are not the only ones. Sometimes God sends mentors, coaches, or friends into our lives to help us find our way out. But the most powerful escape route of all is God's presence. Look at it this way: when temptation knocks at the door, send Jesus to answer it.

August 16

THINK ABOUT GOOD THINGS

Whatever things are true, whatever things are noble, whatever things are just, whatever things are pure, whatever things are lovely, whatever things are of good report, if there is any virtue and if there is anything praiseworthy—meditate on these things.
—**PHILIPPIANS 4:8** NKJV

FOR A VARIETY OF REASONS, MEDITATION is a puzzle to many followers of God. One of the main reasons is the mistaken assumption that Christian meditation is complicated.

In a Christian context, meditation is simply quiet, focused thinking about God and His attributes, passages from the Bible, and similar elements of the faith. The hardest part is quieting your spirit, separating yourself from all the commotion around you, and tuning your ear to hear what God is saying through His Word and His still, small voice. It's tempting to give up, shrug your shoulders, and walk away too soon. But if you stay, what amazing blessing there is in His presence. You will return to your life invigorated, inspired, and bathed in His divine glow.

Yes, meditation is a simple process of just blocking out the world around you and experiencing fellowship with God alone. Nevertheless, it does take intentional effort. On occasion, you may find yourself transitioning into Christian meditation as you're reading the Bible or praying or even daydreaming, but you'll discover that most often you need to set aside dedicated time for meditation. Keep it simple, keep it focused, and your time meditating on God may well become a time you eagerly anticipate.

August 17

TOTAL RECALL

O my soul, bless GOD, don't forget a single blessing!
—PSALM 103:2 MSG

THE STORY IS TOLD OF FORGETFUL Scottish writer John Campbell, who lived in the 1700s. One day Campbell was perusing the shelves in a bookstore and found himself enamored by a book. He purchased the tome and continued reading it at home. Suddenly, halfway through the volume, it dawned on the absentminded author that he himself had written the book.

While we may chuckle at the irony of the Scotsman's memory lapse, we can suffer from a type of spiritual forgetfulness. We can go about our days wrapped up in energizing projects and the people we love and overlook God. Not from blatant intent but more from a mental fog.

Sure, we can meet with Him through regular prayer and Bible reflection, but we may be neglecting to stop and truly recall the many ways He proves Himself faithful during each moment of the day. Wouldn't it feel good to call to mind the myriad of good things with which God showers you? Not just the huge answers to prayer, but even the little gifts He tucks in throughout your day. Remembering the expressions of His goodness, mercy, and love will allow you to enjoy your blessings more than once and strengthen your faith in the process.

JUST PEACE

Let justice roll down like waters,
and righteousness like an ever-flowing stream.
—AMOS 5:24 NRSV

WE LONG FOR THE DAY WHEN corruption and violence cease to exist and the peace of God truly reigns. It is the longing that occupies the heart of God; it is His goal. And those whom He considers His true friends are working with Him toward this end.

If you desire to partner with God, then pray to develop His passion for peace on earth. You will begin to realize that the most critical component of peace is justice. Not the responsibility of the courts to deal with criminal acts, but the aspect of justice that works to put things to right within your community.

You begin to realize that injustice can be uprooted—little by little—by doing what is within your power to do for the poor, the oppressed, the helpless, the disenfranchised, and the weak. You develop a determination to do your part to remedy the imbalance of resources that should sustain life for all of humanity, not just for the privileged few. You will find yourself taking the initiative to join God in His mission to relieve the oppression of poverty, abuse, or violence in your community until the day when Christ Jesus comes and justice overtakes evil, making a clean sweep of the Enemy's stronghold.

WHEN GOD OPENS OUR EYES

[Jesus said], "Do not let your hearts be troubled.
Trust in God; trust also in me."
—JOHN 14:1 NIV

THE DEATH OF JESUS TOOK HIS disciples totally by surprise. They didn't expect it. Though He warned them it was coming, they wouldn't hear it. When Jesus died, His disciples experienced sorrow like they had never experienced before. No theology could comfort them. The world might as well have ended as far as they were concerned. When His resurrection was announced, they couldn't wrap their minds around that either. It seemed like a fairy tale, an insult to their grief.

In the middle of this despair, Jesus Himself showed up to take a walk with two of those disciples. Blinded by their grief, they were prevented from recognizing Him. As they poured out their loss to this "stranger," an amazing thing happened. He helped them make sense out of a God, a world, a disaster that seemed to have no sense. The more they talked, the more they realized that what they had just experienced was not the worst thing that ever happened, but the best. Their eyes were opened to the truth.

This is what we need. This is why we linger in God's presence, because He empowers us to see beyond our troubles to the loving and beautiful design of God.

GOD'S OPINION OF YOU

The fear of human opinion disables;
trusting in God protects you from that.
—**PROVERBS 29:25** MSG

WE CAN LIVE OUR LIVES ACCORDING to the dictates of others. But other people's opinions are just that—human opinions. Contrast that with knowing the truth about who you are as a child of God: You are someone who has been loved by God every single day of your life. You are so important to Him that He wants to have a personal relationship with you that includes daily conversation, His guidance for your life, and the joy of spending all of eternity in His loving presence.

Many of the people in your life will come and go; do you really want the opinions that result from fleeting relationships to shape you? Consider instead the amazing opportunity to have your life shaped by the One who created you. Remember this: There's only one opinion that has life-giving, life-transforming properties, and that's God's opinion. What He thinks about you is the only opinion that really matters, and He thinks you're worth dying for. Don't worry if you can't fully grasp that. None of us can. But it's true, whether you can fathom it or not.

Jesus died for you; that's the only opinion you need.

August 21

NO POWER TRIPS

The LORD protects defenseless people.
When I was weak, he saved me.
—PSALM 116:6 GWT

WHEN PEOPLE OF POWER USE THEIR influence to protect the helpless, we applaud. When strength and supremacy are targeted to help and develop, our world is enriched. When these attributes are wielded for selfish gain, they corrupt and tear down. Misguided clout falters into pride and weakness.

We can be grateful that God Almighty never succumbs to power trips. He rules and reigns with matchless command, yet it's His lovingkindness that draws us to Him. He is careful not to further wound a broken heart. He is a defender of those who can't fight for themselves. He uses His authority to heal and rescue.

You can trust Him to lift you up when you've fallen. You can count on Him to brush you off and help you risk again. Though others may run away when you are at your worst, God runs toward you. Your inability activates His ability. He is for you, and gentle with you, when you can go no further.

In this life, you may face foes bigger than yourself and wonder how you will come through. Prepare for that day today by thanking God for His tender, rescuing heart and His in-control arm. He is never too far away to save.

August 22

SIMPLE PRAYER

We do not know how to pray as we should.
But the Spirit himself speaks to God for us, even begs God
for us with deep feelings that words cannot explain.
—**ROMANS 8:26** NCV

WHAT CONSOLATION, KNOWING THAT JESUS TAUGHT us to pray, "Our Father!" It takes all the pressure off when it comes to prayer. We realize that we don't have to prepare a speech, memorize it, and then perform it perfectly. We don't have to worry about proper grammar or eloquence in verbiage. All we must do is open up our hearts and let the Father in.

The intimacy implied in the parent-child relationship is liberating. Isn't it a relief to know that sometimes prayer is simply having a good cry in the presence of God? Sometimes all that needs to be said is summed up in a deep sigh. Sometimes intercession is complete in merely stating a person's name and remaining before the Lord in reverent repose.

The freedom of expression that God welcomes makes prayer the easiest, most enjoyable, most fulfilling, and most desirable conversation you can have in the course of a day. No one comes as far your way as does the Holy Spirit in reaching out to understand the impulses of your heart.

The next time you feel the struggle to pray, simply get before the Lord and confess to Him your weakness in prayer. He will take it from there.

CREATIVE PERSISTENCE

Jesus refused.... Jesus gave in.
—MATTHEW 15:24, 28 MSG

YEARS AGO, A SALESMAN CALLED ON a business owner. An assistant greeted the sales representative and carried his business card back to the owner's office. The owner looked at the card, tore it up, and threw it away. "Get rid of him," he said. She returned to the salesman and said, "I'm sorry, but the owner is too busy to see you today." "That's fine," he replied. "Could I please have my card back?" After conferring with the owner, she stepped back out to the salesman and handed him a nickel. "I'm sorry," she said, "but your card was destroyed. I hope this covers the loss." The salesman smiled. Handing another business card to the assistant, he said, "Tell your boss I sell two cards for a nickel."

In the Bible we read another story of creative persistence. A woman comes to Jesus asking for her daughter to be healed, and twice Jesus dismisses her. But she doesn't quit. There's a place for her at God's table—she knows it deep inside. She asks another way, and her request is granted. Don't give up. Be persistent. Keep asking God for what you need. Feel free to get creative.

FINDING AND KEEPING HOPE

Now hope does not disappoint, because the love of God has been poured out in our hearts by the Holy Spirit who was given to us.
—ROMANS 5:5 NKJV

HAVE YOU EVER LOST HOPE? FEELING hopeless is one of the most emotionally debilitating conditions people experience. But hopelessness is also one of the most avoidable conditions, once you understand what genuine hope is—and you place your hope in God alone.

Too many people confuse hope with one of several poor imitations, such as the kind of "hope" that is little more than wishful thinking or the kind that depends entirely on a specific outcome. By contrast, authentic hope is the confidence that no matter what the outcome, God will see you through all of life's challenges and difficulties. That's not wishful thinking; that's a certainty.

Think of it this way: You have everything to gain by holding on to the hope that in God's hands everything will one day make sense, and that you will endure to the end. That requires a shift from insisting upon a particular way you think things should go to deciding that no matter how things go, God will be your constant companion and source of comfort.

Placing your hope in God alone offers you the assurance that regardless of the circumstances, you can always be at peace, because He will always be with you.

August 25

LIVING WORDS

Your word I have treasured in my heart,
that I may not sin against You.
—Psalm 119:11 nasb

GETTING LIFE RIGHT MEANS PURPOSELY READING and understanding the rule book. God set the guidelines for a meaningful, peace-filled life and recorded them in His Word. Reading the Bible explains what God likes and dislikes, what behaviors foster joy, what choices lead to disaster, and which ones produce contentment. Examine His written directives, and then read them again. Dig deeper to understand and apply what you discover. Ponder and tuck the Bible's truths into your heart and bring them out later in the day to consider some more.

Someone once said that God's Word is the only book in the Library of Congress that's alive. It is packed with energizing truths. When you're confused, the Bible clears your perspective. When you're upset, His words calm you down. When you face weighty decisions, God's wisdom is your guiding light. When you meditate on Bible verses, your life realigns with God's best for you. The Bible centers you and brings you back into balance.

Some days you may nibble on spiritual nuggets from God's Word, other days you may savor a seven-course meal. Each new day is your invitation to pull out your Bible and let its guiding principles and living words nourish you.

TRANSLATING PRAYER

*God can see what is in people's hearts. And he knows
what is in the mind of the Spirit, because the Spirit
speaks to God for his people in the way God wants.*
—ROMANS 8:27 NCV

IF YOU'VE EVER BEEN TO A foreign country on business and needed to communicate with others in professional situations, you've likely experienced the benefits of having a translator. Translators have a sobering responsibility. They shoulder the weight of interpretation, not merely of words but of context and emotion. How amazing to process meaning in one language while converting it with appropriate inflection into another.

One thing that aids in translation is the body language and facial expressions of the person attempting to communicate. The language of the physical body speaks for itself. A smile translates alike in any tongue. Enthusiasm, anger, frustration, satisfaction, all find their expression in similar gestures no matter what language.

In an astounding way, the Spirit of God enters your heart as an interpreter to discern your motives, your heartaches, your concerns, your desires, and your praise, converting your thoughts and petitions into the very words that He wants to hear you speak. He perfectly translates your longings and needs into prayers.

And most wonderful of all, you can access the Spirit's profound interpretive role at any time. Knowing that He has made conversation with God so simple and so effective, you'll find yourself praying more—and praying powerfully.

August 27

OUR RETURN

You shall know that I am the LORD...when I forgive you all that you have done, says the Lord GOD.
—**EZEKIEL 16:62-63** NRSV

ONE OF THE MOST FAMOUS STORIES in the Bible is the parable of the prodigal son. Jesus shares how a young man takes his family inheritance, goes off on his own, squanders his wealth with reckless living, and ends up in utter poverty. Realizing that the pigs he's feeding for a living have it better than he does, he decides to go back home. But he can't go back as a son because he has disgraced the family name. Perhaps, however, his father will allow him to be a servant. Not sure of the outcome, the young man starts for home. On the way, he rehearses the speech in his mind. *I'm not worthy to be your son*, he says over and over again. But from a long way off his father saw him and came running to meet him. "I'm not worthy to be your son," he began. But the father wasn't listening. His son had returned!

The parable, of course, is an illustration of our relationship with God. The moment we turn back to Him and humble ourselves in His presence, He stops listening to our faults and sets the table for a celebration.

SELFLESSNESS PERSONIFIED

When you do things, do not let selfishness or pride
be your guide. Instead, be humble and give more honor
to others than to yourselves.
—**PHILIPPIANS 2:3** NCV

GOD CALLS US TO A LIFE of selfless living. But what does it mean to be truly selfless? And how can you go about practicing selflessness in your daily life?

One of the best ways to learn anything is by example, and the very best example of selflessness is Jesus Himself. During His three years of ministry on earth, He gave of His time and His gifts so people could be healed of their diseases and infirmities, delivered from the evil that plagued them, and set free to live victorious lives amid an oppressive culture. And then He performed the ultimate selfless act: He gave His life on the cross so others, including you, could have victory in this life and spend eternity with God.

To be truly selfless requires caring more about others than you care about yourself—meeting their needs first whenever possible, taking care of them when it's inconvenient for you, and so forth. You find the ability and desire to practice selflessness where you find the power to do anything God calls you to do—in His presence as you spend time learning about Him, learning from Him, and asking Him to make those changes that will make you more like Christ.

BY DESIGN

Thank you for making me so wonderfully complex!
Your workmanship is marvelous—how well I know it.
—PSALM 139:14 NLT

HAVE YOU EVER SAT BENEATH A tree in the summer and looked up? Think about the intricacy of the leaves, how they connect to the tree. Consider the texture in the bark, and picture the way the sun shines on the veins of the leaf. You can almost hear the sap flowing.

It's an easy conclusion to think that only God could make something like that. Something so marvelously complex. Each part fits together into a beautiful whole. The tree has its place in the landscape. Even in the wild it towers majestically above the earth.

When it comes to thinking about yourself, do you see yourself as made by the same hand? The One who made the trees made you. If you admire the workmanship of the tree, you can also appreciate His artistry in you. You are marvelously complex. All your parts fit together into a beautiful whole.

You're much more intricate than a tree, but the One who lovingly made nature also made you. You can rest in the wonder of His artwork. If God put all that energy into something that cannot even talk, He surely put even more creative zeal into you. In this moment, revel in the wonder of God's workmanship—you.

August 30

DON'T WORRY, JUST WAIT

Since the first day you began to pray for understanding and to humble yourself before your God, your request has been heard in heaven. I have come in answer to your prayer.

—**DANIEL 10:12** NLT

ONCE WE'VE DEVELOPED THE HABIT OF daily time with God, we find ourselves longing more and more for the hour to roll around again. The delight we experience in intimacy with the Lord compels us to seek Him with more and more passion and frequency. And we delight to discover that He is as anxious to be with us as we are to be with Him.

One of the most thrilling discoveries comes with having asked the Lord for understanding and then receiving the insight for which we asked. The first time it occurs, it staggers us somewhat. We are tempted to question whether it might just be coincidence. It happens again, causing us to suspect that something intentional is going on. A third time, and we begin to catch on to the faithfulness of God in response to those who seek Him.

The Scriptures indicate that the very moment you register an inquiry before the Lord, His response is dispatched in the heavens. Depending upon the situation, it could take weeks or even years before the answer is perceptible to you, or it could be instantaneous, even as you ask. The important thing is—you can relax. His answer is on its way.

THE CHILD WITHIN

Let the children come to me. Don't stop them!
—MATTHEW 19:14 NLT

MADELEINE L'ENGLE ONCE SAID, "I AM still every age that I have been. Because I was once a child, I am always a child." By this she did not mean that we should act childishly. Instead, we embrace that child inside us. That four-year-old filled with wonder is still inside. We can celebrate that part of ourselves without compromising our maturity as adults.

There is another reason for embracing the child within. All of us were wounded as children. There are no exceptions. When we reach stages in our spiritual journey when we find that we can't move forward, when we run into a brick wall when trying to overcome issues in our lives, it may well be time to take another look at that wounded child within.

The child within is the root; the issues we face are the fruit. If the root is healthy, the fruit is healthy. But if the root is damaged, the fruit will suffer.

Could it be that Jesus wants us to bring to Himself the hurting child within? That Jesus wants to take that wounded child inside us into His arms and speak words of comfort, of clarity, of encouragement? Those words will transform our lives.

LIVING A FLEXIBLE LIFE

I know how to live on almost nothing or with everything.
I have learned the secret of living in every situation,
whether it is with a full stomach or empty, with plenty or little.
—**PHILIPPIANS 4:12** NLT

WHAT DO YOU THINK OF WHEN you hear the phrase "spiritual maturity"? Most likely, you consider a person to be spiritually mature if she has a good grasp of the Bible, a close relationship with God, and some evidence of a life that's characterized by prayer.

But there are many other evidences of spiritual maturity, some you can see and some that you can't—like living a life so flexible that you can thrive in any environment where God places you. If God wants you to stay put even though you had hoped to move, that's fine. If He calls you to leave your comfortable neighborhood to do mission work in a dirty, noisy city, that's fine too. Spiritually mature people are willing to do whatever God wants them to do.

Spiritual maturity is ultimately cultivated in the presence of God. It's in His presence that you learn true wisdom and genuine trust, which are essential elements in wise decision making. Some of those decisions will involve a certain measure of risk: only God knows what you should decide. Those choices that are in His will are worth the risk—and only by spending time with Him will you know which ones they are.

September 2

CALLING THE SHOTS

We know that in all things God works for the good of those who love him, who have been called according to his purpose.
—ROMANS 8:28 TNIV

TYPICALLY AT A MOVIE'S END, PEOPLE exit the theater barely noticing the film's rolling credits. Name after name flies by, people invisible to the moviegoer but critical to the success of the film. The dozens of off-camera workers include gaffers, grips, best boys, makeup artists, hairstylists, and special effects crews. And the director guides the whole team, creating art out of a mass of personalities, talents, and film.

Wouldn't it be nice some days to have a crew around you? Someone writes your dialog or tells you where to stand so the light hits you just right. Best of all, a director calls the shots so everything that looks messy now eventually comes out looking spectacular.

God really is at work in your life behind the scenes. He is your crew and director, invisible, yet actively transforming commotion into beauty. Trust His judgment the way the actors trust the director. Actors don't always know the reasons why the director orders certain scenes, but when they perform according to the instructions, the production succeeds. Ask yourself if your faith firmly trusts the guidance of your master director. He knows best how to call the shots and bring beauty to life.

September 3

THE MINISTRY OF ANGELS

Angels are only servants—spirits sent to care
for people who will inherit salvation.
—**HEBREWS 1:14 NLT**

THE MINISTRY OF ANGELS IS A MYSTERY to humans. They play an active role in the interchange between heaven and earth, but one that is largely imperceptible to us. The population of angels in the heavens is a number so great that it is beyond human calculation. It is possible that there are several attending to you at any given moment, particularly when you are in difficulty.

Does it really matter? Actually, it does. Knowing that the Lord has made provisions for you through angels helps you be more open to their ministry, more cooperative with their efforts. Just believing in the role of angels increases your spiritual receptivity to the aid that God provides.

Though rarely visible, angels minister grace and mercy to you in times of weariness and distress. Two battalions of angels showed up to ensure Jacob's crossing to Canaan because of his brother's threats. An angel assisted in Peter's release from prison one night in answer to the prayers of his faithful friends.

Angels carry burdens from you to God and return again with messages and deliverance from God to you. Although you may feel all alone when you're without resources or human companionship, don't worry—you're surrounded by angels.

September 4

WHERE DO WE FIND SECURITY?

God spoke…"Once again I will shake not only the earth but the heavens also." This means that all of creation will be shaken and removed, so that only unshakable things will remain.
—HEBREWS 12:26-27 NLT

ON AUGUST 1, 2007, A BRIDGE extending across the Mississippi River, collapsed killing 13 and injuring 145. An ensuing investigation revealed that the structures supporting the bridge's weight were only half as thick as they should have been. To prevent future tragedies like this, investigators recommended improvements in how bridges are tested and inspected.

A bridge must support the weight of those who cross it. Similarly, our spiritual security system must hold up under any weight. God will challenge our security if we don't find it in Him. A rich man came to Jesus hoping to find eternal life. But Jesus called on him to give up his wealth because he was trusting in money instead of God. Jesus also confronted those who counted on their own self-righteousness for security before God.

In your time alone with God, you may need to wrestle with the question: *Where do I find my security?* Having your security called into question by God can make you squirm. But you don't want to cross a bridge wondering if it will support your weight. Nor do you want to face an uncertain future without the assurance that you stand on the foundation that cannot be shaken: Jesus Christ.

THE WEALTH OF WISDOM

Happy are those who find wisdom, and those who get
understanding, for her income is better than silver,
and her revenue better than gold.

—**PROVERBS 3:13-14** NRSV

DID YOU KNOW THAT SPENDING TIME alone with God is the secret to obtaining great wealth? That is, unless wealth is only to be measured in monetary and material terms.

Wealth, in any culture, is measured by what is most highly valued. Where chronic drought and famine occur, the wealthy are those who have plenty of food to eat. Where knowledge is considered the greatest commodity, those who accumulate multiple academic degrees are viewed as prosperous. In the world of racing, the owner of the fastest car is the one to be envied.

But in the kingdom of God, one of the most valuable assets is the wisdom that only comes from spending time with Him. Wisdom is the enlightened perspective developed through spiritual training and experience of God. It is born of revelation, sustained by insight, and applied with understanding. Only God can disseminate true wisdom, and He does so generously for those who ask.

Wisdom is the inevitable outcome of an authentic encounter with God in prayer and in worship. In worship, you experience the humbling awareness of God's otherness; while in prayer, you bend your will to His sovereignty and power. The combination of humility and submission makes the perfect ground for wisdom to take root and grow.

September 6

SOLD OUT?

Wherever you go, I will go; and wherever you lodge,
I will lodge; your people shall be my people,
and your God, my God.
—RUTH 1:16 NKJV

REAL COMMITMENT SEEMS RARE THESE DAYS. Jobs are valued as long as they further the career path. Friendships work when they don't drag you down. Divorce rates remain high. Overall, there's an attitude that says, "I'll continue on as long as…" rather than, "I'm in it for the long haul."

True commitment with others starts by receiving the commitment God gives you. Think about it—He doesn't quit on you when you don't serve His purposes very well. He meets your needs day by day without wavering. And have you ever gone to Him and found Him unavailable? As you soak in His presence every day, you experience freedom from the fear of loss that keeps the heart in a perpetual state of anxiety.

A committed relationship demands you take the risk of the unexpected. God has risked that with you. He's made it clear that He will remain faithful regardless of what you do. Think about your commitment to Him. Is it just for today or for all your tomorrows?

Life's ventures are full of curves. Consider before you reach the unexpected places whether your devotion to God is one of being sold out or "as long as…."

September 7

FEASTING ON GOD'S WORD

Yes, he humbled you by letting you go hungry and then feeding you with manna...to teach you that...we live by every word that comes from the mouth of the LORD.

—DEUTERONOMY 8:3 NLT

WHAT BRINGS FULFILLMENT IN LIFE? IT is a question that has relevance only for humans. Pear trees don't ponder the issue. Neither do giraffes, puffer fish, crows, or bumblebees. In fact, most plants fulfill their reason for existence simply by being a source of food for other creatures, while animals, sea creatures, insects, and birds fulfill their role by being part of the food chain—eating or being eaten.

As a human, you won't find fulfillment in merely satiating your appetite for food. In fact, you won't be truly fulfilled by gratifying any of your physical appetites. Created in the image of God, your fulfillment is derived from a meaningful connection with the source of your existence. In other words, your significance comes from knowing God.

God's Word to you is the essential catalyst for your relationship with Him and for your ultimate happiness. In the same way that His words brought the creation into existence, His Word has the power to sustain life, but even more, to bring your life into its greatest potential.

God's Word provides an abundance of understanding and insight. It is a virtual fountain of wisdom concerning how to live effectively among people and how to please the Lord.

BEING GOOD

The Holy Spirit produces this kind of fruit in our lives:
love, joy, peace, patience, kindness, goodness, faithfulness,
gentleness, and self-control.
—**GALATIANS 5:22-23** NLT

CAN YOU CONSTRUCT A CANTALOUPE? CAN you build a banana? Can you assemble an apple? Of course not! Fruit is not manufactured. Fruit is grown by virtue of its organic connection to the branch, the vine, the tree, the root.

Throughout the Bible, God describes the fruit of His presence in our lives. That fruit includes good moral character, love, kindness, and so on. Many people have misinterpreted this to mean that God is mainly interested in us being "good." We should therefore devote ourselves to improving the moral fiber of our lives. But that's not how it works. Remember, these things are fruit. We cannot fabricate fruit. The best we could hope for would be a cheap imitation.

Rather it is our connection to Jesus Himself that results in our being "good." Think about it. If we were totally at peace, filled with joy, overflowing with contentment and gratitude, how much attraction would temptation have? What could sin offer?

God wants you. As you spend time in His presence, He wants to fill your life, heal your heart, share His great love for you. Let Him do that, and watch the transformation that takes place inside!

CULTIVATING CONFIDENCE

We should not be like cringing, fearful slaves, but we should behave like God's very own children, adopted into...his family, and calling him "Father, Father."
—ROMANS 8:15-16 TLB

LIGHTNING STRIKES WITH A LOUD CLAP of thunder. A startled little girl lunges into her father's arms crying, "Daddy, hold me!"

The many moments that a child spends in the loving embrace of her earthly father creates a bond of trust that nothing can sever. It is no different with God.

Morning by morning, we can awaken with a conscious appreciation of life, giving thanks to God in prayer for our existence, even feeling a sense of anticipation about what the day will bring.

Day by day, we can make a conscious effort to live our lives in such a way that we reflect the goodness of the Lord. Our integrity and authenticity will be a direct result of seeking counsel and guidance in His Word.

Evening by evening, we can wind down the day with a calm resolve that comes from knowing God well enough to trust Him with the details of life. We can retire from the day expressing a sense of gratitude and peace in worship.

And when the storms of life come—and come they eventually do—you'll discover that you've cultivated the intimacy with God that allows you to turn to Him with complete trust—without fear—and cry out, "Father, hold me!"

ULTIMATE POWER SOURCE

Who is the King of glory? The LORD, strong and mighty;
the LORD, invincible in battle.

—PSALM 24:8 NLT

DO YOU EVER FEEL AS IF the world is presenting challenges that you simply aren't equipped to handle? Maybe you are being convicted to confront an unfair situation at work or to report an injustice or a crime to which you were the sole witness. Maybe you are in an abusive relationship and now realize that your safety, and the safety of others, is at risk if you don't speak up. Life has a way of putting us in scenarios that give us no choice but to take action.

The good news is that you have an ally in God. As tender and personal as His love is for you, He is also a powerful protector, your champion, a warrior on your behalf. God can shift circumstances, open doors, bring the right people along to help you in what seems like an impossible situation. He can also give you courage you couldn't muster on your own.

Yes, He is a compassionate Father and Comforter. But He is also the God of the universe, the King of Glory, mighty and just. He will give you strength. All you have to do is ask. What can you do today to tap into God's power and might?

September 11

TRUE NORTH

The LORD is my light and my salvation—whom shall I fear?
The LORD is the stronghold of my life—of whom shall I be afraid?
—**PSALM 27:1** NIV

WE LIVE IN AN AGE OF turbulence. Our world seems to perpetually reel from terrorist attacks, natural disasters, wars, and economic meltdowns. It seems like down is up and up is down as all the things we once assumed offered security and stability start to wobble and are exposed as fragile illusions.

Unsettled times tend to reveal the best and worst in people's character. Those we assumed were towers of strength crumble in the face of change and hardship, while others face challenges with genuine grace and faith. Throughout history, resiliency and the human spirit have lifted countless men and women to press on, but only fortitude of faith in God brings prevailing triumph in tragedy.

The Bible reminds us that our hope is in Christ alone. While people and institutions fail, God's love is eternal and unchanging—unaffected by world events or even death. If nothing else, ongoing upheavals in our world show just how much we need Jesus, the stabilizer of our faith in disorienting times. Pause today to give your uneasy feelings to your strong and steady God. Ask Him to keep you pointed to true north regardless of which way the winds of change blow.

OVERCOMING FEAR

Do not panic; don't be afraid.

—JEREMIAH 51:46 NLT

LIKE MANY PEOPLE, KIM WRESTLED WITH anxiety. Over time, her panic attacks grew worse and worse until she experienced panic almost around the clock. Well-meaning people tried to give her Bible passages on fear, but standing in front of the mirror quoting verses on courage only made things worse. Desperate for help, she turned first to medication, then to counseling, and finally to prayer ministry.

In prayer ministry, while waiting before God, she began to put together the connections between painful experiences in the past, damaging lies, and ongoing panic. As she faced these realities in God's presence, He shared with her the freeing truth about her past, her present, and her future. Often that truth was simple: *You're okay now. It's over.* Things changed. The monster grip of panic over her life was broken, and her experience brought her into a much deeper relationship with Christ.

Kim's experience points the way for any of us who wrestle with fear or anxiety. How do you get rid of fear? You take Jesus to the scariest places inside. Once He is there, those things can never trouble you in the same way again. Whether we do this alone or with the help of a professional, the presence of Jesus is the ultimate answer.

September 13

GOD THE GIVER

He who did not spare his own Son,
but gave him up for us all—how will he not also,
along with him, graciously give us all things?
—ROMANS 8:32 NIV

As the gracious giver, god withholds nothing for the sake of those whom He created—those for whom He risked everything. Why would He? Our deliverance has already cost Him that which He valued most highly—His Son.

Does that mean that all we have to do is figure out the right formula for asking and we'll get everything we ever wanted? Does it mean if we can only prove how worthy we are, we can have anything we ever dreamed of having? Neither is true.

The key to understanding God's generosity lies within the word "Father." God's lavish gifts are determined by the wise and discerning heart of a father. He knows what we need and what we don't—what we can handle and what we can't.

God's way of giving begins in the quiet place of trust that develops between you as you learn to live in His presence. You go to Him daily, seeking to understand Him—His motives, His desires, His character, His actions. As you come to know Him, you start to think like Him. His concerns become your concerns. And before you know it, you realize that the things He most wants for you are the things you most want!

September 14

BELONGING TO GOD

Don't you know that your body is a temple that belongs to the
Holy Spirit? The Holy Spirit, whom you received from God,
lives in you. You don't belong to yourselves.
—1 CORINTHIANS 6:19 GWT

WE LIVE IN AN I-FOCUSED CULTURE, where individuality and personal choices are celebrated from birth on. Choices empower. Choices foster control. Choices are often fun. In a typical day you are free to choose what to wear, what to eat, and whether you will exercise or not. Most days it's up to us to make dozens of selections that affect our well-being, from the mundane to the monumental.

Yet with all the freeing privileges of ordering your daily life, do you know that you're really not as independent as you might think? God is actually a part of your individuality equation. As much as you'd like to claim complete autonomy at times, you are forever connected to your Creator.

You belong to God, and belonging to Him is a liberating revelation. He is right there to help you make sound decisions about your life, your relationships, your work, your future. As your ever-present consultant, He longs to be a part of your choices. So as you go about today, why not stop and listen to God's reassuring voice? He delights in your individuality and in your recognition that you are joined to Him forever.

GOD OF ALL GODS

The LORD your God is the God of gods and Lord of lords.
He is the great God, the mighty and awesome God,
who shows no partiality and cannot be bribed.
—DEUTERONOMY 10:17 NLT

WE ARE LIVING IN AN AGE in which it is considered politically correct to acknowledge that everyone is entitled to their own gods. It is no longer acceptable to promote the God of the Bible in public because someone might be offended by the suggestion that He is above all other gods.

How can you witness to the truth about God if you can't promote Him as God supreme? One very effective way is to reflect His character in your own actions and behavior. Ironically, God's superiority is best demonstrated in His humility and compassion. So when you treat all people with respect and consideration regardless of their race, economic status, religious beliefs, or education, you are witnessing to the indiscriminate love of God for all mankind. When you conscientiously consider the environment—your responsible use of the earth's resources—you are mirroring God's intense love for His creation. When you show compassion for animals—feeding the birds in winter, caring for a stray—you shed light on God's careful concern for His creatures.

What makes Him great is His lavish love. What makes Him known is the love of His people.

TWO SLEEPERS

Jonah had gone below deck,
where he lay down and fell into a deep sleep.
—JONAH 1:5 NIV

THE BIBLE TELLS US THE STORIES of two men who slept on a boat during a storm. The first man was Jonah, a prophet. God wanted him to walk into the capital city of an enemy nation and warn them of impending judgment. Jonah couldn't bring himself to do it, so he ran away from God. He took passage on a ship headed in the opposite direction, and as it set sail, he went below deck and fell into a deep sleep. While he slept, a terrible storm tossed the ship.

The other sleeper was Jesus. It was time to cross the lake. A group of experienced fishermen were at the helm. Jesus fell asleep. After He did, a furious storm threatened to swamp the boat.

Both men were sleeping. Both needed to be awakened. But there the similarity ends. Jonah was sleeping the sleep of escape. He was trying to push God out of his life. Jesus was sleeping within the embrace of His Father.

Storms enter our lives. If we are running from God, like Jonah, a storm can stop us dead in our tracks. But if we linger in God's presence, like Jesus, a storm merely reveals our great calm within.

THE NAKED TRUTH

He said, "Naked I came from my mother's womb,
and naked I shall return there. The LORD gave and the
LORD has taken away. Blessed be the name of the LORD."
—JOB 1:21 NASB

O F ALL THE BILLIONS UPON MEGA-BILLIONS of babies born
on this planet, including furry animal babies, none of these
infants arrived dressed in clothes. No little cherub-cheeked child or
pink-nosed critter entered this world decked out in a cuddly little
outfit with matching booties. We all make our earthly debut
buck naked.

We all started out on equal footing with our possessions—nothing.
Yet some of us were instantly showered with a fancy nursery and a
college education fund, while others of us were fortunate to have a
ragged blanket to wrap around us. Life just isn't fair in doling out
similar material blessings to everyone.

Lest we start spinning too fast in comparing ourselves with the
proverbial Joneses, God reminds us that He is the one ultimately in
charge of dispersing assets and talents and looks and status. It is up
to God to give and to take away. We don't typically appreciate this
until we actually lose something or someone. Regardless of how much
we accumulate in life, whether tangible belongings or relationships or
even Bible knowledge, we are to hold all things in a loose grip and
steadily thank God for each one.

KEEPING YOURSELF IN PERSPECTIVE

Do not think of yourself more highly than you ought,
but rather think of yourself with sober judgment,
in accordance with the measure of faith God has given you.
—ROMANS 12:3 NIV

SOMEONE ONCE SAID THAT HUMILITY IS not a matter of thinking less of yourself, it is rather the freedom from thinking about yourself at all.

Freedom. It has a nice ring to it. How does spending time with God set you free from self?

Being alone with God is an exercise in attentiveness. God speaks! And especially to those who want to hear. Listening for the voice of God helps to quiet your own thoughts. Imagine that you are simply sitting in your backyard, taking in the beauty of nature. Perhaps you can sense God communicating with you through creation, pointing out to you the vastness of the universe and how diligently He cares for it every day. You sense your smallness in comparison to the enormity of God's concerns. In direct contrast, you focus in on a small sparrow perched on your fence post and realize that God is as diligent over that one little bird as He is over you. Likewise, God is as diligent over you as He is the population of the entire continent.

Spending time with God lends perspective in big and small ways. It helps you keep in perspective that the world really does revolve around Him.

FINDING GOD

No one has ever seen God. But God, the one and only Son,
is at the Father's side. He has shown us what God is like.

—JOHN 1:18 NIrV

HOW DO YOU FIND GOD? IF that task were left up to us, we would be in trouble. How could we hope to know anything about Him even if we spent a thousand lifetimes searching? It would be like counting the fish in the Pacific Ocean one by one, hoping we didn't miss any. The universe is so vast and our capabilities so small that we could never explore it from one end to the other in hope of discovering the Creator.

Here we learn the truth. No one has ever seen God. Our eyes aren't big enough. Our hearts can't take Him in. Our lives aren't long enough to see the Almighty, unless He wants to be seen.

But God does want to be seen. He wants to be discovered. He wants to fill our souls with the understanding of Him. And He knows you can't pour the ocean into a drinking glass. So instead, He gives us a drink from the Water of Life. God is not at the end of our search; we are at the end of His. He found us.

In our time alone with Him, we can rejoice that God made Himself known to us.

REAL-LIFE SUPERHERO

Job answered GOD: "I'm convinced: You can do anything and everything. Nothing and no one can upset your plans."
—JOB 42:1-2 MSG

MANY SUPERHERO FANS WILDLY APPLAUD IRON Man, who first debuted in a 1963 Marvel comic book. There's just something enthralling about affluent, ingenious engineer Tony Stark donning his high-tech suit of armor to take on the world's criminals. It's hard to not cheer for Iron Man, Superman, Captain America, and all the other avengers looking out for the safety and serenity of mankind.

While these fictional conquerors appear invincible, they are actually quite puny compared to God Almighty. God lives in the reality of our daily battles with the world's most dastardly terrorist ever—Satan. Without batting an eye, God pulverizes the wicked schemes of the Enemy, who continually attempts to thwart God's good purposes.

As you come before your real-life Superhero, do you take time to consider that nothing can upset His plans or circumvent Him from doing anything and everything He wants to do? God may not have a theme song or wear a gleaming techno suit, but He is the only one powerful enough to protect and defend you from your true enemy. There's just something enthralling about the Almighty coming to your rescue.

September 21

GOD'S AGENTS

*Make every effort to live in peace with all men
and to be holy; without holiness no one will see the Lord.
See to it that no one misses the grace of God.*

—HEBREWS 12:14-15 NIV

THE PEOPLE OF GOD ARE AGENTS of peace! Bringing peace into every situation, God's friends can be trusted to act in the best interests of others no matter what it costs them personally. If you are in relationship with God, your presence brings His presence to bear wherever you go. His comfort and consolation will come through your willingness to extend it.

The people of God are agents of holiness! This is more than merely being reduced to moral purity. It is a life-giving, life-sustaining way of being in the world. Holy people are those who are fully alive to God and who thrive on bringing others into His embrace and abundance. If you are a friend of God, your presence nurtures life just as His does.

The people of God are agents of grace! Those who belong to the Lord ooze with compassion for the fallen, the weak, the oppressed, the wounded, and the weary. If you are God's representative, you apply grace and forgiveness wherever it is needed with no strings attached. Freely you have received, and freely you give.

Be aware of your role as one who represents the Lord as an ambassador of His peace, holiness, and grace.

September 22

APPRENTICED FOR ETERNITY

We have this treasure in jars of clay to show that this all-surpassing power is from God and not from us.
—2 Corinthians 4:7 NIV

GOD TRUSTS US. THINK ABOUT IT. God is 100 percent trustworthy, but are we?

God places in our hands His most precious treasures, His children. Parents have nearly absolute power over their children's lives in their formative years. God grants us that power, looking to us to shelter, guide, and inspire children so they can become men and women of God. Even if we are not parents, God places in our hands the care of one another. Will we protect each other, honor each other, encourage each other? God charges us with the responsibility of making disciples of the nations and transforming our world.

Clearly we are not up to the task, but God entrusts the assignment to us nonetheless. Why would He do that? Doesn't it seem reckless?

Could it be that He delights in accomplishing the impossible through us bumbling, stumbling human beings? Could it be that God is calling us into a moment-by-moment relationship with Him where we look to Him for the wisdom and strength to carry out these important assignments? Could our time alone with Him be a time to receive coaching for the new day? Could it be that we are being apprenticed for eternity?

September 23

SILENCE IS GOLDEN

*They sat on the ground with him for seven days
and seven nights. No one said a word to him,
because they saw how great his suffering was.*

—JOB 2:13 NIV

SOME POSSESS THE GIFT OF GAB, while others find chit-chat excruciating, particularly when talking to strangers. Even if we're known for an eloquent tongue, there are just moments when life renders us speechless. Perhaps you've experienced some of these moments: the first look at a newborn, a generous surprise gift, a sunset over the ocean, the last breath of a loved one. Small everyday beauties and life-altering transitions alike can leave us searching for words. God intended language to be both spoken and unspoken. Surely even He pauses, without words, in awe of His creation.

One of the times we could all do with fewer words is when we encounter a hurting friend. Our natural tendency is the attempt to buoy those we care about with inspiring epiphanies, but so often our well-tended speeches lag into hollow platitudes. You know what it's like to be brought lower by a loved one who rambles on and who can't relate to your needs and your feelings.

Gratefully, God is never like this. He knows just when to nudge you through His Word and when to just sit with you in silence, letting your tears speak. How is He communicating with you this day?

THE WILL TO FORGIVE

You shall not take vengeance or bear a grudge against
any of your people, but you shall love your neighbor
as yourself: I am the LORD.
—LEVITICUS 19:18 NRSV

D O YOU EVER HOLD A GRUDGE? Most of us will qualify our response: "Well, not normally, but when…."

There is a very curious thing that surfaces when you are pursuing a relationship with God. You discover that it is difficult to accomplish His will while harboring a record of wrongs against another. In other words, you will find it almost impossible to fulfill your role in God's mission of love if you have bitterness in your heart toward someone.

So what are you to do if you cannot get the resentment out of your heart? How do you manage your feelings? First, bring the situation into your conversation with the Lord and tell Him how you feel. Don't worry about trying to fix your feelings; God's understanding heart can handle the truth. Once everything is out in the open, you can talk about the course of action you should take. Wait for the Spirit's counsel concerning how to treat the person with whom you are in conflict.

What will His counsel be? To speak to your opponent warmly, drawing him or her into your good will, just as you would want someone to do for you. Don't worry, your heart will soon catch up with your words.

LIFE'S LESSONS

The LORD is a shelter for the oppressed,
a refuge in times of trouble.
—PSALM 9:9 NLT

WHERE DO WE LEARN LIFE'S REAL lessons? Usually it is not when the crowds are cheering, money is in the bank, and we feel great. Rather, we learn lessons when a friend disappoints us, the job ends, the report from the doctor isn't good. It's in these difficult times that we find that we need to turn to Someone greater than ourselves.

Are you in the middle of one of those challenging times right now? First of all, know this: Even when others don't understand, God does. He is here, ready right now to listen to everything that is in your heart. God is the best listener in the universe. But He is more than that. He will share life-changing truth with us if we are willing to listen. That truth can come in many forms: a phone call from a friend, a new discovery from the Bible, a circumstance with God's unmistakable fingerprints on it, a quiet internal conviction that He is speaking.

None of us enjoy going through hard times, but most of us can point back to these trials as the time when we grew the most as people. Take the journey with God, and know that you will emerge triumphant.

September 26

HEARING AND EYE EXAMS

My ears had heard of you but now my eyes have seen you.
—JOB 42:5 NIV

FOR YOU TO HEAR, YOUR EARS capture sound waves and translate these fluctuations into an electrical signal that your brain can understand. Your eyes are similarly complex and require a chemical reaction to convert light into electrical impulses that your brain reads as vision. Both your sense of hearing and sight rely on well-designed components working smoothly together.

In a spiritual sense, you were also intricately wired for keen hearing and sight. God formed you with an innate capacity for tuning in to His sounds and His sights. But sometimes you can depend a bit too much on the things people tell you about God instead of listening to Him yourself. You can also lean too strongly on what others tell you about seeing God work in their lives instead of looking for Him yourself.

To keep your hearing crisp for the resonance of God in your life and your eyesight sharp for the landscapes of God in your life, why not sit still for a little checkup? Ask the Master Audiologist and Ophthalmologist to remove anything that is blocking you from hearing from Him and seeing Him in your own day-to-day life. The good news is, He'll reveal Himself so you can't miss Him.

HOLINESS THAT INSPIRES PRAISE

I will walk with you and be your God,
and you will be my people.
—LEVITICUS 26:12 NCV

EVERYONE UNDERSTANDS THE INDIVIDUAL MOTIVE AND benefit involved with being in relationship with God: personal holiness and eternal reward. Those who are in relationship with Him find it easy to engage in the worship that comes from within their grateful hearts. However, you may not know that there is an outward-looking aspect of your relationship and worship that is intended to benefit those who do not know Him.

Walking with God in intimate relationship does produce personal holiness, but far from separating you from others, it transforms you into a truly human being bearing God's image among the rest of humanity. It makes of you a deeply passionate member of the human race filled with love, compassion, mercy, generosity, peace, patience, gentleness, and joy.

When those who are most truly human live out their true identity, their lives appropriately reflect the character of God and cause others to give Him glory, sometimes unwittingly. What happens then in worship is that they gather up the praises even of those who do not know Him and bring it all to the Lord, the Creator, who is worthy to be praised.

Being God's people is a far greater calling than we could have imagined.

MAKING OUR WAY CLEAR

The LORD directs the steps of the godly.
He delights in every detail of their lives.
—**PSALM 37:23** NLT

HAVE YOU EVER WATCHED ANTS? ANTS often have an interesting way of walking. They take a few steps, and then they stop. They take a few more steps, and then they stop.

The Christian life functions much the same way. We take a few steps, and then we stop to get more direction for our journey. Then we correct our course if we need to, and take a few more steps. It's much like driving through the fog. When we drive through the fog, we don't take anything for granted. We don't know what the next two hundred yards of road will bring. So we slow down and drive according to the visibility ahead.

This step-by-step, day-by-day process is how God works. He could, of course, give us our entire life plan, complete with contingencies, early on. But He doesn't. He clears enough fog so that we can find our way forward a little bit. Then we look back to Him. Our time alone with God affords us the opportunity to clear the fog, to get the course corrections we need, to get back on track and stay on track. Looking to God makes our way clear.

VENDING MACHINE GOD?

Even when He heard that Lazarus was sick, He still stayed
two days longer in the same place where He was.
—JOHN 11:6 AMP

GOD'S WAYS ARE A MYSTERY. HE'S like the wind—you don't see where He comes from, but you know when He's arrived. His timing is always perfect. Yet sometimes perfect is frustrating, like the times when everything is getting bad, and you know just one word from this all-powerful Friend would solve it…and He doesn't move. The truth is, He is not a vending machine where you put in a prayer and suddenly get your way.

God's unpredictability doesn't make Him easy to live with, especially when you want Him to fix your trouble and He doesn't. Your heart whispers, "Why?" And despite your desire to trust Him, sometimes you find there's a nagging feeling of betrayal hovering around the edges of your heart.

As challenging as it is waiting on God's timetable, would you really respect a God who would be at your beck and call? If you could predict God's actions, maybe you'd think you could run the universe. You can't anticipate what God will do, but you can rely on His heart. You can count on His unchanging character. You can depend on His goodness.

When you can't see His hand, keep trusting His heart.

RESONATING WITH REVELATION

They said to each other, "Didn't our hearts burn within us as he talked with us on the road and explained the Scriptures to us?"
—LUKE 24:32 NLT

HAVE YOU EVER HAD AN EXPERIENCE of déjà vu? Feeling as if you've already witnessed what is currently happening, you anticipate what's next just as it is occurring. It is a peculiar phenomenon of the human brain beyond our ability to control.

In a remotely similar manner, the revelation of God through Scripture can resonate somewhere deep within us, as if we had anticipated it all along. The truth about God, about creation, about His interaction and intentions toward mankind grips us with a depth of meaning and fulfillment that brings clarity to every dimension of life. It causes us to exclaim, "Of course! That makes sense of everything!"

Since you were created in the image of God, there is a template for a God-connection that exists at the core of your being. It resonates with the truth about God and with the goodness that characterizes Him. It causes the sensation of familiarity. This familiarity manifests itself in a warm and welcome assurance, like an old and trusted friend. It is alive and vibrant, touching something within you that ignites somewhere in your inner being and brings you fully alive.

An encounter with God's living Word is a life-generating experience.

October 1

BEING REAL

Don't be too good or too wise! Why destroy yourself?
—ECCLESIASTES 7:16 NLT

WHAT KIND OF CHILDREN DOES GOD want? Real ones. The wonderful thing about God is that we don't need to put on a show in order to be accepted by Him. In fact, a show would get in the way. God likes hanging out with us just as we are, without pretense, without facades.

What kind of prayers does God want? Real ones. Learning to punctuate our prayers with flowery religious language doesn't earn us any merit badges with God. But honesty connects our hearts with His. Getting real with God opens the door to genuine transformation in our lives.

Keep in mind that heaven is not populated with religious fakes. Instead, it is filled with real people who took their real struggles to God day after day. Something miraculous happens when we pursue God with this kind of honesty. At first, we are overwhelmed to know that God likes us just the way we are. But the longer we spend time with Him, the more we discover that we are changing. It's not so much that we have tried to change. Instead, He is rubbing off on us and we are becoming like Him.

October 2

CHECKIN' IN

The Israelites sampled their provisions
but did not inquire of the LORD.

—JOSHUA 9:14 TNIV

ONE OF THE MOST CHALLENGING AREAS of deepening in your relationship with God is learning to trust Him above yourself. Let's be honest, we learn from a young age to be independent, to trust our five senses and our own thoughts. In this world, we get good at what we do by having confidence in our own decisions. In this competition called life, we think we have to trust ourselves more than anyone else.

But there's a difference between having the self-confidence to make a sound decision and having the God-confidence to ask for input. Remember, God's knowledge base is way beyond your scope. Being all-knowing, He has access to information you don't have. You've no doubt experienced the backlash from a decision you thought was just fine, but the results proved dreadful. Being outside of time, God can see implications of decisions, even the seemingly unimportant ones, that would never occur to you.

Discover His limitless knowledge for yourself. You can start right now. Ask Him for guidance and direction. He is waiting to give it. His insight could save you a lot of grief down the road. And, when you check in with God, be sure to follow His lead.

GOSSIPING THE GOSPEL

Then those who revered the LORD spoke with one another.
The LORD took note and listened, and a book
of remembrance was written before him of those who
revered the LORD and thought on his name.
—MALACHI 3:16 NRSV

HAVE YOU EVER BEEN CAUGHT SAYING something good behind someone's back? You could say you were "guilty" of good gossip. The person about whom you spoke so favorably is blessed to know that you go about sharing your respect and admiration for them. Imagine the things that God hears said about Him because people never stop to consider that He listens—good and bad.

Some people make the mistake of thinking that God only listens to us when we intentionally address Him in prayer. Yet the Scriptures make it plain that He is capable of listening to the deepest secrets of our hearts, much more the conversations in which we engage.

Consider then what God hears you say behind His back and how that affects your relationship with Him. How much conversation do you entertain that is spiritual in nature? Where does it lead and what does it produce?

Those whose hearts are full of God cannot help speaking about Him in ways that inspire others. They bless the Lord because of their sincere love and gratitude, as well as their authentic joy in helping others come to know Him. Their hearts are full of gossip about God, and He's listening.

October 4

LETTING GO

Cast your bread upon the waters,
for you will find it after many days.
—ECCLESIASTES II:I NKJV

ON JANUARY 8, 1956, MISSIONARY JIM Elliot and his four companions were speared to death on the banks of the Curaray River in Ecuador, South America, as they tried to make contact with the Huaorani people. At first, the world was shocked and saddened. But, as reporters began to dig deeper into this story, they came across this October 28, 1949, entry in Jim's prayer journal: "He is no fool who gives what he cannot keep to gain that which he cannot lose."

That simple statement inspired a whole new generation to weigh life and death in the balance and to conclude that eternal gain far outweighs temporary loss.

Why do we let go? Because we learn that there are some things we cannot keep, even when we wish we could. In our time alone with God, we give to God all those things we are not capable of holding on our own. Our dreams. Our hopes. Our children. Our very lives. When our hands are finally empty, our eyes are opened to discover that everything we gave away is now safe, waiting for us in the hands of our eternal Father.

October 5

LOGICAL LOVE

I tell you, "I will not force out the people in this land.
They will be your enemies,
and their gods will be a trap for you."
—JUDGES 2:3 NCV

A POPULAR PARENTING COURSE TITLED "PARENTING with Love and Logic" is designed to help parents raise their kids to be responsible adults. The premise is to present simple choices that give children a taste of reality by offering consequences. The consequences help them develop their own inner voice that asks them, "How much pain will this cause me?" before they engage in a behavior. The parent remains the good guy; the child's decisions become the bad guy. The parent empathizes and feels sad for poor choices but doesn't rescue the child from the consequence of a bad decision.

Like a great parent, God does not always rescue His children from the consequences of their poor choices. He'll warn us, teach us, and train us, but if we deliberately move away from His plan, He won't rescue us from the pain. He's simply raising us in a logically loving way.

Pause for a moment and ponder if God is trying to get your attention regarding something. There may be a direction He wants you to move in or an attitude He's nudging you to drop. Before you have to experience the consequences of your choice, listen to His urging.

LOVING YOUR ENEMIES

When someone gives you a hard time, respond with the
energies of prayer, for then you are working out of your true
selves, your God-created selves.

—MATTHEW 5:44 MSG

WHEN PEOPLE MISTREAT YOU, IT'S NATURAL to want to strike back—wrong for wrong. A spontaneous desire for revenge sometimes threatens to break out in retaliation because of the innate sense of justice with which we were created.

God has counseled His friends to consider another alternative in response to unprovoked wrongs. He has commissioned and empowered His people to turn the intense emotional energy that usually expresses itself in retaliatory measures into passionate prayer for the sake of the wrongdoer. How strange. Yes, but how powerful!

If you seek the counsel of God when wronged by another, you'll be reminded that what is at stake is the precious and precarious place of healthy human relationships within the created order. Any rift in the fabric of humanity translates into a breach in God's glory. Having been created in His image, mankind was meant to live in community, reflecting God's love and unity for His purposes. He has entrusted us with this loving community.

Go to God when wronged and request that He help you forgive the wrong committed. You'll discover true intimacy with Him when you pray for the one who wounded you, because He understands suffering. You'll find that mercy trumps judgment and heals broken hearts.

October 7

THE VACUUM PRINCIPLE

Don't be drunk with wine, because that will ruin your life.
Instead, be filled with the Holy Spirit.
—EPHESIANS 5:18 NLT

WHAT'S THE EASIEST WAY TO TAKE the air out of a drinking glass? Simple. Fill it with water. If we tried to remove the air without putting something in its place, what would happen? The glass would shatter, not strong enough to hold an airless vacuum.

Spiritually speaking, we are the same way. By ourselves, we are empty containers. We are designed to be filled with something. Apart from God, we humans turn to all sorts of things to fill up the emptiness inside. But none of those things fully satisfy.

God understands this. That's why He invites you to be filled with His Spirit. God, in the person of His Holy Spirit, wants to live inside you. He wants to fill every "room" in your "house." He wants to be your comfort. When He enters painful places in your heart, you find peace. When He enters confused places in your heart, you find clarity. When He enters grieving places, you find joy. When He enters your frustrating experiences, you discover a patience that takes hard things and makes them easy. When He enters your relationships, you experience love. As you invite the Holy Spirit in, you become whole.

October 8

LESS IS MORE

*The LORD said, "Gideon...I can't let you win
with this many soldiers. The Israelites would think
that they had won the battle all by themselves
and that I didn't have anything to do with it."*
—JUDGES 7:2 CEV

SOME DAYS YOU HAVE FEWER RESOURCES than you think you need to win the day. You get up in the morning wishing you had a few more minutes of sleep, a bit more energy, and more gas in the tank. The decisions you must make would be easier with more information. You're feeling a bit off your game.

That can be a good thing. When you have less, you're stretched to find resources. God longs for you to rely on His resources for victory. His supply is limitless, but it's easy to forget that when you have all you need.

When people struggle through something together, it brings them closer. A group of soldiers is forever bonded after facing intense challenges together, relying on each other's strengths to win the battle. God wants you to win. And He wants you to have the joy of seeing Him personally come through for you.

In a quiet moment today, take stock of your resources. If you see you're coming up short on what it takes to overcome, believe that God wants victory for you and He wants to prove afresh His might in your life.

HONORING GOD IN YOUR WORK

We rebuilt the wall, and all the wall was joined together
to half its height; for the people had a mind to work.
—Nehemiah 4:6 nrsv

TWO WOMEN RECEIVED THEIR PERFORMANCE REVIEWS on the same day. The manager commented later, "They are both very talented and intelligent women, but their performance is as different as night and day."

"To what would you attribute the dissimilarity?" the human resources director inquired.

"It's simple," he responded. "One of them comes in asking herself how much work she can get done; the other comes to work asking how much she can get by with."

From the beginning, God designed our role to be a productive one. Man was given a job in Eden—he was made to work. Seeking instruction from the Word of God, you find that you honor Him in your willingness to work and in your commitment to excellence related to work. Furthermore, you discover that God honors those who demonstrate a good, honest work ethic not merely in terms of accomplishments, but among people.

He is Himself an innovative and productive being. Having been created in God's image means that you are to reflect His nature and character in every dimension of your life. Your talents and energies, when put to work, are to be a blessing to others and a glory to God. Work as if He were your boss.

October 10

A DIFFERENT PERSPECTIVE

The commandments I give you today must be in your hearts.
—DEUTERONOMY 6:6 NIRV

IN OUR TIME ALONE WITH GOD, we will often find ourselves pondering God's instructions and commandments as found in the Bible. It's important that we process our feelings about these commandments with Him. Keep in mind that there are two ways to look at the commandments of God. First, we can look at them and say, "What fun is God spoiling? What privilege is He taking away?" The serpent tempted Eve by convincing her that God was out to deny her something that was rightfully hers.

But there is another way to look at God's commandments. We can ask, "What was God seeking to protect when He issued this command?" This turns everything around. God cares about the same things we care about. We want our families to be safe. We want our work to mean something. We want our marriages to last. We want justice. We want to be happy. Guess what? All of these things and more are put in place and protected by the commandments of God. As we process our feelings about these commandments with God, it's important to be honest with Him, and it's also important to see the heart behind the instruction.

BECOMING A PERSON OF INTEGRITY

I'll not deny my integrity even if it costs me my life.
I'm holding fast to my integrity and not loosening
my grip—and, believe me, I'll never regret it.
—JOB 27:5-6 MSG

IF YOU'VE EVER KNOWN SOMEONE WHO is honorable in everything she says and does, you know what an admirable—and rare—trait integrity is. But integrity doesn't come upon a person on the spur of the moment. It grows and develops and ripens to maturity in the background of that person's life—most likely, in the presence of God.

The most difficult decisions of life are made in God's presence. It's there that you draw on His strength and wisdom to make a commitment to live a life that's pleasing to Him and brings honor to His name. In His presence, you make the ultimate decisions that make specific decisions easier. Once you've decided that you will live an authentic, transparent life, for example, you won't be tempted to fake it at work to make yourself look better. You've already decided to live a life of integrity, and wearing a mask to hide who you really are doesn't fit into that life.

Becoming a person of integrity apart from God is an effort that's destined to fail. A disciplined, responsible, committed life characterized by unfailing honesty and trustworthiness—integrity—is tested in the world but is born and bred in the presence of God.

THE CELEBRATION OF OBEDIENCE

*Go and celebrate with a feast of rich foods and sweet drinks,
and share gifts of food with people who have
nothing prepared. This is a sacred day before our Lord.*
—**NEHEMIAH 8:10** NLT

D ID YOU KNOW THAT GOD LOVES to throw parties? If you were brought up to think of Him as austere and unapproachable, you are in for a wonderful surprise. He is, in fact, the author of celebration.

What kinds of things cause God to call for a celebration? When, with willing hearts, God's people joined Him in His mission to rescue, reconcile, and restore His people, His purpose, His cities, and His reign on the earth, His response was overwhelming joy and He regularly threw parties to give it expression.

There were parties for celebrating the grain harvest and marriage. Parties for consecrating the tabernacle and the priests. There were parties to celebrate birth and parties to commemorate deliverance from bondage. There was even the weekly celebration of Sabbath—rest.

So how can you get in on the celebration and experience the joy He's planned for you? By committing yourself to God's purposes and spending time with Him, getting to know your role in what He is about here on earth. You'll quickly discover the joy that resides in God's heart when His people get involved in celebrating what He is doing. You'll also discover that the party never ends!

A BIGGER HOME

I go to prepare a place for you.

—JOHN 14:2 NASB

HAVE YOU EVER WANTED A BIGGER house? Have you ever wanted more room to have fun with your family, or entertain guests, or work on projects, or whatever? Most of us have at some point. And most of us are encouraged to know that Jesus is preparing a place for us in heaven.

But did you know that God is also preparing a place for Himself?

Where does God live? He lives inside you. The Bible tells us that we are God's house. Think of this from His perspective. How does a great big God have room to live inside a little tiny person? Doesn't it get cramped in there? Does He have space to stretch?

God doesn't need more land. But He does need more real estate in our hearts. That's why He puts experiences in our lives designed to give Him more space. Every time we open the door to Him in a way that we never have before, we give Him more room—room to enjoy us and room for us to enjoy Him. This is the adventure of getting to know God. This is part of the reason He grants us everlasting life—He's building a bigger home inside us.

October 14

SIMPLE FAITH

He has shown all you people what is good.
And what does the LORD require of you? To act justly
and to love mercy and to walk humbly with your God.

—**MICAH 6:8** TNIV

KNOWING WHAT GOD WANTS, KNOWING HOW to please Him, can seem mysterious at times. Sometimes it seems there is so much to learn, so much to become, and so much to keep straight. Perhaps a "Life of Faith 101" course, with syllabus, would make it easier to navigate!

God gets it. Several times in the Bible He distills what life is all about—and it's usually pretty simple. He highlights things like love God, love people, trust God; obey Him and you'll be blessed or disobey and it brings a mess. Sometimes the bigger the idea, the simpler it really is. God isn't trying to make you follow a complicated rule system. He's building a family. He's developing a relationship with you.

God wants what's best for you, and He leaves some signposts along the way to help make it easier for you. He has given you a few simple ideas to help you walk in His ways and get along in His world. He wants you to do what you know is right. He reminds you to love others and to remember that He is Lord over all.

October 15

GETTING IN THE GAME

Ezra praised the LORD, the great God, and all the people
chanted, "Amen! Amen!" as they lifted their hands.
Then they bowed down and worshiped
the LORD with their faces to the ground.
—NEHEMIAH 8:6 NLT

EVEN IF YOU AREN'T ACCUSTOMED TO wearing a chunk of cheese on your head or waving a big foam finger in the air, you are probably a fan of some sport and have a favorite team. You enjoy watching and cheering enthusiastically from the sidelines.

Your relationship with God is not a game. It is business of the most serious nature. But that doesn't mean you shouldn't let your enthusiasm erupt and your zeal spill over. The good fight of faith is far more exciting than any sporting event could ever be. Still there are some things we can learn from our passion for sports.

First of all, enthusiasm grows when you are keenly aware of what is going on in the game. Keep up with what God is doing, and stay abreast of the conflict in which He is engaged. Learn to identify His opponents and their strategies. Second, see yourself as part of the team, even if your role is encouraging from the sidelines. Keep up with what your teammates are doing and how you can use your talents most effectively. Third, talk about the game, fanning the flame of enthusiasm through spirited conversation.

And don't forget the best part. God has already guaranteed the win!

October 16

WHEN TEMPTATIONS
LOSE THEIR POWER

When you are tempted, he will show you a way out.
—1 CORINTHIANS 10:13 NLT

TWO CHILDREN WERE FIGHTING. WHEN THE dad separated them, he asked the older brother, "Can you think of any reasons why it might not be a good idea to pound on your little sister?" The boy immediately ticked off a list of reasons why he shouldn't be fighting.

The dad was amazed. *He knows this speech better than I do*, he thought to himself. Then he tried a different question. "Can you give me any reasons why you think you *should* beat up your sister?" Here the conversation completely changed tone. Tearfully, the young boy recounted the many injustices he felt that he had endured and the lack of support he felt he was getting from the adults around him.

From that conversation emerged a deeper understanding between the father and the son, an understanding that helped the son outgrow this pattern of fighting with his sister.

When we are tempted, God looks to us to share what's really going on in our hearts. When we do this, we create room for Him to forge a new understanding and a deeper relationship with us so those temptations begin to lose their power in our lives.

KEY TO SUCCESS

*I answered them by saying, "The God of heaven will
give us success. We his servants will start rebuilding."*

—NEHEMIAH 2:20 NIV

THE SELF-HELP BOOK INDUSTRY EXPLODED ON the scene
in the 1970s and has grown exponentially since. Store shelves
are full of books on losing weight, gaining confidence, finding love,
managing stress. One of the most popular subjects of all time is
how to be successful. Do you want success on the job? Or success in
relationships? Do you want to be a successful entrepreneur? Or a
successful parent? These books promise that you too can can triumph
and achieve.

The tips and techniques offered are helpful, but most miss the key
ingredient. God is the author of success. Follow His ways and you will
have victory in life. Go your own way and you will not.

God considers you His partner. You're His hands and feet on
earth, the visible to His invisible, working under His direction and
inspiration to change your corner of the world. So, hone your skills.
Make your work the best it can be. Work hard but leave the results to
God because, as overseer of the universe, He can promote you at the
right time.

Success and victory are God's to give. Timing and results are in
God's hands. The quality of the job is in yours.

GRACE THAT AMAZES

*The grace of God that brings salvation
has appeared to all men.*
—TITUS 2:11 NIV

GRACE IS STILL AMAZING! THE GRACE of God first amazes us because He reached down to rescue humanity while we were still so undeserving.

The grace of God continues to amaze us as we discover that in this newfound faith, we have also found family—a community of committed people who love the Lord and His people with authentic love.

The grace of God further amazes us as we find ourselves involved in a relationship with God through which He reveals Himself to us in deeply personal ways. He meets us in moments spent in His Word, sharing insights about Himself and about humanity that we had not known. He converses with us in prayer in ways that bring true peace and great joy.

And the grace of God amazes us when we discover that He gives wisdom to live by. The counsel of His Word combined with the inner impulse of His Spirit trains our consciences to discern right from wrong, especially valuable when wrong appears right.

Grace is a profound gift of life to mankind that brings the original intent of our existence to fulfillment—to bear the image of God on the earth, and thereby to fill the earth with God's glory.

A DIRECT RELATIONSHIP

There is only one go-between for God and human beings.
He is the man Christ Jesus.

—1 TIMOTHY 2:5 NIRV

DO YOU REMEMBER YOUR JUNIOR-HIGH OR middle-school days? Girl likes boy. Girl is too chicken to tell boy. Girl gets somebody else to drop the hint. Does boy like girl? Girl needs to find out, but can't ask. So girl gets a friend to ask a friend who asks the boy. It was heavy stuff at the time. But imagine a married couple trying to act that way! A marriage can't function with intermediaries. If husbands or wives want to know where they stand, they need to ask directly.

God wants to move us out of a middle-school relationship with Him into a marriage-level relationship. He wants a personal, intimate connection with each of us. He wants to talk with us directly without always relying on someone else to carry the message.

What does that direct communication look like? It looks a little different for each person. For some it means receiving new insights from the Lord as they read their Bible. Some experience a sense of God's presence as they go about their day. Some hear a quiet voice in their hearts and have tested it enough to know it comes from above. Discover which way works for you!

BE ALL YOU CAN BE

*You, Lord, are a shield around me, my glory,
and the One who lifts up my head.*
—Psalm 3:3 hcsb

Several years ago the army's campaign and recruiting slogan proclaimed, "Be All You Can Be. Army." It was one of the most successful marketing campaigns in history. It touches the heart desire at the core of all of us—achieving our potential.

You want to know you are leaving a significant mark in this life. You long to know that you have achieved your potential and lived your best for the good of others. As a God-follower, you are connected with the most notable coach and motivator of all time. God inspires superior work. He inspires you to excellence in all you do. He stirs creative endeavors everywhere.

When God made you, He didn't stop at your physical body. He made your soul and spirit. He put dreams and desires in you that He wants you to accomplish. He is able to inspire your creativity so you'll reach new levels. He is able to guide and direct you in ways that make you the best "you" you can be.

All around you are God-sparks firing your potential. There may be a small change you could make today that will cause one of those sparks to catch fire in your spirit. Listen. Connect.

October 21

BRIDGING THE GAP

*If he has done you any wrong or owes you anything,
charge it to me.*

—**PHILEMON 1:18 NIV**

THOSE WHO HAVE RECEIVED THE GRACE of God find great joy in giving grace to one another. It does the heart good to return to another the lavish generosity from which you have benefited so fully. And the reconciliation and restoration of our personal relationships results in much glory to God as a witness to others that this grace is real and is effectively bringing unity among the community of faith.

Having become accustomed to giving and receiving forgiveness, there is one thing further that you can do to delight the heart of God. When you discover a rift in a friendship that doesn't involve you, you may find an amazing opportunity to become a catalyst for healing. You can become a bridge that spans the rift and holds a relationship together until reconciliation comes.

Consulting first with God alone in prayer, seek from Him the discernment with which to understand the dilemma. Only God can really know both sides of the issue. Continue in prayer, petitioning Him for the wisdom to speak words to one or both parties that inspire reconciliation, rekindling respect and reminding them both of the other's worth in God's perspective.

Your faithful words may help remove a mountain of resentment.

BRING BACK THE BOUNCE

They are like trees planted along the riverbank,
bearing fruit each season. Their leaves never wither,
and they prosper in all they do.
—PSALM 1:3 NLT

THE ANTI-AGING MARKET IS BURSTING AS the Baby Boomer generation hits middle age. Daily, this generation is redefining age limits. The thirst for the Fountain of Youth is never quenched. The market responds with science-based supplements that support optimal hormone levels and increase the declining energy-builder B12. Anti-wrinkle creams boast an all-day facelift. Gyms attract a bursting enrollment for people age forty and above. This maturing generation is all about health, energy, and vitality.

The search for vitality expands beyond the physical to the inner realm of the spirit. While you can apply a cream to lift the corners of your eyes, only an inner liveliness will regenerate the spark of the eye.

Walking along the winding road of life with the King of the universe creates an inner verve unmatched by supplements or anti-aging creams. The energy of His life flows through you as you make little conscious choices to go His way wherever you go. This translates into a sense of well-being only longed for but never attained without God.

If you want to bring back the bounce in your step or reignite a sparkle in your eyes, plan a few moments in the presence of Life Himself.

FIXIN' TO FIGHT

Do not be afraid of them. Remember the Lord,
great and awesome, and fight for your brethren,
your sons, your daughters, your wives, and your houses.
—NEHEMIAH 4:14 NKJV

THERE WILL BE TIMES IN YOUR life when you face the unthinkable: when your worst fear comes to life and you feel circumstances conspiring against you. Fear will threaten to overtake you. All light of hope will fade or barely flicker.

Refuse to give in to this fear. Giving in to trepidation shuts down your mind. Instead, fix your thoughts not on the threat but on the One who is all-powerful and stands with you. Fix your mind on God. And fight.

Some treasures are worth the fight. God decided you were one of them. He moved heaven and earth to save you, battled all the powers of hell arrayed against Him, and defeated the last enemy—death—to win your soul. God is a fighter. You are worth the fight. Your family, your home are worth the fight.

When you're up against fright and worry, focus your thinking on God's mighty power working for you. Remember His deliverance in your life in times past and count on Him to help now. Refuse to give up. Refuse to believe the despair. Fill your mind with His majestic authority. Seek His help. Then stand and fight.

GOD'S GREAT HEART

The Lord bless you, and keep you; the Lord make His face shine on you, and be gracious to you; the Lord lift up His countenance on you, and give you peace.
—**Numbers 6:24-26 nasb**

ARE YOU AWARE OF GOD'S DESIRE to fill your life with an abundance of good things?

God wants to bless you. It is His greatest joy to give lavishly and generously to those whom He loves—and His love is indiscriminate. Are you receptive to God's blessing, aware that in relationship with God you are also in a position to experience His abundance?

God cares for you. Even concerning the smallest details of your day, it matters to the Lord that things are well with you. Did you know that He is with you to bless you when things go wrong, as well as when things go right?

God gives you peace. Though this world is a troubled place, the Lord provides the calm that allows you to pillow your head at night, confident that you'll arise in the morning. Do you trust Him when your peace is disturbed?

God is attentive to you. He doesn't miss anything. Are you reciprocally attentive to Him? God prospers you. He rewards and applauds your efforts. Do you return thanks?

God smiles on you. Observant and always looking for the best in you, God looks for reasons to rejoice over you. Did you know that you bless His heart with joy?

OUR ROLE

If it is leadership, let him govern diligently.
—ROMANS 12:8 NIV

OUR TIME ALONE WITH GOD WILL take many different forms. Sometimes we will be filled with wonder and gratitude. Sometimes we will be pouring out our hearts, desperate for an answer to a pressing need. But sometimes our time with God will be a conference between two leaders: God as the supreme ruler of the universe, and us as leaders within our own sphere of influence.

God designed us to rule. As rulers, we speak life and blessing and hope into other lives. We bring safety and wisdom. We envision. We show people the way out of hopelessness. We empower people. We inspire. We engage and stay in relationship even when it gets messy. We draw out the strengths of those around us. We strategize. We convey momentum. We pioneer. We break sinful patterns.

We lead in education, media, arts, entertainment, industry, commerce, family, government, and, yes, in religion. Does that mean if you have a job as a clerk or a janitor that you can't lead? Of course not! You lead anytime you use your influence to bring good into your world.

Let God use your time alone with Him to strengthen you as a leader.

October 26

UNDERCOVER BOSS

When all our enemies heard of it…they lost their confidence;
for they recognized that this work had been accomplished
with the help of our God.

—NEHEMIAH 6:16 NASB

GOD IS A GREAT MANAGER. HE is ready to help His people. The almighty God desires your success. When asked, He gets in the middle of the muddled times, carrying you through the muck until you are on solid ground again. He infuses your work with life. People see it. Those who love life are drawn to your cause. They know there's more to you and your work than meets the eye, and they can see God reflected in your passion and purpose.

God enjoys empowering you. He loves seeing a good plan succeed. Invite Him into your latest project. Work in a way that honors Him. It's so easy to cut a corner or leave out a detail, but God doesn't—and He loves excellence in His people.

Humbly recognize God's authority over everything and His amazing management ability. Imagine that He's right by your side as you labor. Dedicate your best to each minute of your work. Your attitude and trust invite God to move in and do something greater than you could do on your own.

WILLING TO TRUST

*My servant Caleb has a different attitude
than the others have. He has remained loyal to me,
so I will bring him into the land he explored.*
—NUMBERS 14:24 NLT

WHAT DOES IT MEAN TO BE faithful to God? Does it mean perfect performance in terms of morality? How about perfect church attendance? Could it mean a perfect habit of prayer?

God's Word indicates that He doesn't measure faithfulness with checklists or record-keeping ledgers. God considers faithfulness not as a contract-keeping agreement, but in the context of covenant relationship.

When you are responsive to the needs of people, the Lord interprets your actions as faithfulness. He is more interested in how much compassion you have in your heart than in how many times you've been to church this year. God takes more notice of your courage to speak out against injustice than He does your carefully selected wardrobe.

In fact, God is more concerned with your willingness to trust Him than He is any part of your performance. Your loyalty to God is determined by your faith in His promises, particularly when it requires waiting through bleak and troubled times. When your vision is blurred by adversity and time seems to drag on and on, your ability to hang on to the promises of God brings Him much joy and results in great glory.

Faithfulness isn't measured in perfection and performance, but in endurance.

THE LINE IN OUR HEARTS

You will know the truth, and the truth will make you free.
—JOHN 8:32 NASB

EACH OF US HAS A LINE inside our hearts. On one side of the line, we have said yes to God. On the other side, we haven't yet said yes. That line is in a different place for each of us, and it's there for different reasons. The line is where growth takes place. This is great news, because it means that every day can be an adventure with Jesus.

In the places where we have said yes, we've discovered that Jesus is true to His word, that He can be trusted. But in the places where we haven't trusted Him, we mistakenly believe that something bad will happen to us if we do, that we are somehow better off saying no. These lies hold us back.

The good news is this: Jesus specializes in freeing us from those lies that hold us back. He really wants to work with us, helping us discover the liberating truths that will cause those painful lies to lose their power in our lives. As we come back to this line in our time alone with God, we will make our greatest discoveries and experience our deepest transformation.

October 29

STOP, DROP, AND PRAY

Turn all your anxiety over to God because he cares for you.
—1 PETER 5:7 GWT

Y OU CAN ALWAYS CHURN WITH ANXIETY about something—illness, loss, a financial setback, terrorism. Anxiety is a common stressor for many of us, even if it's just a tiny nagging whisper. At times you may find yourself waking up in the middle of the night with a daytime concern now magnified. What can be done with budding panic at three in the morning?

Anxiety creeps in where control issues have left the door ajar. It hooks in to that part of you that wants circumstances to go your way and keeps you obsessing about the outcome. When you're ready to let go of handling distress on your own, pour out your heart to God. He totally understands what you need. He knows and is compassionate about what's bothering you. You can count on Him to act.

Just a simple request will do, nothing formal or fancy. There's no ritual or perfect prayer wording required. You can tell God in elaborate detail or just get to the point. When you're done, thank Him for all His wonderful blessings and for who He is. Then let Him move while you move calmly forward with your day.

October 30

WARMTH FOR THE WINTER

For this very reason, Christ died and returned to life so that he might be the Lord of both the dead and the living.
—**ROMANS 14:9** NIV

EVERY AUTUMN, NATURE BEGINS A GRADUAL descent into a dormant state resembling death, evidenced by the barren trees and the wilted roses. Yet there is a sweetness about the melancholy of fall that stirs hope within our hearts and fills us with a warmth unaffected by the chilly autumn air. What is it that warms and cheers us while winter reaches toward us with frosty fingers? It is our confidence that spring is on its way!

The whole creation witnesses to the glory of God. Furthermore, the creation illustrates in vivid imagery the most incredible love story ever told: the sacrificial death and victorious resurrection of Jesus.

Spending time with God in creation has great value as you find your meditation on nature affirming the good news about Jesus. Death stalks us all, just as winter stalks the natural world. But the power of absolute love overcame the power of death, and when Jesus rose from the grave, He brought the rest of us with Him—a future reality held in trust by faith.

God is God, in the barrenness of winter just as surely as in the spring. And Jesus is Lord, just as surely in death as in life!

HIDING

The Lord God called to Adam and said to him,
Where are you?

—GENESIS 3:9 AMP

ON A FIRST DATE WE DRESS up and try to make a good impression. We don't tell all of our secrets at that first meeting, nor do we reveal all of our flaws. But in a marriage we come out of hiding to see each other as we really are, the good and the bad.

God wants to move past the "first date" kind of relationship into the sort of intimacy where we feel free to reveal everything that's going on inside. When it comes to our ongoing relationship with God, our single biggest need is to come out of hiding. This is where God takes the initiative. Instead of waiting for us to "dress up" for Him, God comes looking for us. Much of life is God wooing us out of the shadows. He doesn't violate us. He doesn't drag us into the light. He doesn't expose us. Instead, He gently awakens us to the truth.

God already knows all our secrets. What we want to hide He knows about already. Jesus is not here to condemn but to restore us as children of God. Jesus is here. He will touch us, and we will be clean.

POINT OF PRAISE

LORD, our Lord, how majestic is your name in all the earth!
You have set your glory above the heavens.
—PSALM 8:1 TNIV

PRAISE IS A SPIRITUAL WEAPON. IT'S your sharp sword to cut through the confusion of your day. Praise stirs up conditions related to God's world. All day long angels sing praise to God, and now you are doing the same on earth. That releases His life into the circumstances around you, and it rallies your own spirit and initiates energy within your will.

Praise lifts your eyes from your own situations the way looking at a sky filled with stars makes you feel grounded in the universe. No longer are you the center. There is someone bigger than you. And that Someone is approachable, powerful, and compassionate toward you.

Telling God what you love about who He is raises you out of listless attitudes and pressing problems. When you ponder God's authority, His greatness, and His awesome power, the burdens weighing on you drop away. In the updraft of praise, your spirit finds its wings to soar.

Worship and praise are not for God's benefit. They are for yours. They secure and reassure something deep within you. They activate your spirit, calm your anger, and destroy discouragement.

Praise will lift you up, higher and higher.

STEADY ON

LORD, how long will You continually forget me?
How long will You hide Your face from me?
—PSALM 13:1 HCSB

FEELING FORGOTTEN AND INVISIBLE TO GOD and to people you care about hurts. Pain isolates and cocoons you from the world, whether its source is emotional or physical. When trouble comes your way, it may seem like a gray curtain is drawn around you. You can see out, but you don't feel anyone can see in.

Believe it or not, even Jesus had that feeling. As He was on the cross, He cried out asking why the Father had turned away. You can be assured that the Son of God understands how your abandonment feels since He experienced this emotion Himself.

There will be dark times of the soul when you'll feel alone, as if even God Himself has left you. In the midst of that darkness, stay steady. Keep on doing what you know to be right. Keep on spending time with God every day, meditating on a verse or two to strengthen your faith. Hang on to your trust in God. The light is coming back as sure as the sun rises after the darkness of night. In time, you will stand victorious in the Spirit, knowing that even if your feelings indicated otherwise, God never deserted you.

November 3

RESTORING THE JOY

Why are you in despair, O my soul? And why have you become disturbed within me? Hope in God, for I shall again praise Him for the help of His presence.

—PSALM 42:5 NASB

HOW'S YOUR ENERGY? ARE YOU FEELING in tune with God and with yourself, or is this a day when things feel a little off? Some days you must give yourself a good talking to just to get out the door. Your head starts filling with cynical thinking and out goes your joy. It's a challenge to find peace.

Those negative ideas are straight from the pit. They don't help or energize you, but they sure do paint your day gray. They're often believable enough to sound like truth, but if you only focus on that negativity, it will weigh you down, steal your dreams, and discourage your heart. And the more you believe it, the worse your day will seem.

Instead of listening to the lies, grab those thoughts and replace them with uplifting statements that are true and good! Refuse to dwell on thoughts of failure. You are an overcomer, connected to the almighty God. He is able to turn your situation around in a heartbeat, and all it costs you is faith. Hang on to your hope. Re-center, and remember who you are as God's child. Remember that He is a life-giver. And when you do, you'll have plenty to be glad about again.

FORGIVENESS THAT FORGETS

I have not achieved it, but I focus on this one thing:
Forgetting the past and looking forward to what lies ahead,
I press on to reach the end of the race.
—**PHILIPPIANS 3:13-14** NLT

AMONG THE MANY BENEFITS OF SPENDING time with God, one of the most exhilarating is the freedom that He provides in forgetting past mistakes. Everyone has skeletons in their closet that they wish they had the power to evict. Only God can effectively deal with the memories that haunt us, that hunt us down in moments of solitude and rob us of our peace.

How does He do it? How does God help you to forget the past? He does it by giving you a new identity—a brand-new beginning. You become a new creation with a redeemed history and a brilliant new future.

Spending time with God in His Word, you discover that your way of thinking is being renewed. You find yourself preoccupied with learning how to love more adequately, how to be more generous, how to rejoice even in the midst of adversity.

Spending time with God in meditation, you find that your desires change. You long to please Him, you discover great delight in obedience, and you experience the joy of serving others.

Memories are healed, in part because you become so wrapped up in God you find it hard to recall what life was like before you knew Him.

November 5

SURPRISED BY THE SPIRIT

"Not by might nor by power, but by my Spirit,"
says the LORD Almighty.

—ZECHARIAH 4:6 NIV

SPENDING TIME ALONE WITH GOD AFFORDS you many unexpected surprises. For instance, you discover that the goal is not to be first, number one, king of the hill, or boss of the universe. The goal is to be last, humble, the servant of all. The Spirit of God teaches you to put your own interests aside and find true joy in putting others first.

Another surprise is found in the awareness that losing is finding, that giving is getting, that dying is living, and that weakness is strength. God's ways seem to be radically inverted from the way the world reasons. His values seem completely paradoxical: He wins the ultimate battle by surrendering His life—even rescuing His executioners.

How do you translate God's inverted way of thinking into a world like ours? You allow His Spirit to lead you.

The Spirit of the Lord is present within you. He takes up residence in your heart in order to counsel you, guide you, and surprise you with courage—the kind of courage it takes to live the life He has laid out for you, particularly as His Spirit reveals to you the biggest surprise of all: that the ultimate power is the power of love.

WHERE'S THE POWER?

"Sir," Gideon replied, "if the LORD is with us,
why has all this happened to us? And where are all the
miracles our ancestors told us about?"
—JUDGES 6:13 NLT

THE TROUBLE WITH TROUBLE IS THAT it brings up so many things we try to keep pushed down, far away from the "nice zone." When difficult things still happen to us after we've tried to follow all of God's ways, we might wonder, *Does Christianity work? If the Lord is with me, why is all this happening to me?* This is a variation on, *Where is God when it hurts?*

The real underlying question is: If God is all-powerful, why doesn't He just make this go away? It's disturbing to think that He is watching our mess and seemingly choosing to let us squirm. What happened to all those stories of miracles we heard in Sunday School? Were those just fairy tales? If they were real, where's the power?

God doesn't flinch at your honest questions. He is always ready for real interaction with His people. And getting real with God often leads to a release of His power. He is right there in your trouble, fighting for your freedom. "Where's the power?" can precede, "Wow, God, You're amazing!" An honest ownership of your scariest questions can lead to a breakthrough.

IN THE ZONE

Who may enter your presence on your holy hill?
Those who lead blameless lives and do what is right,
speaking the truth from sincere hearts.
—PSALM 15:1-2 NLT

YOU KNOW YOU'RE IN THE ZONE when you're completely focused, your actions feel effortless, and everything clicks. It's like staying in the sweet spot when you fish, in peak performance as an athlete, or optimal focus as a student. You need to find ways to stay balanced, because there's always something to pull you out of your zone. You invest valuable time and energy in staying fine-tuned to keep on task.

When you really feel like you're clicking with God, you are in your "God zone." There's life, peace, and joy in that zone. How do you keep that going? Obey God. Do what's right. Speak truthfully.

Obeying God is God-language for "I love You, Lord, and I want to respect and model Your ways." Doing what is right is turning to His Word each day for direction and wise steps. Speaking truth is being loyal to God's integrity with your words because God is truth; He never lies. Ever. A lie moves you away from His authentic presence.

Through obedience, doing what's right, and speaking truth, you can invest in your "God zone." It's worth it. Just between God and you, are you in the zone today?

THE POWER OF WORDS

A man who lacks judgment derides his neighbor,
but a man of understanding holds his tongue.
—**PROVERBS 11:12** NIV

IN THE BEGINNING, GOD CREATED LIGHT with just a word. Though the concept of light existed in His mind, it wasn't until the word was uttered that it actually came into being. Likewise, God created most of the cosmos by giving voice to what was already in His vast mind.

Words are so powerful! They have the power to create or to alter the state of reality in which we live. Words can build people up or destroy them. Words can bring great joy and blessing to a person's heart, or they can bring deep despair and a loss of hope. Words can encourage and inspire, or they can provoke anger and fear.

Being trained by God's Spirit in discernment is critical to fulfilling your role among mankind. Knowing what words to use and when to use them is one of the most important things you learn by spending time with God. He will teach you to have an understanding heart in order to know how to help others—particularly concerning when to listen and when to speak. In fact, speaking to God first about a matter will effect good judgment.

The wisdom of timely words is inestimable, and the power to bless invaluable.

WITH ALL MY HEART

My brothers who went up with me made the hearts of the
people melt with fear. I, however,
followed the LORD my God wholeheartedly.
—JOSHUA **14:8** NIV

WHOLEHEARTEDLY" MEANS WITHOUT RESERVE, without reservation, with all your heart. Society shines with examples of wholehearted living. These dedicated individuals come from all career fields and walks of life—from pop superstars to missionaries to the soldiers defending our freedom. Maybe you know one of these stellar folks. They excel in politics and in medicine, in the church and in Little League. Students, teachers, janitors, truck drivers, parents, and grandparents are all part of the wholehearted who strive for their best in their work and for the people in their lives.

Living with full engagement, committing targeted energy to your assignment, is a deliberate choice. Living with all your heart takes commitment to a passion bigger than yourself. It means knowing what matters deeply to you and sticking with that in the storms and challenges of life. It means following your course even when your closest friends go another way.

In the pause of this moment, consider your life today. Imagine living it wholeheartedly. Imagine following God without fear, confident in His faithfulness. Feel the freedom. God urges His people to follow Him wholeheartedly because in living without reservation there is freedom. And in that freedom, you're truly alive.

DYNAMIC DUO

I know the LORD is always with me.
I will not be shaken, for he is right beside me.
—PSALM 16:8 NLT

THE NAMES WILBUR AND ORVILLE WRIGHT were carved in history when their airplane flew a full thirty minutes at Kitty Hawk, North Carolina, in 1909. These brothers, five years apart, initiated several ventures before going into the flight business. They'd become a dynamic duo building a printing press, starting a newspaper, and creating a bicycle company. Wilbur and Orville's bicycle endeavor turned so successful it financed their aviation research and development. Wilbur proved studious and Orville a mischief maker. The Wright brothers continually leaned on each other in uncharted territory and found strength to overcome setbacks.

God longs to be this steady partner for you. He is always ready to spur you on, encourage you, and support you when needed. Whether the skies are cloudy or clear, He wants to see you spread your wings and fly.

What would it take for God and you to be a stronger dynamic duo? Is there anything in your relationship that hinders you from consulting Him more? Is there anything to keep you from leaning on Him fully? Talk to Him about any hesitancies you may have about being in tandem with Him. As your ever-present partner, He sticks even closer than a brother. And He's ready to help you soar.

November 11

HONORING VETERANS OF LIFE

Rise in the presence of the aged, show respect for the elderly
and revere your God. I am the LORD.
—LEVITICUS 19:32 NIV

WHILE READING SCRIPTURE, YOU'LL NOTICE A distinct contrast in the way God venerates the aged and the way that our culture treats them. We applaud and celebrate veterans of war, but what about veterans of life? Don't we owe honor and respect to those who have survived the ravages of living?

God retains the aged among us to teach us the kind of wisdom that only comes with time and experience. It is a generous act of mercy that allows us the privilege of age, and living among the elderly community brings out certain virtues in us that need to be nurtured.

Take the time to contemplate in prayer what a difference dealing with the aged could make in your character. For instance, you will cultivate humility as you learn to listen to those who have lived through the things you are currently experiencing. You stand to learn a great deal about sacrifice in dealing with the weakness and feebleness of the aged. And furthermore, God nurtures tenderness within the community when you take the time to dignify the elderly by taking care of their needs.

Honoring the aged with compassion will enrich your life, deepen your character, bless the elderly, and please the Lord.

November 12

DESPERATE PRAYERS

Lord, your dear friend is very sick.
—JOHN 11:3 NLT

OFTEN THE MORE DESPERATE WE ARE, the more needy we are, the more simple our prayers become. And that is just as it should be. "Help!" is a perfectly good prayer when we are in urgent need of God's intervention. There comes a time when it's best to dispense with theology and bring our raw need to God.

Simple prayers work—not because they are simple, but because they are mixed with faith. We know we have nowhere else to turn. We know God cares. We know He is our only hope.

But what happens if these desperate prayers are not answered according to our expectation? This happened to a family that was very close to Jesus. The brother was sick, and the sisters begged Jesus to come and heal Him. But Jesus lingered where He was for another couple days—long enough for the brother to die. This story didn't end with tragedy, however. Jesus showed up after all hope was gone and raised their brother from the dead.

That's what it's like to depend on God. We bring our urgent needs to Him. But even if all we hope for is destroyed, God never runs out of options.

SAFE HOUSE

The LORD is my rock and my fortress and my deliverer;
my God, my strength, in whom I will trust; my shield
and the horn of my salvation, my stronghold.
—**PSALM 18:2** NKJV

A SAFE HOUSE IS SET UP in law enforcement for people in distress or perceived danger. In the spy business, it's a safe haven when the heat is on. These places are designed to shield until the danger goes away.

At some point, you've probably needed a safe house, a place to regroup and pull it together without outside pressures or extra stress. Just out of college with no job, Mom and Dad's might have been the safe house, or a friend's apartment floor. Your safe house might be a woodsy cabin or a downtown hotel—a respite where you feel protected while you figure out how to go on from here.

God is like a safe house. He likes to shelter you from trouble. He gives peace in the midst of drama. He covers you. He gives you space to think and regroup. There's something great about God' protection, like a house in a storm. A roof over your head and walls around you won't stop the rain or halt the thunder, but it sure keeps you dry in the midst of it. Open the door and come on in.

GLAD TO KNOW GOD'S WILL

Be joyful always; pray continually; give thanks in all circumstances, for this is God's will for you in Christ Jesus.
—1 Thessalonians 5:16-18 NIV

How can you know God's will for your life? It is a question often asked by those diligently seeking to follow where He leads. Can you with certainty know that you are fulfilling your calling—the purpose for which you exist? Abraham knew. Moses knew. Isaiah knew. Peter and Paul knew. Can you know?

Yes, you can know. But since it won't come to you in the form of direct correspondence such as a certified letter from heaven or a message left on your phone by God, you'll probably discover it like most other people do—little by little, as the revelation unfolds itself in relationship with Him.

There is, however, a disposition of the heart that will help. There is a posture that will increase your receptivity and make a radical difference in accurately discerning God's will. If you will develop a consistent and frequent habit of prayer—concentrating your energies on what God has done with praise and gratitude in your heart, no matter how trying your circumstances—you will find the eyes of your heart opened wide to what He is doing in the present and a clearer vision of where He is leading you.

THE JOY OF GIVING

Giving, not getting, is the way.
Generosity begets generosity. Stinginess impoverishes.
—MARK 4:24 MSG

ONE OF THE MOST DELIGHTFUL EXPERIENCES in life is watching a child voluntarily give a treasured item to someone else—maybe his mother or a special friend. The sheer joy he radiates can't help but be contagious. And yet, his act of selflessness can also be bittersweet to those adults who realize that such joyful, unselfish giving—at one time perhaps a characteristic of their childhood—has become foreign to them.

If you can identify, there's good news. God can and will restore that spirit of joyful giving if you will trust Him with everything you have—everything. Not just your abundance, not just those things you wouldn't mind giving to someone else, but everything. Once you've given your very life to Him, giving Him control over your possessions shouldn't be a problem. And if He tells you to give some of those possessions away, well, they're no longer yours anyway.

According to 2 Corinthians 9:7, "God loves a cheerful giver." He wants you to enjoy sharing what you have with others, just like He shares all He has with you. He won't coerce you. It will always be your choice, but one He is always pleased to see you make.

WHERE ARE YOU, GOD?

My God, my God, why have you deserted me?
Why are you so far away? Won't you listen to my groans
and come to my rescue?

—PSALM 22:1 CEV

THERE'S A THEORY THAT EVERYTHING, FROM national disasters to personal tragedies, occurs in "threes." That may or may not be true, but we've all felt at times like we were being assaulted with bad news. A hailstorm of trials descends…illness, job loss, unexpected death. *A person can only take so much*, you think, and you cry out to God. But He's silent.

You might conclude He's not listening, or worse, He's turned His back on you. Even Jesus, as He hung on the cross, thought His Father had abandoned Him. Your limited human perspective makes you think, *Well, if He* really *loved me, He'd take me out of this misery* right now.

God has not left you alone. He *is* compassionate and His timing is perfect. It's just not *your* timing. Want to understand the big picture? Study the stories of the Old Testament. Note how God works through unlikely people and inexplicable events to bring about amazing outcomes and unexpected blessings in the lives of the faithful.

As you wait on God's answers, lean on His Word and His promises. He will bring you through this—and out the other side.

FANNING THE FLAME

Do not put out the Spirit's fire; do not treat prophecies
with contempt. Test everything. Hold on to the good.
Avoid every kind of evil.

—1 Thessalonians 5:19-22 niv

DRAWING NEARER AND NEARER TO GOD as your friendship deepens, you may have already discovered that every aspect of your inner life has intensified. You feel a burning desire to please Him; you have a craving to understand Him better; you feel a deeper love for others; and you see things with greater clarity and deeper discernment than ever before.

If this describes your experience of God, then keep it up! You're headed in the right direction.

There are a couple of things you should watch for to avoid being derailed. First, remain open to the counsel of the Word and to the teachings of others who walk with God. The Lord's instruction comes through many venues and in unexpected moments. Be attentive and receptive to every opportunity to learn, knowing that He is carefully watching over your progress, as there is much to learn.

Secondly, be diligent in discerning right from wrong. Being open and receptive doesn't equate to being naïve. It is in your best interest to compare any teaching with what is actually written in Scripture. God will give you insight into His truth as you earnestly seek it, and the challenge of research will sharpen your spiritual discernment.

FORGIVING OURSELVES

Who is a God like You, pardoning iniquity and passing over the transgression of the remnant of His heritage?

—**MICAH 7:18** NKJV

SOMETIMES IT IS EASIER TO FORGIVE others than it is to forgive ourselves. Some of us are so conscientious that the slightest slip-up leaves us wallowing in self-condemnation. Some of us feel that we've committed a sin so horrible that even God could not forgive us. Some of us know in our heads that God has forgiven us, but we can't feel it in our hearts.

If this is a struggle for you, here are some questions for you to process in the Lord's presence when you are alone with Him: *If those feelings of guilt and shame could talk, what would they say? What would happen if you stopped punishing yourself? How did these messages become part of your life?* There are no right or wrong answers here, just honest and dishonest ones. The more honest we can be with the Lord, the more He is in a position to transform us. Don't forget to ask Him for the truth about all of this. Who are you really? Jesus needs to answer that for you. Once He does, you will never be the same again.

Forgiving yourself is not only possible, it's easy once you discover what God says about you.

COLOR MY WORLD

*May the words from my mouth and the thoughts
from my heart be acceptable to you, O LORD,
my rock and my defender.*
—PSALM 19:14 GWT

GOD IS BIG ON WORDS. HE has infused words with power. The words you speak produce life or death in your heart and in the lives of people around you. God is also big on the words you think. Thoughts are powerful. They shape your attitudes, your words, and your actions. Change your thoughts, change your words, change your life.

When things get tough, you're probably tempted to get discouraged or depressed. When things are going great, you may be tempted toward pride. Whatever your circumstances, you see everything that's happening through the colored lens of your thoughts, and that perception influences your words. If you change the lens, you'll see the situation differently. Put on a pair of blue-tinted glasses and the world looks blue, and rose-colored lenses make everything glow pink.

God's lens is pure and true. Color your worldview by cherishing your connection with God. Thinking about Him balances trouble with hope and triumph with humility. Be thankful because gratitude builds a wall of defense, no matter the circumstance. Guard your heart with hope. A hopeful heart changes your thoughts, which changes your words, which changes your life.

What color lens are you wearing today?

KNOWLEDGE YOU NEED

*Apply your mind to instruction
and your ear to words of knowledge.*

—PROVERBS 23:12 NRSV

L IVING IN THE INFORMATION AGE, WE have at our fingertips more data than any other civilization in history. The Internet provides endless facts about almost anything. In fact, we have to be careful that we don't get more than the facts.

So how do you determine what kind of knowledge is worthwhile and where to go to obtain it? A beginning place for valid instruction comes from the time you spend alone with God in the Word.

The Scriptures may be read in different ways. Some read the Bible for devotional thoughts upon which to meditate. Some read to mine out timeless truths upon which to base their value system. Some read for the historical benefit. Others read out of duty. And some read only select portions of Scripture, such as the Psalms, to assist in their prayers and worship.

Those who discover the vast amount of insight and wisdom that come from Scripture are those who read the Word as a source of inspiration and instruction. They have found the Spirit of the Lord to be an amazing teacher and counselor.

Your relationship with God will find new depth and dimension when you listen to Him and begin the learning.

EMBRACE SIMPLICITY

Satisfy us in the morning with your unfailing love,
that we may sing for joy and be glad all our days.
—PSALM 90:14 NIV

EMBRACING SIMPLICITY" DOESN'T MEAN LIVING ON a subsistence level. It does mean seeing the material trappings of life as mere adornment—and finding true peace and fulfillment in your relationship with God and in those qualities that He has placed within you.

Most of us realize that mere survival is not what God intended for His people. However, the abundance we enjoy on the outside can blind us to the spiritual abundance God has provided for us. What does that mean? It means that God offers each of us the gifts and grace we need to make the most of the life we've been given and help others do the same without having to rely on material possessions for contentment.

The place to begin is in your personal time alone with God. It is there in His presence that you will see the bigger picture. When viewed from the perspective of eternity, many of the concerns of this material world will diminish in importance. Ask God to give you the grace to live in anticipation of the joys that are to come. When you do, you will find life to be so much simpler.

NEVER FORGET

When your children ask their fathers in the future,
"What is the meaning of these stones?" you should tell
your children, "Israel crossed the Jordan on dry ground."
—JOSHUA 4:21-22 HCSB

WHEN GOD DELIVERS, NEVER FORGET WHAT He's done for you. When He rescues you from danger, remember that day. When He delivers you from a bad work situation, remember that day. When He provides the help you needed, remember that day. And then, share the story.

We tend to have short memories. Even major events are forgotten, as many a wife will attest regarding her husband's memory of anniversaries. Remembering what God has done for you builds your faith. Sharing the story builds faith for others.

Create your own memorials. One of the simplest ways is to keep a journal. Write a log of your journey, the joy and the trouble, and then how God showed up in the middle of it. If it's been a long-awaited moment, celebrate it with friends over a special meal and highlight God's awesome rescue. Or you could make a cairn in your garden, setting stones on top of each other as a memorial. The point is not what you choose to do, but to do something to help you remember in days to come. God is a good God who rescues His people. Remember, and tell the story.

THE RADIANCE OF GOD'S GLORY

His appearance changed from the inside out,
right before their eyes. Sunlight poured from his face.
His clothes were filled with light.

—MATTHEW 17:1-2 MSG

THE GOSPELS—MATTHEW, MARK, LUKE, AND JOHN—contain the record of Jesus' life among men while revealing amazing things about God. The Scriptures themselves claim that Jesus is an exact representation of God. So spending time with Jesus translates into learning more about God.

In other words, the true radiance of God can be seen in Jesus. If you long to see God's glory—to understand what it is and what it does—go to Jesus. You'll find that the way Jesus treated people reflects directly on God's mercy. The words He spoke came straight from God's heart. The way He loved people He learned expressly from His Father. The forgiveness He extended came from the depths of God's grace. The miracles He performed were Spirit-empowered.

By spending time with Jesus, you discover that God is the one who is merciful, and all wisdom comes from God. God is He who loves passionately and forgives absolutely. All power is His. But now for the real surprise.

In Jesus lies the secret of the radiance of God's glory: the radiance of God was revealed in Jesus' willingness to die in order that you might live. In other words, the true nature of glory is sacrificial love.

YOUR OXYGEN MASK

The Spirit of the LORD is upon me, for he has anointed me to bring Good News to the poor.
—LUKE 4:18 NLT

AIRLINE FLIGHTS TYPICALLY BEGIN WITH A standard set of instructions about seat belts, emergency exits, and crash procedures. Somewhere in the middle of those instructions, we hear the words: "If we should experience a sudden loss of cabin pressure, an oxygen mask will appear…. Please secure your own mask before assisting any children who might be with you." The reason for this instruction is clear. The thin air at high altitudes doesn't provide the brain with enough oxygen to think clearly and make good decisions. In order to help a child, you need to think clearly. You need your own oxygen mask on first.

Things work the same way in the Christian life. In order to help others, we need to receive the "oxygen" of God's transforming presence in our own lives first. This empowers us to bring Jesus into the place of need and to speak life into other people. If we neglect this, we can quickly burn out in a world filled with need. First let yourself be loved by God, deeply and completely. It sounds selfish, but it is not. The more you receive God's love, the more you can love others.

November 25

FILLING WHAT'S EMPTY

The LORD is my shepherd, I shall not want.

—PSALM 23:1 NASB

WHAT MAKES FOR A CONTENTED LIFE? Those of us living in a capitalistic society tend to view money and what it can buy as the ultimate solution to every problem. Indeed, money can fix quite a few things, but we've all heard enough stories of miserable millionaires to know that it can't fix a starving soul.

You may experience an initial "high" when you buy the latest high-tech gadget, but the feeling fades quickly. Accumulating possessions can appear to boost status, but in an instant your status can falter. It's the intangibles that fill the empty places within you: community, emotional connection, a sense of purpose.

When you make Jesus the Lord of your life, you gain new perspective on the limitations of the material world and what it can do for you. As you apply principles of Christian living to your life, what you own fades into the background as you find fulfillment and peace through loving and serving others. God may not shower you with earthly wealth, but He does promise you *abundance*, which the dictionary defines as "overflowing fullness." Does it get any better than that?

DEPEND ON HIM

Asa called out to the LORD his God, saying, "LORD, only you can help weak people against the strong. Help us, LORD our God, because we depend on you."
—2 CHRONICLES 14:11 NCV

AT SOME POINT IN YOUR JOURNEY through life, as you progressed day by day in some sort of routine, you may have made the decision to include a time to be with God in a meaningful way. A slight shift in your priorities occurred, with some minor adjustments along the way. Before you knew it, you took up the habit of prayer and reading from Scripture on a daily basis.

As we do this, little by little we begin to realize the effects of that decision, feeling encouraged and enlightened in spirit. In fact, we might even sense that our relationship with God is causing welcome changes within us. Our quiet times are making things go well for us.

But what about when adversity strikes? As we run to God, crying out to Him for help, for wisdom, for strength, and for deliverance, we find both courage and consolation in discovering that He is right there for us—right where we've been accustomed to meeting with Him day after day.

The Lord is faithful to keep your appointment with Him on a routine basis, bringing insight and blessing every day. As you continue to meet with Him, you'll discover that your routine appointment will cultivate an intimacy with God upon which you can depend in troubled times.

GOD'S ARTISTRY

There was not a woman in that country
as beautiful as Job's daughters.
—JOB 42:15 MSG

GOD'S ARTISTRY IS EVERYWHERE: THE MOON reflected in the quiet waters of a lake in the woods, the unrestrained laughter of a child, a bride adorned on her wedding day, a song rising up from a grateful heart, an elderly couple walking hand in hand.

Beauty invites us to celebrate God's goodness in our lives. It catches our attention; it causes us to pause and consider. It elevates us as human beings. It inspires us to care about things that matter. That's why God's fingerprints are found in each of us—not just physical attractiveness, but beautiful thoughts, stories, attitudes, and relationships. All of this points heavenward.

By itself this artistry can be a pathway into the presence of God. Vibrant rainbows and warm smiles, kind words and soothing voices—these are all gifts from God, calling us to Him, reminding us that He isn't finished with us yet. We are each a work in progress. The full wonder of what He is doing in us has not yet been revealed. Something better lies ahead. We are each a masterpiece created by God. The more we linger in His transforming presence, the more His beauty is reflected in our lives.

A SONG IN YOUR HEART

*The Lord is my Strength and my [impenetrable] Shield...and
I am helped; therefore my heart greatly rejoices,
and with my song will I praise Him.*
—PSALM 28:7 AMP

D O YOU NURTURE AN ATTITUDE OF gratitude? Sometimes the
daily grind can erode your joy, making you forget the blessings
and benefits of a life redeemed by Jesus. Whiny teenagers, insensi-
tive spouses, harried commutes, unremitting financial pressures, and
over-scheduled lives create noise—external and internal—that muffles
God's voice. *Thank God for what?* you might wonder to yourself. *All
my stress?*

Often we trudge through life with a dejected gait. If we're not
careful we can start to sound like gloomy Eeyore, Winnie the Pooh's
pal, who resigns much of life to his trademark "Ohhh-kayyy." You, on
the other hand, were created to keep a song in your heart, even if on
some days it's hard to sing.

Each day is an invitation to re-order your life to make room for
gratitude to God. As you settle down for prayer, worship, or Bible
study, begin by spending time thanking God for the little things. Your
ability to read, your home, the people who love you. Contemplate all
the simple things that bring you unexpected joys. In no time, you'll
find yourself refreshed with a grateful heart and moving from a drab
"Ohhh-kayyy" to a delighted "Ohhh-yeaaa!"

November 29

HIS PLAN FOR MY LIFE

*What do you think GOD expects from you? Just this: Live in
his presence in holy reverence, follow the road he sets out for
you, love him, serve GOD...live a good life.*
—DEUTERONOMY 10:12-13 MSG

WHEN YOU LOOK BACK OVER THE past ten years of your life,
what stands out as your most obvious priority? Obtaining a
college degree? Establishing your career? Becoming a family? Just one
big party? Or a long exercise in futility and failure? Whatever it is, it
is worth taking a look backward in order to get a bearing on how to
go forward.

How would today be different if ten years ago you had asked and
answered the question, *What does God want for me over the next decade
of my life?* Would your priorities have been different?

How about asking that question regarding the next ten years. What
difference would that make? In fact, what immediate changes would
have to occur in order to give answer to that question?

It's pretty simple, actually. God wants to have an authentic rela-
tionship with you. He wants your life to be fulfilling and purposeful.
He wants you to recognize how much you need Him and how much
He needs you to help other people find their way to Him. In short,
God wants to lavish His love on you and on others through you. That
should make the next ten years look like a pretty exciting prospect.

WHAT GOD CAN DO

Look instead for what God can do.

—JOHN 9:3 MSG

IN THE SUMMER OF 1994, SEVENTY-THREE-YEAR-OLD Alvin Straight faced a serious challenge. His estranged brother, Lyle, had just suffered a stroke in his home town of Mount Zion, Wisconsin. Alvin knew he needed to go and make things right with his brother, but he had no car, no driver's license, and very little money to make the 240-mile trip. He dealt with these limitations by making the trip on a 1966 John Deere riding lawn mower. Top speed? Five miles per hour. The journey took six weeks. But the outcome was reconciliation with his brother and a story that inspired millions.

Our limitations are God's opportunities. Without the constraints that Alvin Straight faced, there would be no story, no inspiration, and possibly no reconciliation. In the theatrical version of their story, it was only when his brother saw the sacrifice Alvin had made to visit him that he understood the depth of the love between them.

What is holding you back? Hidden inside your weaknesses is an opportunity for God to be strong. When you bring your limitations into God's presence, you invite the impossible. You never know— He just may blow the roof off your expectations and show you His creative, redeeming, miracle-working power.

December 1

SOUL SHOWER

*I made my sins known to you, and I did not
cover up my guilt. I decided to confess them to you, O LORD.
Then you forgave all my sins.*
—PSALM 32:5 GWT

A CLEAN HEART IS A SINCERE heart. Covering up something always backfires because the truth always comes out. Some way, somehow, often when it's least expected, the honest facts will surface. We might as well admit reality and come clean.

Take a soul shower. Clean up all the "dirt" you're carrying in your heart. Let go of the junk other people did to you, and own up to your own. There isn't one of us who hasn't been hurt or hurt someone else. Is it doing you any good to hang on to it? Is it making you any more energetic and alive?

Soul dirt weighs you down more than garden dirt does. You can brush garden dirt off your hands and knees, but there's not a thing you can do to cleanse your own soul.

Yet it only takes a moment to be scrubbed clean. Reflect a bit on your heart. If you find some grime, take it to your loving and forgiving God. Make your confession before Him. Wait for His peace and joy to follow. Then, walk away clean in every way.

December 2

EFFECTIVE PRAYER

I tell you, you can pray for anything,
and if you believe that you've received it, it will be yours.

—MARK 11:24 NLT

THE PRAYER THAT IS OFFERED UP to God in complete trust and then left with the Lord in quiet confidence brings honor to God in the heavens. He derives great joy in responding to the faith that takes hold of what it asks before it receives.

What is the key to that kind of prayer? How do you develop the confidence to pray effectively?

The first lesson in effective prayer is that prayer does not require you to be perfect, sinless, or noble. No one who has experienced power in prayer did so because they attained perfection. The myth of perfection does more to inhibit faith than any other thing. Prayer looks to God, not to the one praying.

Secondly, God listens to you pray because He is faithful. There is no evidence in Scripture that would lead you to doubt that God has heard your prayer. His willingness to listen does not need proof that you are worthy of His audience. In fact, you can be sure that God actually longs to hear from you. He wants you to speak to Him from the very depths of your heart.

Trust in God simply because He is who He says He is.

TEARS IN HEAVEN

Jesus wept.

—JOHN 11:35 NASB

B ORN IN ALBANIA IN 1910, AGNES Bojaxhiu grew up with one
desire: to serve the Lord as a missionary. Her quest eventually led
her to India where, for a while, she lived comfortably as a teacher.
But as famine, war, and disease ravaged that nation, the distress of the
people filled her heart with pain. In response, she left the comfort of
her mission and walked into the slums of Calcutta. At first she had no
home and had to beg for food. But she persisted because she could not
ignore the cries of the poor.

In time, her efforts bore fruit. Others joined her. Together they
started clinics, orphanages, and charity centers that helped many
thousands, first in India and then around the world. Along the way, she
ceased to be known as Agnes Bojaxhiu, and is now remembered by the
world as Mother Teresa.

We can never comprehend human suffering without taking into
account the suffering of God. When we hurt, God hurts. No tear falls
here on earth without God feeling the hurt in heaven. But it doesn't
stop there. Just as Mother Teresa's compassion changed our world, so
also God will provide healing for all who come to Him.

December 4

RAZZLE AND DAZZLE

See, I am doing a new thing! Now it springs up;
do you not perceive it? I am making a way in the desert
and streams in the wasteland.
—ISAIAH 43:19 NIV

OFTEN WE MISS THE SUBTLE MOVEMENTS of God in our daily lives because, without realizing, we expect Him to razzle and dazzle us like the professional athletes who dunk or chip-shot or drag both feet in a corner of the end zone to pull out the winning score. Surely God can pour on the power and turn up the lights to prove Himself victorious and glorious. Yes, He is more than capable of making headline news, but what if He wants to enter our moments in a more understated style?

Perhaps you've witnessed God showing up in people and predicaments like you've never expected. Maybe you've watched the hand of God untangle your problems or heard Him whisper to your heart. Possibly He's spoken to you through specific Bible verses on the very day you needed fresh hope and a renewed perspective.

The Creator of all things is more than ready to razzle and dazzle you a bit to keep you awed by His majesty, but oftentimes He chooses to reveal a new, inspiring thing in ways you'd least expect—such as coming to earth as a babe born in a lowly manger.

December 5

THE WISDOM OF DAILY DEVOTION

*Job answered, "...Should we take only good
things from God and not trouble?"*
—JOB 2:10 NCV

AT THE TOP OF THE MORNING, there is no way of knowing what the day will bring. Most likely you have a plan for the day, but who's to know whether the moments will play out the way you have predicted. One thing is certain: they will play out—whether planned or not.

The most important part of your plan, no doubt, is to begin every day with prayer, committing the day to God. If you start your day this way, you will find that you are more at peace throughout the day, regardless of what happens. There is a marked difference in the disposition of those who rely upon the Lord for daily strength and wisdom. Having entrusted yourself to God, you are calm, confident, and better prepared in every circumstance.

Having begun the day in prayer, you will also find it much easier to return to your conversation with God when things get difficult. Train yourself to turn back to God for guidance in prayer before consulting with anyone else in times of conflict, adversity, or struggle. You will see that you are consistently better equipped to deal with trials when you seek divine guidance before human counsel. At day's end, you are at peace.

December 6

LEAVE THE DOOR OPEN

Sun, stand still.

—JOSHUA 10:12 NIrV

THROUGHOUT THE BIBLE, WE READ STORY after story of great miracles that God performed. At first glance, it would seem like God performed these wonders for the best of the best, the most righteous men and women of the ages. But upon closer examination we discover this isn't necessarily the case. God rearranged the laws of physics to protect a leader who had just made a major bungle. God sent bread from heaven to a community of people who frequently complained about Him. A young man who fell asleep in church, resulting in a fatal fall from a third-story window, was raised from the dead. An argumentative fisherman hauled an impossible supply of fish from the water. And the list goes on.

All of this arms us with hope. God can come through for us, even though we know that we are far from perfect. What can God do for you? Anything! There are no limitations on the power of God. As you spend time in His presence, leave the door open for your supernatural God to show up with a solution to your impossible challenges.

PERSONAL MENTOR

I will instruct you and teach you in the way you should go;
I will counsel you with my loving eye on you.
—PSALM 32:8 TNIV

THE BIG BROTHER/BIG SISTER PROGRAM IS more than one hundred years old. Their passion is helping kids reach their potential through one-on-one relationships with mentors. The mentor is matched to a young person, and by doing activities together and finding common ground, they build a relationship. In an atmosphere of trust, the "Little," as the younger person is called, has someone to turn to for advice, help, guidance, and some fun. The "Big" doesn't pity or show judgment for past decisions, but instead befriends and helps and enjoys the little brother or sister.

In a similar way, God is your personal mentor. Like one of the "Bigs," He isn't judging you for past mistakes, but He'll help you make great decisions from this point forward. He's also readily available to kick back and encourage you to relax.

This week, why not jot down all the ways you can think of that God has given you counsel and pointed you in the right direction. Look up verses in His Word that remind you of His supportive advice and faithfulness. And remember to thank Him for being beside you and enjoying life with you. You'll never find a better friend to turn to anytime.

December 8

THE POWER TO ENCOURAGE

*Let us think of ways to motivate one another
to acts of love and good works.*
—HEBREWS 10:24 NLT

IF YOU ARE LIKE MOST PEOPLE, you care enough to help others when they really need you. There's a feeling of deep gratification that accompanies a good turn. However, you can also help others to help others, causing your own good to multiply exponentially in those around you.

One way to experiment with this exciting potential is to speak to God about those in whom you see the propensity to commit acts of kindness for the sake of others. Pray over them diligently and with a whole heart. Ask the Lord to move on their hearts to create the desire to get involved in actively serving others. Solicit His insight concerning how you might encourage these individuals to step up and step out.

Your own devotion to God and to people in need will fan the flame of those around you. Having the courage to speak out about the blessing and the motivation you find while spending time in God's presence will inspire your friends to want to know more and seek God's blessing for themselves.

It is a thrilling thing to discover that you have the power to ignite those around you to love and good works, all to the glory of God!

December 9

A BETTER GIFT

*Your prayers and gifts to the poor have come up
as a memorial offering before God.*
—ACTS 10:4 NIV

IN 1881, FIFTEEN-YEAR-OLD MATT MILES WANTED just one thing for Christmas: a new rifle. But there wasn't enough money to buy it. Deeply disappointed, Matt was in no mood for extra chores on a bitterly cold Christmas Eve. But he had no choice, so he went outside and helped his dad load more wood on the sled than he thought the horse could pull. His dad gathered up some packages and they set out. After a trip of two miles, they stopped at the home of a widow who had three small children. Inside, they found the family huddled, shivering and shoeless, around a tiny fire that provided no warmth. For the next half hour, they unloaded wood, stoked the fire, and unwrapped packages for the family. Matt's dad had bought shoes for each and candy for the children. The widow could find no words for her gratitude; she simply stood there with silent tears running down her face.

Matt returned home a changed person. The rifle was no longer important. He had received the best Christmas present of his life.

Your acts of kindness are never forgotten by God. He sees. What you have done will always be remembered.

RELENTLESS COMPANION

*If your heart is broken, you'll find GOD right there;
if you're kicked in the gut, he'll help you catch your breath.*
—**PSALM 34:18** MSG

SAMWISE GAMGEE IS THE PLUCKY AND loyal hobbit from J. R. R. Tolkien's *Lord of the Rings* trilogy. Sam's friend, Frodo, has a mission—to journey to the dark land of Mordor to destroy the ruling Ring by throwing it into the volcanic fires of Mount Doom, thus demolishing evil from the land. No matter the adventure or the danger, there's tireless Sam, glued to Frodo's side. It's Sam who hoards their food so Frodo always has nourishment. It's Sam who wields swords in Frodo's defense.

God is your own faithful companion and defender. When you feel like life has knocked the wind out of you and you can barely put one foot in front of the other, God kneels down to lift you up. He carries you when you're too weary to keep forging ahead. He nourishes your heart with soul food and eases your mind with the sweet water of peace. He defends you from whatever comes against you and cheers you in the gloom.

As you consistently slip away from your own arduous missions in life to rest in God's presence, be sure to tell Him about the ominous mountains you face. Then thank Him for helping you press on.

PERSONAL POWER

*God's Way is not a matter of mere talk;
it's an empowered life.*

—1 CORINTHIANS 4:20 MSG

HAVE YOU KNOWN ANYONE WHO APPEARS to possess an unusually vibrant personal power—power by which they accomplish lofty goals and become an inspiration? Someone who also seems to have the intuitive ability to tap into the latent potential of others to help them rise above the status quo? Do these people strike you as blissfully unconcerned about themselves while deeply invested in those around them, possessing the power to bless people who cannot muster the resources to obtain a blessing otherwise?

What is the source of this power?

Ironically, this mastery doesn't come through the channels of empowerment: motivational speeches, support groups, or self-help books. It is derived from an authentic intimacy with God, something readily available to you. This power is derived from time spent contemplating God's truths and integrating them into the fiber of your character through diligent application. It comes through deep and meaningful conversations with God over every aspect of your life. And it is most thoroughly developed in learning to love like God loves.

Would you be interested in obtaining this kind of power?

The place to begin is in asking God to teach you about His love, aware that His lessons will require action.

OUR DESIRES

Who satisfies your desires with good things.
—PSALM 103:5 NIV

"WHAT DO YOU WANT?" AGAIN AND again God will come back to us with this question. How do we answer? Honestly. Do we always know what we want? Not necessarily. Do we sometimes think we know when we don't? Most certainly! We can at times be like the little child who cried and cried because his mother would not buy him cigars.

Our desires are sometimes good and sometimes bad. But inside each desire is something planted by God. The desire to consume a plateful of chocolate chip cookies, for example, might really have little to do with hunger for food and much to do with hunger for the affirmation that God longs to give His sons and daughters. A desire to travel might be the first step in an adventure ordained by God. A desire to help a single mom might be the doorway into a lifelong ministry. God knows exactly what to do with each one of our desires—that's why we bring all of them to Him, no matter how good or how bad we might think they are.

Our desires, placed into God's hands, set us on a wonderful journey of growth and God-discovery.

DIGGING IN

Jonah immediately tried to run away from the LORD by going to Tarshish. He went to Joppa and found a ship.... He paid for the trip and went on board...to get away from the LORD.
—JONAH 1:3 GWT

THE MOTHER KNEW WHAT GOD WAS asking of her—she just didn't want to do it. Her neighbor continued to yell and curse at the mom's sometimes noisy children. She wrestled with God's nudge to not just forgive the neighbor but to also extend a blessing to her.

You, too, may know what it's like when you sense you're supposed to do something but you just don't want to do it. Your heels are digging in. Your jaw is set. Your eyes squint with the fire of determination. No. I won't. Uh-uh. No.

The only thing is, you're saying no to God. Saying no to the Ruler of all just doesn't go over well. Next time you feel like going your own way, take a deep breath and think, *How much will this obstinacy distance me from a close relationship with God?* There's no place to hide that He can't see. So deal with your heart. Ask, "Why am I so set on resisting His plan?" Pour out whatever comes to mind. He already knows your hesitancies.

God is wise. If He's asking you to do something, He has a reason. Your part is needed—now. What He's asking of you matters more than you know.

December 14

LESSONS FROM THE STORM

We are pushed hard from all sides. But we are not beaten down. We are bewildered. But that doesn't make us lose hope. Others make us suffer. But God does not desert us.
—2 Corinthians 4:8-9 nirv

WE WOULD LIKE TO BELIEVE THAT if we do exactly what God requires, everything will always go smoothly. Not necessarily true. Sometimes following God can be inconvenient, difficult, even downright painful. Throughout history, many followers of God have experienced all sorts of trouble and persecution. God does not promise to bail us out of every uncomfortable situation. But He does assure us that He will be with us throughout our difficult times.

One day Jesus and His disciples crossed a large lake in a boat. During the trip, Jesus fell asleep. A sudden storm blew in with such intensity that the disciples were certain the boat would sink and they would drown. They woke up Jesus, who easily rebuked the storm. In moments, all was calm.

The lesson? Without the storm, they never would have experienced the truth: The Master of all nature was there in the boat with them. His name is Jesus.

In your time alone with God, bring to Him all your troubles—those things that concern and hurt you. Don't hold anything back. In this way, you too will experience the truth. Jesus is here. His presence makes all the difference.

December 15

SUFFERING WITH OTHERS

*Praise be to the God and Father of our Lord Jesus Christ,
the Father of compassion and the God of all comfort.*
—2 CORINTHIANS 1:3 NIV

DO YOU KNOW THAT THE LITERAL meaning of the word *compassion* is "suffering with"? To be truly compassionate, a person must take on the sufferings of another. That's a far cry from feeling sorry for someone, which is one of several diluted definitions of compassion used in contemporary culture. Those who truly follow God, however, fortify rather than dilute the literal meaning of the word by expanding it to include attempts to alleviate the suffering. To them, it's not enough to comfort a neighbor who cannot feed his family when you have the means to help provide what is lacking.

Still, there are times when it would seem there is little you can do to lessen another person's suffering. One such occasion is when a friend has lost a loved one. Even then, however, the presence of God that lingers in your life as a result of time spent alone with Him may be the comfort that person needs to make it through the loneliness of grief.

Our God is known for His great compassion. He has truly entered into our suffering, fulfilling the word in the broadest possible sense. Let Him show you how you can walk in the fullness of compassion for those whose lives you touch.

THROUGH YOUR EYES

Many have undertaken to draw up an account
of the things that have been fulfilled among us.
—LUKE 1:1-3 NIV

IN THE BIBLE, WE FIND FOUR separate accounts of the life of Jesus Christ—none of them written by Jesus Himself. Matthew, a former tax collector and one of the twelve disciples, wrote an account targeted to the readers who despised his old profession: the religious Jews. John Mark, a young man from a wealthy family and a missionary dropout, wrote a narrative with the action-oriented Romans in mind. Luke, a medical doctor, wrote the longest chronicle, the one with great attention to stories of healing and other human experiences. John, a fisherman-turned-apostle, wrote a series of essays about Jesus that appeal to the Western philosophical mind. These are the four Gospels—the same Jesus, different approaches; stories in harmony with one another, yet each one is unique.

Why didn't Jesus write His own story? Why did He leave that task in the hands of others? Simple: Jesus wants the world to see Him through the lens of who you are. In God's presence, you gain your own experience with Jesus that you will share with your world. Others will come to know Him because of who you are and the stories you tell.

FREED BY TRUTH

*Lead me in your truth and teach me, for you are the God
of my salvation; for you I wait all the day long.*
—PSALM 25:5 ESV

B LAME, EXCUSES, AND SELF-PITY. RAMPANT SINCE man's
introduction to earth, these attitudes sometimes seem easier than
being honest, but they're like a soul-virus that kills from the inside out.
Blame and excuses cause you to lose your power. Self-pity sidelines
you. Truth, however, empowers and frees you.

Why give up your freedom to choose and get stuck on the sidelines
of life?

Jesus does not cater to excuses. He takes action. He is straight-line
truth and He doesn't let you get away with lying to yourself. Blaming
others and using excuses is really another form of self-deception, like a
little white lie. Yet in God's eyes, all lies are damaging and dangerous.
Jesus called the Devil the father of all lies. You know you want to avoid
that grand deceiver and his messed-up games.

As you pause before God today, maybe it's time to take stock of
how you might be passing the buck to someone else or blaming a
circumstance. Facing an uncomfortable truth is hard. Go eye-to-eye
with the face in the mirror and ask yourself, "What's really going on?"
Facing life with an honest perspective frees you to walk in confidence
and truth.

LABELS

*He settles the barren woman in her home
as a happy mother of children.*
—**PSALM 113:9** NIV

THROUGHOUT THE BIBLE WE READ STORIES of people whose lives were defined by a problem they could not solve. Often these were medical conditions—paralysis, leprosy, blindness, or other chronic issues. No fewer than seven women were labeled "barren" because they were unable to have children.

All of those people were living with a label: "leper," "cripple," "barren." That label defined their existence. But in each case, God tore the label away and gave them a new life. Lepers were cleansed. The paralyzed were given the ability to walk. The eyes of the blind were opened. And some of the most famous people in biblical history, including Isaac, Jacob, Joseph, Samson, Samuel the prophet, and John the Baptist, were born to formerly "childless" women.

What label defines your life? You may have given yourself a label that doesn't fit, such as "fat," "ugly," "stupid," "poor," and so on. No matter what statement may have characterized your life up to this point, God can, in an instant, redefine you. Give Him the opportunity to do that. Bring those negative labels into His presence. Lay them at His feet. Let Him speak His truth over your life. He will show you who you really are in Him.

December 19

KEEP YOUR NEEDS FEW

*My God will meet all your needs according
to his glorious riches in Christ Jesus.*
—**PHILIPPIANS 4:19** NIV

WE TEND TO USE THE WORD "need" loosely, when in reality our needs are far fewer than our words suggest. So what do we really need? And how do we distinguish that from those things we simply want?

Like a good and loving father, God has promised to take care of us. He tells us to come to Him with our requests, open up our hearts to Him, and He will do what is best for us. Like a wise father, He won't indulge us by giving us everything we ask for. But He does promise to supply those things we really need and pour out His abundant blessings on us as well.

Don't waste your time trying to decide between your wants and needs. Make all your requests known to Him. Open your heart and let your hopes and desires flow out to Him. He loves it when you come into His presence and pour out your heart. And you can be sure that He will always answer though it might not be in the way you expect. His provision is always more than enough and always for your best. You will never need more than that.

December 20

BREAKING THE POWER OF FEAR

We can serve God without fear.
—LUKE 1:74 NLT

A MAN GREW UP AFRAID OF dogs. Twice during his childhood he had been on the receiving end of canine aggression. Though neither attack was vicious, they were enough to sear in his brain the message: *Dogs are dangerous.* As a result, his fear of dogs was paralyzing. Even a tiny barking dog would cause him to freeze with fright. But he decided to take his fears into God's presence. Again and again, he brought his various fears to the Lord and reviewed the incidents where they originated. Over time, he noticed that he was beginning to relax around dogs.

One cold winter day he was walking in a park when a Rottweiler came charging toward him. The dog's master was at least a hundred yards away. The Rottweiler grabbed his gloved hand in its teeth. Standing very still, the man called to the dog's owner, "Please take control of your dog." No panic. No paralyzing fear. With God's help, he remained calm despite his extremely precarious situation.

Do you have fears? The more time you spend bringing those fears to God, the more opportunity He has to break the power of those fears in your life.

December 21

THE ALL-ENCOMPASSING COVENANT

May God himself, the God of peace, sanctify you through and through. May your whole spirit, soul and body be kept blameless at the coming of our Lord Jesus Christ.

—1 Thessalonians 5:23 NIV

WHEN YOU ENTER INTO THE COVENANT of marriage, it affects every aspect of your being: your time, your energy, your income, your personal space, your dwelling place, your heart, your body, your future, your relationships, and even your leisure time. Nothing is left untouched by the partnership of marriage.

In the same way, nothing in your life is left untouched by your relationship with God. Every aspect of your life is affected by the compassionate character of the Lord you are learning to love. It begins as an inside job. You sense that your perspective on life, on people, on your job, on money, on time is undergoing a radical change. You welcome the reconstruction of your values and find that you are curiously intrigued with spiritual concerns as never before.

It isn't long before people notice a change in your personality. You seem more sensitive, more engaged with people. You laugh more, cry more, and care more. You are more desirable to be around, and people seek you out in conversation.

Eventually, you discover that your relationship with God is affecting your physical world as well. You feel more alive, make healthier choices, and have more energy than before. God's thorough work in you is an advantage in every way.

WHEN GOD SPEAKS

God does speak—now one way, now another.
—JOB 33:14 NIV

IN THE BIBLE WE READ OF a certain godly man who lost his family, his health, his possessions, his reputation, and the respect of his friends. In bewilderment he looked to God for answers. *Why has this happened to me*, he wondered, *when all my life I've served God?*

At the end of the story, God showed up and spoke to him, but not in the way you might expect. Rather than arriving as a consoling, soothing, healing angel, God spoke out of a howling tornado. He made no attempt to comfort this man, nor did he answer any of his questions. Instead, God spoke about wild things—oxen, donkeys, hawks, eagles, and ostriches. God's response was unexpected, but somehow it worked. The suffering man stood in awe of God. After that, everything was restored to him double.

Elsewhere, a discouraged prophet wanted God to speak from a tornado, but He wouldn't. Instead He spoke in a quiet whisper. One time, God spoke through a donkey. To a young boy, He spoke through an audible voice.

How will God speak to you when you're alone with Him?

That's part of the adventure. He will speak in a way that's unique to you.

December 23

LOOKING FOR A REFUND

*Her husband Joseph was an honorable man and did
not want to disgrace her publicly. So he decided to break
the marriage agreement with her secretly.*
—MATTHEW 1:19 GWT

TODAY THE CHRISTMAS STORY CONJURES UP images of shepherds and angels, a baby in a manger, wise men kneeling with expensive gifts. We hear "Silent Night" in our imagination and smile as we think of snowflakes softly falling and gifts wrapped neatly with a bow.

But it didn't start out that way. It started out with Joseph, an honorable young man, receiving the heart-wrenching news that Mary, the woman he intended to marry, was pregnant with someone else's child. No explanation could cover the facts. The law and custom of the day gave him two choices: have her stoned for prostitution, or quietly break off the engagement.

As we unwrap the gift of life, sometimes we see things we didn't expect. In panic, we want to rush back to the store with the receipt and demand an exchange. Nothing makes sense. God must have it wrong. Life dealt us the wrong set of cards. The beauty of Joseph's story and our own is this: As we enter God's presence to ponder our choices, a whole new way of looking at things opens up before us. Our tragedy is erased. In its place is the wonder of God's perfect plan.

BENEATH THE SURFACE

*About that time Caesar Augustus ordered a census
to be taken throughout the Empire.*

—LUKE 2:1 MSG

THE CHRISTMAS STORY OPENS WITH A seemingly random event: An emperor orders more taxes. This puts into motion Joseph and Mary's difficult trek to Bethlehem where they are greeted as *personae non gratae* and denied access to the only decent lodging in the village.

But beneath the surface, a very different story emerges. Without knowing it, the pagan emperor arranges for the Son of God to be born precisely where the prophets predicted He would arrive. Jesus, from the moment of His birth, identifies Himself with the poor, the oppressed, the downtrodden.

The Christmas story contains many lessons. One of them is this: We need God's presence to interpret for us the seemingly random events of our lives. Without God's perspective, we could easily be lulled into thinking that we are only pawns, victims in a meaningless sea of chance. But as we press into God, we discover that nothing is accidental, everything in our lives has purpose. Every element of our existence is in God's hands and is being used to bring good into our lives. You never know how God is going to use an event to change your life. And you never know what significance a humble circumstance might contain.

THE BIRTHPLACE OF JOY

Do not be afraid. I bring you good news of great joy that will be for all the people.

—LUKE 2:10 NIV

WHAT IS THE FIRST THING GOD does after His Son is born? He throws a party. And whom does He invite? Everyone…even the innkeeper who denied a room to Joseph and Mary. He wanted all of us to be there.

Who needs the good news of Christmas? We all do. Deep inside, we all need to know that God entered our world not as an avenger or a tyrant, but as a vulnerable child. He allowed Himself to become human, fragile, and breakable just like us. He made Himself near. He erased the distance between us. He sat down on the ground and invited us to come and sit beside Him.

This is the message of Christmas, and this is what opens the door for us to spend time alone in God's presence. He understands us. He feels our humanity. We can be real around Him. We are no longer spectators but participants. We are no longer servants but friends. We are invited into His family. We have found our way home.

Through this place of intimacy with God comes everything good that will ever enter our lives or come into our world. Christmas is the birthplace of joy.

QUIET BUT POWERFUL

She gave birth to her first child, a son. She wrapped him
snugly in strips of cloth and laid him in a manger,
because there was no lodging available for them.
—LUKE 2:7 NLT

IN THE 2002 MOVIE VERSION OF *The Count of Monte Cristo*, the count makes a theatrical entrance with fireworks, dancers, and a hot-air balloon. His entrance validated his status in the society of his day. By contrast, the arrival of Jesus seems like an undercover mission. A traveling Jewish woman stops at a cave in Bethlehem to bring a child into the world. Though Jesus outranked Caesar Augustus, He was barely a blip on the Roman radar screen.

Today, Jesus continues to arrive in the lives of people all around the world. For the most part, this still looks like a stealth mission. The media minimize it. Politicians ignore it. Leaders overlook it without understanding that Jesus Christ will transform everything they see.

How does God transform a life, a family, a nation, the world? Quietly. Without fanfare or fireworks. Where He is allowed in, He enters. There the changes happen. Addictions are broken. Marriages are restored. Broken hearts are mended. Ruined lives are restored. New hope is uncovered.

In our time alone with God, this is what we pray for. This is what we invite. This is what we experience—the quiet but powerful birth of Jesus within us.

TREASURES

Mary kept all these things like a secret treasure in her heart.
—LUKE 2:19 NIrV

WHEN AMY HANSON WAS CHRISTMAS SHOPPING as a teenager, she came across an aging homeless man holding a box of matches in a trembling hand. Struck by that image, she couldn't bring herself to walk by. Emptying her pockets of all her shopping money, she gave him everything she had. Years later, working as a journalist, she traveled to Southeast Asia where she met children who lived in landfills, surviving by scavenging and selling anything that seemed to be of value. Again, the image was too much for her. She returned home and raised funds to help these children climb out of poverty. To the world, these children were throwaways. But to Amy, they were precious. No wonder Amy's mother gave her the nickname "Treasure."

Children sometimes play the game of searching for buried treasure. Our time alone with God is something like that game, but far better because we have the opportunity to uncover something or someone that God treasures. God will put in your heart something or someone that you will find precious. This all happens for a reason. It becomes your opportunity to make a difference. What you treasure can change your world.

LOVING GOD BY LOVING OTHERS

Now, vigilantly guard your souls: Love GOD, your God.
—JOSHUA 23:11 MSG

TO LOVE GOD IS THE FIRST and greatest commandment in Scripture. But how do you love a God you cannot see?

The Word of God addresses this dilemma by putting skin on the object of love: You demonstrate your love for God by loving others in authentic and intentional ways. How clarifying, yet how challenging!

Doesn't it make sense, then, to develop the habit of bringing the issue of love into your quiet time with God—seeking insight from God about this most crucial command?

You'll find that God will call you to love by helping others when they are in need. And with His counsel, you will become more discerning about others' needs. He will also lead you into opportunities to love that don't come easily. It is natural to love those close to you—family, friends, and coworkers. God will call you to consider taking your love for Him beyond your familiar boundaries.

God may give you a loving word to speak to someone else by giving good counsel in conflict or bringing a word of encouragement in the midst of despair.

The opportunity to express your love for God presents itself daily in a constant stream of people who crave human connection.

December 29

THE GREAT COMMUNICATOR

I waited patiently for the LORD.
He turned to me and heard my cry.
—PSALM 40:1 NCV

WE'RE A PLUGGED-IN WORLD. WE'RE CONNECTED to computers, iPods, and Wiis. Most of us engage with Twitter, Facebook, or texting. We leave voicemail and e-mail. We Skype and chat at the speed of light. Yet in spite of all these plug-ins, there's loneliness. All this availability and we still call silently for someone to hear our hearts. Sometimes it's hard to be heard when there's so much to say.

It's about true connection.

Getting an audience for the language of your heart is key. You want to be heard, your world acknowledged, and help sent quickly. If your friends are busy or wrapped up in their own lives, the art of listening can turn into the art of information management. Where do you go to be heard?

Fortunately, you are connected to the Great Communicator. God perceives the yearnings of your heart. He is never too busy for you. You won't be sent to His voicemail. And He always responds right on time; never early, but never too late. Consider checking in with Him throughout your day just to say hello. God is always up for your instant message…and He'll answer at the speed of light.

STAYING STRONG

*When the devil had finished all this tempting,
he left him until an opportune time.*
—LUKE 4:13 NIV

IN A WAR, THE OPPOSING GENERALS carefully study each other's weaknesses in order to find a way to exploit them. When and where is the enemy most vulnerable? That's where the attack will come. This strategy can allow a small and weak army to do considerable damage to a larger, well-equipped army.

In the same way, it is good for us to know our own strengths and weaknesses. If we know when we are strong and when we are vulnerable, it will help us to guard against temptations and failures. Those weak moments can come when we aren't taking care of ourselves. One pastor said, "Sometimes the most spiritual thing you can do is get a good night's sleep." Weak moments can come when we aren't nurturing our most important relationships, including family, marriage, and God.

All of the disciplines work together to keep you strong. Prayer, Bible study, healthy relationships, sleep, exercise, a balance of work and rest, good nutrition—all have a place in your life. Apart from God, these disciplines won't do enough. But as God is invited into them, you will find the strength to prevail in your spiritual battles.

December 31

THE WAY BACK

*The town harlot, having learned that Jesus was a guest
in the home of the Pharisee, came with a bottle of very
expensive perfume and stood at his feet, weeping.*
—LUKE 7:37-38 MSG

AS A YOUNG MAN, JOSH MCDOWELL set out to disprove the
Bible and discredit the Christian faith. Like many others who
have set out to do the same, he encountered Jesus, and his life was
never the same. He went from being a skeptic to being one of the
foremost advocates for Christianity. But his story doesn't end there.
Growing up in a small town where everybody knew that his father was
an alcoholic, Josh's heart was filled with anger and shame. But as the
presence of Jesus filled his life, all that hatred drained away and was
replaced by love. His father couldn't believe the transformation in Josh.
He welcomed Jesus into his life, put away the bottle, and lived sober
from that point on.

This story, multiplied millions of times, provides living proof that
Jesus offers what no one else can: a way out and a way back. All of us
have failed, but none of us is so far gone that Jesus cannot redeem our
lives and turn them into something beautiful. No one is too far gone.
Even those who have fallen a thousand times are welcome in the arms
of Jesus.

A plan for Bible reading to take readers through the New Testament and Psalms twice a year, and through the rest of the Bible once each year.

JANUARY

1st	Genesis	1	Matthew	1	Ezra	1	Acts	1
2nd	Genesis	2	Matthew	2	Ezra	2	Acts	2
3rd	Genesis	3	Matthew	3	Ezra	3	Acts	3
4th	Genesis	4	Matthew	4	Ezra	4	Acts	4
5th	Genesis	5	Matthew	5	Ezra	5	Acts	5
6th	Genesis	6	Matthew	6	Ezra	6	Acts	6
7th	Genesis	7	Matthew	7	Ezra	7	Acts	7
8th	Genesis	8	Matthew	8	Ezra	8	Acts	8
9th	Genesis	9–10	Matthew	9	Ezra	9	Acts	9
10th	Genesis	11	Matthew	10	Ezra	10	Acts	10
11th	Genesis	12	Matthew	11	Nehemiah	1	Acts	11
12th	Genesis	13	Matthew	12	Nehemiah	2	Acts	12
13th	Genesis	14	Matthew	13	Nehemiah	3	Acts	13
14th	Genesis	15	Matthew	14	Nehemiah	4	Acts	14
15th	Genesis	16	Matthew	15	Nehemiah	5	Acts	15
16th	Genesis	17	Matthew	16	Nehemiah	6	Acts	16
17th	Genesis	18	Matthew	17	Nehemiah	7	Acts	17
18th	Genesis	19	Matthew	18	Nehemiah	8	Acts	18
19th	Genesis	20	Matthew	19	Nehemiah	9	Acts	19
20th	Genesis	21	Matthew	20	Nehemiah	10	Acts	20
21st	Genesis	22	Matthew	21	Nehemiah	11	Acts	21
22nd	Genesis	23	Matthew	22	Nehemiah	12	Acts	22
23rd	Genesis	24	Matthew	23	Nehemiah	13	Acts	23
24th	Genesis	25	Matthew	24	Esther	1	Acts	24
25th	Genesis	26	Matthew	25	Esther	2	Acts	25
26th	Genesis	27	Matthew	26	Esther	3	Acts	26
27th	Genesis	28	Matthew	27	Esther	4	Acts	27
28th	Genesis	29	Matthew	28	Esther	5	Acts	28
29th	Genesis	30	Mark	1	Esther	6	Romans	1

| 30th | Genesis | 31 | Mark | 2 | Esther | 7 | Romans | 2 |
| 31st | Genesis | 32 | Mark | 3 | Esther | 8 | Romans | 3 |

FEBRUARY

1st	Genesis	33	Mark	4	Esther	9–10	Romans	4
2nd	Genesis	34	Mark	5	Job	1	Romans	5
3rd	Genesis	35–36	Mark	6	Job	2	Romans	6
4th	Genesis	37	Mark	7	Job	3	Romans	7
5th	Genesis	38	Mark	8	Job	4	Romans	8
6th	Genesis	39	Mark	9	Job	5	Romans	9
7th	Genesis	40	Mark	10	Job	6	Romans	10
8th	Genesis	41	Mark	11	Job	7	Romans	11
9th	Genesis	42	Mark	12	Job	8	Romans	12
10th	Genesis	43	Mark	13	Job	9	Romans	13
11th	Genesis	44	Mark	14	Job	10	Romans	14
12th	Genesis	45	Mark	15	Job	11	Romans	15
13th	Genesis	46	Mark	16	Job	12	Romans	16
14th	Genesis	47	Luke	1:1–38	Job	13	1 Corinthians	1
15th	Genesis	48	Luke	1:39ff	Job	14	1 Corinthians	2
16th	Genesis	49	Luke	2	Job	15	1 Corinthians	3
17th	Genesis	50	Luke	3	Job	16–17	1 Corinthians	4
18th	Exodus	1	Luke	4	Job	18	1 Corinthians	5
19th	Exodus	2	Luke	5	Job	19	1 Corinthians	6
20th	Exodus	3	Luke	6	Job	20	1 Corinthians	7
21st	Exodus	4	Luke	7	Job	21	1 Corinthians	8
22nd	Exodus	5	Luke	8	Job	22	1 Corinthians	9
23rd	Exodus	6	Luke	9	Job	23	1 Corinthians	10
24th	Exodus	7	Luke	10	Job	24	1 Corinthians	11
25th	Exodus	8	Luke	11	Job	25–26	1 Corinthians	12
26th	Exodus	9	Luke	12	Job	27	1 Corinthians	13
27th	Exodus	10	Luke	13	Job	28	1 Corinthians	14
28th	Exodus	11–12:21	Luke	14	Job	29	1 Corinthians	15

March

1st	Exodus	12:22ff	Luke	15	Job	30	1 Corinthians	16
2nd	Exodus	13	Luke	16	Job	31	2 Corinthians	1
3rd	Exodus	14	Luke	17	Job	32	2 Corinthians	2
4th	Exodus	15	Luke	18	Job	33	2 Corinthians	3
5th	Exodus	16	Luke	19	Job	34	2 Corinthians	4
6th	Exodus	17	Luke	20	Job	35	2 Corinthians	5
7th	Exodus	18	Luke	21	Job	36	2 Corinthians	6
8th	Exodus	19	Luke	22	Job	37	2 Corinthians	7
9th	Exodus	20	Luke	23	Job	38	2 Corinthians	8
10th	Exodus	21	Luke	24	Job	39	2 Corinthians	9
11th	Exodus	22	John	1	Job	40	2 Corinthians	10
12th	Exodus	23	John	2	Job	41	2 Corinthians	11
13th	Exodus	24	John	3	Job	42	2 Corinthians	12
14th	Exodus	25	John	4	Proverbs	1	2 Corinthians	13
15th	Exodus	26	John	5	Proverbs	2	Galatians	1
16th	Exodus	27	John	6	Proverbs	3	Galatians	2
17th	Exodus	28	John	7	Proverbs	4	Galatians	3
18th	Exodus	29	John	8	Proverbs	5	Galatians	4
19th	Exodus	30	John	9	Proverbs	6	Galatians	5
20th	Exodus	31	John	10	Proverbs	7	Galatians	6
21st	Exodus	32	John	11	Proverbs	8	Ephesians	1
22nd	Exodus	33	John	12	Proverbs	9	Ephesians	2
23rd	Exodus	34	John	13	Proverbs	10	Ephesians	3
24th	Exodus	35	John	14	Proverbs	11	Ephesians	4
25th	Exodus	36	John	15	Proverbs	12	Ephesians	5
26th	Exodus	37	John	16	Proverbs	13	Ephesians	6
27th	Exodus	38	John	17	Proverbs	14	Philippians	1
28th	Exodus	39	John	18	Proverbs	15	Philippians	2
29th	Exodus	40	John	19	Proverbs	16	Philippians	3
30th	Leviticus	1	John	20	Proverbs	17	Philippians	4
31st	Leviticus	2–3	John	21	Proverbs	18	Colossians	1

APRIL

1st	Leviticus	4	Psalms	1–2	Proverbs	19	Colossians	2
2nd	Leviticus	5	Psalms	3–4	Proverbs	20	Colossians	3
3rd	Leviticus	6	Psalms	5–6	Proverbs	21	Colossians	4
4th	Leviticus	7	Psalms	7–8	Proverbs	22	1 Thessalonians	1
5th	Leviticus	8	Psalms	9	Proverbs	23	1 Thessalonians	2
6th	Leviticus	9	Psalms	10	Proverbs	24	1 Thessalonians	3
7th	Leviticus	10	Psalms	11–12	Proverbs	25	1 Thessalonians	4
8th	Leviticus	11–12	Psalms	13–14	Proverbs	26	1 Thessalonians	5
9th	Leviticus	13	Psalms	15–16	Proverbs	27	2 Thessalonians	1
10th	Leviticus	14	Psalms	17	Proverbs	28	2 Thessalonians	2
11th	Leviticus	15	Psalms	18	Proverbs	29	2 Thessalonians	3
12th	Leviticus	16	Psalms	19	Proverbs	30	1 Timothy	1
13th	Leviticus	17	Psalms	20–21	Proverbs	31	1 Timothy	2
14th	Leviticus	18	Psalms	22	Ecclesiastes	1	1 Timothy	3
15th	Leviticus	19	Psalms	23–24	Ecclesiastes	2	1 Timothy	4
16th	Leviticus	20	Psalms	25	Ecclesiastes	3	1 Timothy	5
17th	Leviticus	21	Psalms	26–27	Ecclesiastes	4	1 Timothy	6
18th	Leviticus	22	Psalms	28–29	Ecclesiastes	5	2 Timothy	1
19th	Leviticus	23	Psalms	30	Ecclesiastes	6	2 Timothy	2
20th	Leviticus	24	Psalms	31	Ecclesiastes	7	2 Timothy	3
21st	Leviticus	25	Psalms	32	Ecclesiastes	8	2 Timothy	4
22nd	Leviticus	26	Psalms	33	Ecclesiastes	9	Titus	1
23rd	Leviticus	27	Psalms	34	Ecclesiastes	10	Titus	2
24th	Numbers	1	Psalms	35	Ecclesiastes	11	Titus	3
25th	Numbers	2	Psalms	36	Ecclesiastes	12	Philemon	1
26th	Numbers	3	Psalms	37	Song of Songs	1	Hebrews	1
27th	Numbers	4	Psalms	38	Song of Songs	2	Hebrews	2
28th	Numbers	5	Psalms	39	Song of Songs	3	Hebrews	3
29th	Numbers	6	Psalms	40–41	Song of Songs	4	Hebrews	4
30th	Numbers	7	Psalms	42–43	Song of Songs	5	Hebrews	5

MAY

1st	Numbers	8	Psalms	44	Song of Songs	6	Hebrews	6
2nd	Numbers	9	Psalms	45	Song of Songs	7	Hebrews	7
3rd	Numbers	10	Psalms	46–47	Song of Songs	8	Hebrews	8
4th	Numbers	11	Psalms	48	Isaiah	1	Hebrews	9
5th	Numbers	12–13	Psalms	49	Isaiah	2	Hebrews	10
6th	Numbers	14	Psalms	50	Isaiah	3–4	Hebrews	11
7th	Numbers	15	Psalms	51	Isaiah	5	Hebrews	12
8th	Numbers	16	Psalms	52–54	Isaiah	6	Hebrews	13
9th	Numbers	17–18	Psalms	55	Isaiah	7	James	1
10th	Numbers	19	Psalms	56–57	Isaiah	8–9:7	James	2
11th	Numbers	20	Psalms	58–59	Isaiah	9:8–10:4	James	3
12th	Numbers	21	Psalms	60–61	Isaiah	10:5ff	James	4
13th	Numbers	22	Psalms	62–63	Isaiah	11–12	James	5
14th	Numbers	23	Psalms	64–65	Isaiah	13	1 Peter	1
15th	Numbers	24	Psalms	66–67	Isaiah	14	1 Peter	2
16th	Numbers	25	Psalms	68	Isaiah	15	1 Peter	3
17th	Numbers	26	Psalms	69	Isaiah	16	1 Peter	4
18th	Numbers	27	Psalms	70–71	Isaiah	17–18	1 Peter	5
19th	Numbers	28	Psalms	72	Isaiah	19–20	2 Peter	1
20th	Numbers	29	Psalms	73	Isaiah	21	2 Peter	2
21st	Numbers	30	Psalms	74	Isaiah	22	2 Peter	3
22nd	Numbers	31	Psalms	75–76	Isaiah	23	1 John	1
23rd	Numbers	32	Psalms	77	Isaiah	24	1 John	2
24th	Numbers	33	Psalms	78:1–37	Isaiah	25	1 John	3
25th	Numbers	34	Psalms	78:38ff	Isaiah	26	1 John	4
26th	Numbers	35	Psalms	79	Isaiah	27	1 John	5
27th	Numbers	36	Psalms	80	Isaiah	28	2 John	1
28th	Deuteronomy	1	Psalms	81–82	Isaiah	29	3 John	1
29th	Deuteronomy	2	Psalms	83–84	Isaiah	30	Jude	1
30th	Deuteronomy	3	Psalms	85	Isaiah	31	Revelation	1
31st	Deuteronomy	4	Psalms	86–87	Isaiah	32	Revelation	2

JUNE

1st	Deuteronomy	5	Psalms	88	Isaiah	33	Revelation	3
2nd	Deuteronomy	6	Psalms	89	Isaiah	34	Revelation	4
3rd	Deuteronomy	7	Psalms	90	Isaiah	35	Revelation	5
4th	Deuteronomy	8	Psalms	91	Isaiah	36	Revelation	6
5th	Deuteronomy	9	Psalms	92–93	Isaiah	37	Revelation	7
6th	Deuteronomy	10	Psalms	94	Isaiah	38	Revelation	8
7th	Deuteronomy	11	Psalms	95–96	Isaiah	39	Revelation	9
8th	Deuteronomy	12	Psalms	97–98	Isaiah	40	Revelation	10
9th	Deuteronomy	13–14	Psalms	99–101	Isaiah	41	Revelation	11
10th	Deuteronomy	15	Psalms	102	Isaiah	42	Revelation	12
11th	Deuteronomy	16	Psalms	103	Isaiah	43	Revelation	13
12th	Deuteronomy	17	Psalms	104	Isaiah	44	Revelation	14
13th	Deuteronomy	18	Psalms	105	Isaiah	45	Revelation	15
14th	Deuteronomy	19	Psalms	106	Isaiah	46	Revelation	16
15th	Deuteronomy	20	Psalms	107	Isaiah	47	Revelation	17
16th	Deuteronomy	21	Psalms	108–109	Isaiah	48	Revelation	18
17th	Deuteronomy	22	Psalms	110–111	Isaiah	49	Revelation	19
18th	Deuteronomy	23	Psalms	112–113	Isaiah	50	Revelation	20
19th	Deuteronomy	24	Psalms	114–115	Isaiah	51	Revelation	21
20th	Deuteronomy	25	Psalms	116	Isaiah	52	Revelation	22
21st	Deuteronomy	26	Psalms	117–118	Isaiah	53	Matthew	1
22nd	Deuteronomy	27–28:19	Psalms	119:1–24	Isaiah	54	Matthew	2
23rd	Deuteronomy	28:20ff	Psalms	119:25–48	Isaiah	55	Matthew	3
24th	Deuteronomy	29	Psalms	119:49–72	Isaiah	56	Matthew	4
25th	Deuteronomy	30	Psalms	119:73–96	Isaiah	57	Matthew	5
26th	Deuteronomy	31	Psalms	119:97–120	Isaiah	58	Matthew	6
27th	Deuteronomy	32	Psalms	119:121–144	Isaiah	59	Matthew	7
28th	Deuteronomy	33–34	Psalms	119:145–176	Isaiah	60	Matthew	8
29th	Joshua	1	Psalms	120–122	Isaiah	61	Matthew	9
30th	Joshua	2	Psalms	123–125	Isaiah	62	Matthew	10

JULY

1st	Joshua	3	Psalms	126–128	Isaiah	63	Matthew	11
2nd	Joshua	4	Psalms	129–131	Isaiah	64	Matthew	12
3rd	Joshua	5–6:5	Psalms	132–134	Isaiah	65	Matthew	13
4th	Joshua	6:6ff	Psalms	135–136	Isaiah	66	Matthew	14
5th	Joshua	7	Psalms	137–138	Jeremiah	1	Matthew	15
6th	Joshua	8	Psalms	139	Jeremiah	2	Matthew	16
7th	Joshua	9	Psalms	140–141	Jeremiah	3	Matthew	17
8th	Joshua	10	Psalms	142–143	Jeremiah	4	Matthew	18
9th	Joshua	11	Psalms	144	Jeremiah	5	Matthew	19
10th	Joshua	12–13	Psalms	145	Jeremiah	6	Matthew	20
11th	Joshua	14–15	Psalms	146–147	Jeremiah	7	Matthew	21
12th	Joshua	16–17	Psalms	148	Jeremiah	8	Matthew	22
13th	Joshua	18–19	Psalms	149–150	Jeremiah	9	Matthew	23
14th	Joshua	20–21	Acts	1	Jeremiah	10	Matthew	24
15th	Joshua	22	Acts	2	Jeremiah	11	Matthew	25
16th	Joshua	23	Acts	3	Jeremiah	12	Matthew	26
17th	Joshua	24	Acts	4	Jeremiah	13	Matthew	27
18th	Judges	1	Acts	5	Jeremiah	14	Matthew	28
19th	Judges	2	Acts	6	Jeremiah	15	Mark	1
20th	Judges	3	Acts	7	Jeremiah	16	Mark	2
21st	Judges	4	Acts	8	Jeremiah	17	Mark	3
22nd	Judges	5	Acts	9	Jeremiah	18	Mark	4
23rd	Judges	6	Acts	10	Jeremiah	19	Mark	5
24th	Judges	7	Acts	11	Jeremiah	20	Mark	6
25th	Judges	8	Acts	12	Jeremiah	21	Mark	7
26th	Judges	9	Acts	13	Jeremiah	22	Mark	8
27th	Judges	10–11:11	Acts	14	Jeremiah	23	Mark	9
28th	Judges	11:12ff	Acts	15	Jeremiah	24	Mark	10
29th	Judges	12	Acts	16	Jeremiah	25	Mark	11
30th	Judges	13	Acts	17	Jeremiah	26	Mark	12
31st	Judges	14	Acts	18	Jeremiah	27	Mark	13

August

1st	Judges	15	Acts	19	Jeremiah	28	Mark	14
2nd	Judges	16	Acts	20	Jeremiah	29	Mark	15
3rd	Judges	17	Acts	21	Jeremiah	30–31	Mark	16
4th	Judges	18	Acts	22	Jeremiah	32	Psalms	1–2
5th	Judges	19	Acts	23	Jeremiah	33	Psalms	3–4
6th	Judges	20	Acts	24	Jeremiah	34	Psalms	5–6
7th	Judges	21	Acts	25	Jeremiah	35	Psalms	7–8
8th	Ruth	1	Acts	26	Jeremiah	36 & 45	Psalms	9
9th	Ruth	2	Acts	27	Jeremiah	37	Psalms	10
10th	Ruth	3–4	Acts	28	Jeremiah	38	Psalms	11–12
11th	1 Samuel	1	Romans	1	Jeremiah	39	Psalms	13–14
12th	1 Samuel	2	Romans	2	Jeremiah	40	Psalms	15–16
13th	1 Samuel	3	Romans	3	Jeremiah	41	Psalms	17
14th	1 Samuel	4	Romans	4	Jeremiah	42	Psalms	18
15th	1 Samuel	5–6	Romans	5	Jeremiah	43	Psalms	19
16th	1 Samuel	7–8	Romans	6	Jeremiah	44	Psalms	20–21
17th	1 Samuel	9	Romans	7	Jeremiah	46	Psalms	22
18th	1 Samuel	10	Romans	8	Jeremiah	47	Psalms	23–24
19th	1 Samuel	11	Romans	9	Jeremiah	48	Psalms	25
20th	1 Samuel	12	Romans	10	Jeremiah	49	Psalms	26–27
21st	1 Samuel	13	Romans	11	Jeremiah	50	Psalms	28–29
22nd	1 Samuel	14	Romans	12	Jeremiah	51	Psalms	30
23rd	1 Samuel	15	Romans	13	Jeremiah	52	Psalms	31
24th	1 Samuel	16	Romans	14	Lamentations	1	Psalms	32
25th	1 Samuel	17	Romans	15	Lamentations	2	Psalms	33
26th	1 Samuel	18	Romans	16	Lamentations	3	Psalms	34
27th	1 Samuel	19	1 Corinthians	1	Lamentations	4	Psalms	35
28th	1 Samuel	20	1 Corinthians	2	Lamentations	5	Psalms	36
29th	1 Samuel	21–22	1 Corinthians	3	Ezekiel	1	Psalms	37
30th	1 Samuel	23	1 Corinthians	4	Ezekiel	2	Psalms	38
31st	1 Samuel	24	1 Corinthians	5	Ezekiel	3	Psalms	39

September

1st	1 Samuel	25	1 Corinthians	6	Ezekiel	4	Psalms	40–41
2nd	1 Samuel	26	1 Corinthians	7	Ezekiel	5	Psalms	42–43
3rd	1 Samuel	27	1 Corinthians	8	Ezekiel	6	Psalms	44
4th	1 Samuel	28	1 Corinthians	9	Ezekiel	7	Psalms	45
5th	1 Samuel	29–30	1 Corinthians	10	Ezekiel	8	Psalms	46–47
6th	1 Samuel	31	1 Corinthians	11	Ezekiel	9	Psalms	48
7th	2 Samuel	1	1 Corinthians	12	Ezekiel	10	Psalms	49
8th	2 Samuel	2	1 Corinthians	13	Ezekiel	11	Psalms	50
9th	2 Samuel	3	1 Corinthians	14	Ezekiel	12	Psalms	51
10th	2 Samuel	4–5	1 Corinthians	15	Ezekiel	13	Psalms	52–54
11th	2 Samuel	6	1 Corinthians	16	Ezekiel	14	Psalms	55
12th	2 Samuel	7	2 Corinthians	1	Ezekiel	15	Psalms	56–57
13th	2 Samuel	8–9	2 Corinthians	2	Ezekiel	16	Psalms	58–59
14th	2 Samuel	10	2 Corinthians	3	Ezekiel	17	Psalms	60–61
15th	2 Samuel	11	2 Corinthians	4	Ezekiel	18	Psalms	62–63
16th	2 Samuel	12	2 Corinthians	5	Ezekiel	19	Psalms	64–65
17th	2 Samuel	13	2 Corinthians	6	Ezekiel	20	Psalms	66–67
18th	2 Samuel	14	2 Corinthians	7	Ezekiel	21	Psalms	68
19th	2 Samuel	15	2 Corinthians	8	Ezekiel	22	Psalms	69
20th	2 Samuel	16	2 Corinthians	9	Ezekiel	23	Psalms	70–71
21st	2 Samuel	17	2 Corinthians	10	Ezekiel	24	Psalms	72
22nd	2 Samuel	18	2 Corinthians	11	Ezekiel	25	Psalms	73
23rd	2 Samuel	19	2 Corinthians	12	Ezekiel	26	Psalms	74
24th	2 Samuel	20	2 Corinthians	13	Ezekiel	27	Psalms	75–76
25th	2 Samuel	21	Galatians	1	Ezekiel	28	Psalms	77
26th	2 Samuel	22	Galatians	2	Ezekiel	29	Psalms	78:1–37
27th	2 Samuel	23	Galatians	3	Ezekiel	30	Psalms	78:38ff
28th	2 Samuel	24	Galatians	4	Ezekiel	31	Psalms	79
29th	1 Kings	1	Galatians	5	Ezekiel	32	Psalms	80
30th	1 Kings	2	Galatians	6	Ezekiel	33	Psalms	81–82

OCTOBER

1st	1 Kings	3	Ephesians	1	Ezekiel	34	Psalms	83–84
2nd	1 Kings	4–5	Ephesians	2	Ezekiel	35	Psalms	85
3rd	1 Kings	6	Ephesians	3	Ezekiel	36	Psalms	86
4th	1 Kings	7	Ephesians	4	Ezekiel	37	Psalms	87–88
5th	1 Kings	8	Ephesians	5	Ezekiel	38	Psalms	89
6th	1 Kings	9	Ephesians	6	Ezekiel	39	Psalms	90
7th	1 Kings	10	Philippians	1	Ezekiel	40	Psalms	91
8th	1 Kings	11	Philippians	2	Ezekiel	41	Psalms	92–93
9th	1 Kings	12	Philippians	3	Ezekiel	42	Psalms	94
10th	1 Kings	13	Philippians	4	Ezekiel	43	Psalms	95–96
11th	1 Kings	14	Colossians	1	Ezekiel	44	Psalms	97–98
12th	1 Kings	15	Colossians	2	Ezekiel	45	Psalms	99–101
13th	1 Kings	16	Colossians	3	Ezekiel	46	Psalms	102
14th	1 Kings	17	Colossians	4	Ezekiel	47	Psalms	103
15th	1 Kings	18	1 Thessalonians	1	Ezekiel	48	Psalms	104
16th	1 Kings	19	1 Thessalonians	2	Daniel	1	Psalms	105
17th	1 Kings	20	1 Thessalonians	3	Daniel	2	Psalms	106
18th	1 Kings	21	1 Thessalonians	4	Daniel	3	Psalms	107
19th	1 Kings	22	1 Thessalonians	5	Daniel	4	Psalms	108–109
20th	2 Kings	1	2 Thessalonians	1	Daniel	5	Psalms	110–111
21st	2 Kings	2	2 Thessalonians	2	Daniel	6	Psalms	112–113
22nd	2 Kings	3	2 Thessalonians	3	Daniel	7	Psalms	114–115
23rd	2 Kings	4	1 Timothy	1	Daniel	8	Psalms	116
24th	2 Kings	5	1 Timothy	2	Daniel	9	Psalms	117–118
25th	2 Kings	6	1 Timothy	3	Daniel	10	Psalms	119:1–24
26th	2 Kings	7	1 Timothy	4	Daniel	11	Psalms	119:25–48
27th	2 Kings	8	1 Timothy	5	Daniel	12	Psalms	119:49–72
28th	2 Kings	9	1 Timothy	6	Hosea	1	Psalms	119:73–96
29th	2 Kings	10	2 Timothy	1	Hosea	2	Psalms	119:97–120
30th	2 Kings	11–12	2 Timothy	2	Hosea	3–4	Psalms	119:121–144
31st	2 Kings	13	2 Timothy	3	Hosea	5–6	Psalms	119:145–176

NOVEMBER

1st	2 Kings	14	2 Timothy	4	Hosea	7	Psalms	120–122
2nd	2 Kings	15	Titus	1	Hosea	8	Psalms	123–125
3rd	2 Kings	16	Titus	2	Hosea	9	Psalms	126–128
4th	2 Kings	17	Titus	3	Hosea	10	Psalms	129–131
5th	2 Kings	18	Philemon	1	Hosea	11	Psalms	132–134
6th	2 Kings	19	Hebrews	1	Hosea	12	Psalms	135–136
7th	2 Kings	20	Hebrews	2	Hosea	13	Psalms	137–138
8th	2 Kings	21	Hebrews	3	Hosea	14	Psalms	139
9th	2 Kings	22	Hebrews	4	Joel	1	Psalms	140–141
10th	2 Kings	23	Hebrews	5	Joel	2	Psalms	142
11th	2 Kings	24	Hebrews	6	Joel	3	Psalms	143
12th	2 Kings	25	Hebrews	7	Amos	1	Psalms	144
13th	1 Chronicles	1–2	Hebrews	8	Amos	2	Psalms	145
14th	1 Chronicles	3–4	Hebrews	9	Amos	3	Psalms	146–147
15th	1 Chronicles	5–6	Hebrews	10	Amos	4	Psalms	148–150
16th	1 Chronicles	7–8	Hebrews	11	Amos	5	Luke	1:1–38
17th	1 Chronicles	9–10	Hebrews	12	Amos	6	Luke	1:39ff
18th	1 Chronicles	11–12	Hebrews	13	Amos	7	Luke	2
19th	1 Chronicles	13–14	James	1	Amos	8	Luke	3
20th	1 Chronicles	15	James	2	Amos	9	Luke	4
21st	1 Chronicles	16	James	3	Obadiah	1	Luke	5
22nd	1 Chronicles	17	James	4	Jonah	1	Luke	6
23rd	1 Chronicles	18	James	5	Jonah	2	Luke	7
24th	1 Chronicles	19–20	1 Peter	1	Jonah	3	Luke	8
25th	1 Chronicles	21	1 Peter	2	Jonah	4	Luke	9
26th	1 Chronicles	22	1 Peter	3	Micah	1	Luke	10
27th	1 Chronicles	23	1 Peter	4	Micah	2	Luke	11
28th	1 Chronicles	24–25	1 Peter	5	Micah	3	Luke	12
29th	1 Chronicles	26–27	2 Peter	1	Micah	4	Luke	13
30th	1 Chronicles	28	2 Peter	2	Micah	5	Luke	14

DECEMBER

1st	1 Chronicles	29	2 Peter	3	Micah	6	Luke	15
2nd	2 Chronicles	1	1 John	1	Micah	7	Luke	16
3rd	2 Chronicles	2	1 John	2	Nahum	1	Luke	17
4th	2 Chronicles	3–4	1 John	3	Nahum	2	Luke	18
5th	2 Chronicles	5–6:11	1 John	4	Nahum	3	Luke	19
6th	2 Chronicles	6:12ff	1 John	5	Habakkuk	1	Luke	20
7th	2 Chronicles	7	2 John	1	Habakkuk	2	Luke	21
8th	2 Chronicles	8	3 John	1	Habakkuk	3	Luke	22
9th	2 Chronicles	9	Jude	1	Zephaniah	1	Luke	23
10th	2 Chronicles	10	Revelation	1	Zephaniah	2	Luke	24
11th	2 Chronicles	11–12	Revelation	2	Zephaniah	3	John	1
12th	2 Chronicles	13	Revelation	3	Haggai	1	John	2
13th	2 Chronicles	14–15	Revelation	4	Haggai	2	John	3
14th	2 Chronicles	16	Revelation	5	Zechariah	1	John	4
15th	2 Chronicles	17	Revelation	6	Zechariah	2	John	5
16th	2 Chronicles	18	Revelation	7	Zechariah	3	John	6
17th	2 Chronicles	19–20	Revelation	8	Zechariah	4	John	7
18th	2 Chronicles	21	Revelation	9	Zechariah	5	John	8
19th	2 Chronicles	22–23	Revelation	10	Zechariah	6	John	9
20th	2 Chronicles	24	Revelation	11	Zechariah	7	John	10
21st	2 Chronicles	25	Revelation	12	Zechariah	8	John	11
22nd	2 Chronicles	26	Revelation	13	Zechariah	9	John	12
23rd	2 Chronicles	27–28	Revelation	14	Zechariah	10	John	13
24th	2 Chronicles	29	Revelation	15	Zechariah	11	John	14
25th	2 Chronicles	30	Revelation	16	Zechariah	12–13:1	John	15
26th	2 Chronicles	31	Revelation	17	Zechariah	13:2ff	John	16
27th	2 Chronicles	32	Revelation	18	Zechariah	14	John	17
28th	2 Chronicles	33	Revelation	19	Malachi	1	John	18
29th	2 Chronicles	34	Revelation	20	Malachi	2	John	19
30th	2 Chronicles	35	Revelation	21	Malachi	3	John	20
31st	2 Chronicles	36	Revelation	22	Malachi	4	John	21